MAX GALLO

The Night of Long Knives

Translated from the French by Lily Emmet

HARPER & ROW, PUBLISHERS

New York • Evanston • San Francisco • London

This book was first published in France under the title *La Nuit des Longs Couteaux*.

STANDARD BOOK NUMBER: 06-011397-9

Designed by Yvette A. Vogel

CONTENTS

Illustrations are grouped in a section after page 118.

The night has been unruly; where we lay
Our chimneys were blown down; and, as they say
Lamentings heard i' the air; strange screams of death,
And prophesying with accents terrible
Of dire combustion and confus'd events
New hatch'd to the woeful time.
—SHAKESPEARE, Macbeth, II, 3

How escape thoughts of Richard III?
Never, since the time of Lancaster and Tudor,
Have we witnessed such a tale of fire and death.
—BERTOLT BRECHT,
The Resistible Ascension of Arturo Ui

It was no secret that this time the revolution would have to be bloody; when we spoke of it, we called it "The Night of Long Knives."

—ADOLF HITLER, July 13, 1934

I was responsible for the German nation; consequently, it was I alone who, during those twenty-four hours, was the Supreme Court of Justice of the German people.

In every time and place, rebels have been killed. . . . I ordered the leaders of the guilty shot. I also ordered the abscesses caused by our internal and external poisons cauterized until the living flesh was burned.

—ADOLF HITLER, July 13, 1934

FOREWORD

What follows is an historical narrative. I have tried to recreate events not only in terms of general causes and political mechanisms, but also by evoking the attitudes, thoughts and faces of the various actors and by describing the skies and landscapes which set the scene of those tragic days. I have chosen this approach to extend the rigorous and somewhat abstract limits of analysis, and, above all, to recreate a climate, a regime and a time which, as Brecht observed, irresistibly suggest Shakespearean tragedy.

I have used several sources to reconstruct this narrative: the archives of the Institute of Contemporary History in Munich, public documents relating to various trials, newspapers of the time, memoirs of the various protagonists, and historical studies relating to the events themselves and to the Third Reich. I have also spoken to all the participants I was able to find—great or small—who would agree to answer my questions, and I have visited the places where the actions occurred.

FOREWORD

I have mixed all these elements together, organizing them in a scenario in which time shifts both forward and backward, the past flowing into the present, the present moment containing the past.

The reader must decide whether the puzzle and the entirety of this historic day are clearly reconstructed here. This book must be taken for what it is intended to be—a narrative account. I would like to thank my friend, the German scholar Jacques Celerne, for the help he has given me.

Max Gallo

Saturday, June 30, 1934; late afternoon. An SS firing squad draws up to the courtyard of the Stadelheim Prison, Munich. Gruppenführer (Major General) Sepp Dietrich walks rapidly through the prison corridors. Behind the cell doors, men who until yesterday had been his comrades or superiors have been waiting several hours for their fates to be decided. Sepp Dietrich knows that they are going to die. Averting his eyes, he will shout to each of them: "The Führer has condemned you to death for high treason. Heil Hitler!"

Ignoring their cries and curses, he will order the next door opened. Already, the first prisoner is being dragged to the courtyard, and the SS officer commanding the Black Guard firing squad shouts into the rosy June light: "By order of the Führer: ready, aim, fire!"

Edmund Schmidt, Gruppenführer of the Sturmabteilung (Storm Troopers), Cell 497: shot.

Hans Joachim von Spreti-Weilbach, Standartenführer (Colonel) SA, Cell 501: shot.

Hans Peter von Heydebreck, Gruppenführer SA, Cell 502: shot.

Hans Hayn, Gruppenführer SA, Cell 503: shot.

August Schneidhuber, Obergruppenführer (Lieutenant General) SA, Munich police prefect, Cell 504: shot.

Some hours later in a neighboring cell, a man with a scarred face will be killed by two SS officers: Ernst Roehm, Minister of the Reich, one of the founders of the Nazi Party, and Chief of Staff of the SA. Simultaneously in Berlin, assassins will murder General von Schleicher, former Chancellor of the Reich, and his wife. Schleicher's assistant at the War Ministry, General von Bredow, is also killed. A single gunman will murder Director Erich Klausener in his office at the Ministry of Communications, firing a bullet into his back.

Many others will fall as well—including Edgar Jung, private secretary to Franz von Papen, Vice Chancellor of the Reich, and Gregor Strasser, a companion of Hitler's since the early days. All the victims, humble or illustrious, are murdered between Saturday, June 30, 1934, and Monday, July 2—that long night of German history, the Night of Long Knives, which witnesses the destruction of men once Hitler's closest allies and friends—Strasser and Roehm, Generals Schleicher and Bredow.

In the Third Reich, as in the rest of the world, many conflicting hypotheses will be developed to explain the assassinations. It will be noted that death at the hands of the Nazis has taken place—as it will many times in the future—over a weekend, when most responsible officials have abandoned their capitals, leaving empty ministries in the hands of a few subordinates. All prominent figures are likely to be unreachable for several hours at least. Nazi death strikes like lightning on spring and summer weekends while editors sleep peacefully, with their Sunday editions already made up since major events are unlikely. The big cities are empty; everyone's guard is down; public life is in a state of suspended animation.

Across Europe on Saturday, June 30, and Sunday, July 1, 1934, the weather is hot and sunny. At Nogent the gleaming river reflects boating parties and clusters of dancers—the joyous crowds of summer. In the parks of London the grass is thick and soft: people walk barefoot; couples lie down on it.

There are throngs along the shores of Berlin's lakes; buxom women and blond children. The Nazi flag ripples above the beaches in the warm breeze. That Saturday in Berlin the radio announces a temperature of 86 degrees, but no public mention is made of the firing squads and bullets which have decimated the ranks of the Sturmabteilung, the Army of the SA, until Saturday evening.

On the afternoon of Sunday, July 1, Berlin is calm, and people are out walking or sitting in the cafés as on any other fine summer Sunday. Unter den Linden is crowded with strolling couples. It is impossible to find a table at Kranzler's café, and the white beer flavored with raspberry syrup (a Berlin specialty) flows freely.

The lack of public concern seems almost excessive. The evening papers announce a few deaths, and truckloads of Schutzstaffel—the SS Black Shirts—are seen on the streets, although no one notices them or questions their presence. The Führer gives an elegant party in the gardens of the Chancellory. Everything seems peaceful.

Foreign diplomats and journalists, anxiously alert despite the apparent calm, try to find out what is happening, to understand it. Questionnaires flow from their offices and ministries. How many people have been killed? Why? How? Has X been killed, or Y, the former Chancellor? Shock, surprise and outrage are freely expressed. André François-Poncet, the French Ambassador, dined only a few days ago with Captain Roehm, Chief of Staff of the SA, but François-Poncet is on vacation in Paris, and can only give the Foreign Minister his personal impressions of the fifty-seven-year-old Munich-born SS leader who entered the Party at the same time as Hitler, and who helped the future Chancellor take his first steps in politics.

"I had no idea of Roehm's political maneuvers," said François-Poncet. "I had no idea of the ferocity of his conflict with Hitler. I always felt an extreme repugnance toward Roehm, and avoided him as much as I could, despite the eminence of his position in the Third Reich. Finally, the Chief of Protocol, Count von Bassewitz, felt called upon to reproach me for this, and at his insistence I agreed to meet Roehm at an evening party. Our meeting was barely cordial, our interview without interest."* Now Roehm has been killed.

People muttered the names of generals, of one in particular who had been Chancellor, and the names of high functionaries. Sometimes, mixed in with the luminaries, an unknown is mentioned: the body of a Jew has been found, or an innkeeper. Then again, one of the founders of the Party: Gregor Strasser himself.

All have been murdered without explanation by gangs of killers, glacial, passionless, methodical. They are killed in front of their own doors, before witnesses. Sometimes a wife, too, pays with her life for a hasty gesture. The bodies are left where they fall—in the entry of a ministerial office, by the side of a road, or half sunk in the water of some woodland swamp. After a few hours, the police arrive and take the body away—or it is discovered by chance many days later. People have been killed in Munich, in Berlin, in Silesia. Execution squads have been at work in barracks courtyards. Should the victims be counted in the tens? In the hundreds? Some die shouting "Heil Hitler!"; others, cursing. Some are killed in their beds; others are dragged into cellars to have their throats cut. Have the Nazis begun to devour themselves, during this long night, just as the inexorable law of revolution seems to dictate?

In Rome Baron Pompeo Aloisi, Mussolini's private secretary, is very perplexed. Less than a fortnight earlier in Venice, he was present at the first meeting between the Duce and the Führer. Nothing at that time suggested an imminent upheaval. Despite

---

* André François-Poncet, *Souvenirs d'une ambassade à Berlin.* Paris, 1946.

occasional rumors, the SA seemed as always one of the principal bulwarks of the regime. Had not the Brown Shirts and their leader, Captain Roehm, helped Hitler seize power, and did they not now control the streets of German cities? On the first of July, Aloisi notes in his diary: "The repression has been very severe. Of the thirteen corps commanders of the SA, seven have been shot." As fresh information reaches Aloisi in his privileged position, his astonishment grows. Otto Strasser, the brother of Gregor, will call the killings "a German Saint Bartholomew." Mussolini makes no secret of his disgust. "The arrests," Aloisi told him, "were accompanied by revolting scenes." The Duce, with his Latin pride in virility, has already emphasized this aspect: "One of the characteristics of the revolt is that the majority of its leaders were pederasts, beginning with Roehm."

André François-Poncet, the most elegant and witty of the ambassadors to Berlin, felt that there was "something repulsive" about Roehm. The French Ambassador, whose sense of dignity bordered on the haughty, whose manners and intelligence were equally polished, had accepted an invitation to dine with Roehm. There was nothing clandestine about the evening. The dinner was catered by Horcher, manager of one of Berlin's finest restaurants. François-Poncet awaited the arrival of Captain Roehm. "He came, accompanied by six or seven young men of striking beauty and elegance. The chief of the SA introduced them to me as his aides-de-camp." But once the surprise had worn off, François-Poncet quickly grew bored. "The meal was dreary, the conversation insignificant. I found Roehm heavy and apathetic. He livened up only to complain about his health and his rheumatism, which he proposed to treat at Wiessee. On my way home, I cursed our Amphitryon, blaming him for the dullness of the evening." But later, thinking again of this dinner, and of his host, the banker Regendanz, François-Poncet added: "He and I were the only survivors of that evening—and he escaped only because he managed to flee to England."

On December 2 Hitler had brought Roehm into the cabinet as Minister Without Portfolio. He is seen everywhere in his SA uniform, reviewing units of the immense army of two and a half million men which he has built up. He parades around exuding a provocative pride. The most innocuous words in his mouth become harsh and violent, almost shocking—an effect, perhaps, of his ugliness, which far surpasses ordinary human ugliness. His skull is always shaved, and his fat, coarse face is marked by a wide scar down the side of his nose and chin. The end of his nose, the product of plastic surgery, is a caricature—red and round, with a pointed tip. Yet somehow, in that coarse, violent physiognomy there is also the look of a grotesque baby. Roehm, with his animal face and bulging stomach which his SA belt seems scarcely able to contain, is immensely visible, surrounded by handsome young men with smooth cheeks, melting eyes, their profiles designed for medallions, their hands impeccably manicured, their uniforms tailored with maximum elegance.

Roehm stares with open insolence, and the calm arrogance of authority, at anyone who speaks to him. "I am a soldier," he says, "and I look at the world from a soldier's point of view, from a point of view intentionally military. It is the military element in any situation which interests me."

His face and his scars are his credentials, his decorations, the signature of his life. In 1908 he was a second lieutenant. By 1914 he was in Lorraine, an officer at the front, dragging his men through mud, cold and fire. On June 2, 1916, as a captain, he set out for the assault on Thiaumont, part of the belt of fortifications at Verdun. He was seriously wounded and disfigured for life, his skin marked forever with the signs of his military vocation. He served on the Rumanian front, the French front, and then through the Armistice and its shame. He was among those who joined Colonel Ritter von Epp of the Freikorps to go on fighting after the Armistice, so that four years of combat should not have been in vain. As an officer of the reduced Armistice Army, he organized the Bavarian Civil Guards to crush the "Reds"—those Spartacists who believed that in a beaten and humiliated Germany they could re-enact the Russian Revolution. During the twenties, through the fogs of the Bavarian winter, Roehm armed and drilled this militia-police. On behalf of the Army, he entered the German Workers' Party, the future Nazi Party. There, in that atmosphere of displaced fanaticism, he met a veteran of the Franco-German front, a pale and puny man with a look of exaltation in his eyes, fired by nationalist passion and visionary ambition, a magnetic orator who spoke in short, sharp bursts: Adolf Hitler.

Roehm chose this man to be Party propagandist, and on July 1, 1934, he is killed by two SS officers acting on the orders of that same man, now Chancellor of the Reich. Six months before, on December 31, 1933, Roehm received a letter from his Führer which the press made public. Goering, Goebbels, Hess and Himmler were among the others—twelve in all—who received similar letters from the Chancellor that day, commemorating a year in office with expressions of gratitude to his faithful comrades. The letter to Roehm rang with blunt sincerity.

> MY DEAR CHIEF OF STAFF:
> I have been able to lead the struggle of our National Socialist movement and Revolution because of the SA, which crushed the Red Terror. If the task of the Army is to protect our country from external enemies, it is the task of the SA to assure the victory of the National Socialist Revolution on the domestic front, the existence of the National Socialist State and the unity of our people. When I called you to your present post, my dear Chief of Staff, the SA was passing through a serious crisis. It is above all thanks to you and your help that this political instrument became, within a few years, the force which allowed me to wage the final battle for power, and drive our Marxist adversaries to their knees. That is why, at the end of this year of the National Socialist Revolution, I must thank you, Ernst Roehm, for the inestimable services you have rendered to nationalism and the German

people. You must know that I am grateful to destiny,
which has allowed me to call such a man as you my
friend and brother-in-arms.

With all my friendship and gratitude,

Yours,

ADOLF HITLER

Among the twelve Nazi leaders singled out for these letters,
Roehm alone was addressed by the affectionate diminutive "du."
"I am grateful to destiny"—Hitler's words. Six months later,
Roehm is murdered on Hitler's orders. So much for destiny.

HITLER'S SPEECH

Ernst Roehm, summarily executed: A traitor to the Nazis and
the Führer? Or was he betrayed by a Machiavellian leader who
surrounded him with attentions only to ensure his damnation, as
in a Shakespearean drama where murder, hypocrisy and treachery
form the substance of intrigues for power?

Two weeks after Roehm's execution, on Friday the thirteenth
of July, a crushing heat hangs over the German capital. The Reichstag has been called to an evening session. By seven o'clock the
official cars of uniformed Nazi deputies are driving up to the Kroll
Opera, in that quiet and airy section of Berlin west of the Königsplatz, between the Tiergarten and the Spree. The men walk to the
Opera House, which is built in the heavy neo-classic style of the
late nineteenth century. Parliament has met there since the Reichstag fire of February 27, 1933. White and black uniforms mingle
together; there is a continuous exchange of Nazi salutes. It is a
meeting of vigorous men in their fifties with short hair, loud
voices and self-assured gestures. Since January 30, 1933, they have
been victorious. And since the thirtieth of June, 1934, they have
been the survivors of the first Nazi purge.

When Hitler comes in, guarded by the SS against possible
assassination, and walks to the speaker's platform, everyone stands

and salutes. André François-Poncet notices that he looks drawn and pale. Goering, as titular President of the Reichstag, opens the session at eight o'clock, immediately yielding to the Führer, who is already standing at the rostrum. In that operatic setting, with the boxes and orchestra seats occupied by uniformed deputies, the Chancellor stands, nervously clutching the lectern which has been placed in front of him. Then he extends his arm in a clenched-fist salute.

"Deputies! Men of the German Reichstag!" he begins.

André François-Poncet remembers that his voice was harsher than usual, that his words were flung out like blows. For Adolf Hitler, making a speech is an act of violence.

He has come before this, "the most highly qualified forum in the nation," he begins, "to present to our people . . . explanations of events which will, I hope, remain in our history for all eternity, a memory as instructive as it is tragic."

Outside in the Tiergarten, along the cool avenues of trees around the Königsplatz, crowds gather, listening to the radio broadcast of the speech.

"My explanations will be frank and blunt," Hitler goes on, "with the exception of a few reservations imposed by the interests of the Reich and by a sense of decency."

Every Berliner listening outside the Opera that Friday, July 13, 1934, already knows a certain amount. The "revolting scenes" mentioned by the Italian diplomat Aloisi have been graphically described by some of the newspapers. These executions have been, in part, an act of purification: purification by blood and death.

"It was no longer simply a question of Roehm's intentions," barks Hitler, "but also of his attitude, which reflected his growing alienation from the Party. All the principles which make up our greatness had lost their meaning for him. The life the Chief of Staff and a certain number of other leaders had begun to lead was intolerable from the point of view of National Socialism. The question was no longer that he and his friends had violated every decency, but rather that the contagion was widespread, and was affecting even the most distant elements."

Captain Roehm, once addressed as "du" by the Chancellor as his oldest and most faithful friend, has been transformed into this focus of discord, an "abscess" which must be destroyed. The Chancellor's voice becomes hoarser and hoarser. "Mutinies are judged by their own laws," he shouts. ". . . I ordered the leaders of the guilty shot. I also ordered the abscesses caused by our internal and external poisons cauterized until the living flesh was burned. I also ordered that any rebel attempting to resist arrest should be killed immediately. . . ."

". . . shot . . . until the living flesh was burned . . . killed immediately." Hilter's words, like sharp bursts of gunfire, suggest the violence which marked that night, less than two weeks earlier. "The action was completed during the night of Sunday, July 1," the Chancellor adds, "and normal conditions have been re-established."

Furiously clutching the lectern of the Kroll Opera, Hitler continues his speech of justification. In the hall, the deputies respond with long and violent applause. Inspired by the passion he has unleashed, Hitler speaks faster and faster.

His voice is hoarse and harsh. "I am prepared to assume before history responsibility for the decisions I have had to take to save what is most precious to us: the German people and the German Reich."

The audience rises with a single movement as the first wave of applause breaks. The Nazi deputies in the great hall lit by glittering chandeliers approve by acclamation the decisions which the Führer has claimed before history as his own.

Outside, the crowds stand and watch the deputies leaving, clapping and saluting as they catch sight of the dignitaries: Hitler, Goering, Himmler and Hess. Then the city retires for the night. The Supreme Court of Justice of the German people has spoken.

But the decisions which led to the executions and assassinations arose out of another long story, culminating on another Friday—June 29, 1934—at Bad Godesberg on the Rhine. It was there on a hotel terrace, against the background of a stormy evening, that the Night of Long Knives began.

PART ONE

Night on the Rhine

Friday, June 29, to Saturday, June 30, 1934

1

Friday, June 29, 1934
Bad Godesberg: Hotel Dreesen

2:00–9:00 P.M.

The Ruhr lies some sixty miles to the north of Bad Godesberg. Sometimes, when the damp, bitter, northeast wind sweeps down the Rhine Valley, it carries the gray, Ruhr smoke, smelling of sulphur and carbon monoxide, as far as Godesberg.

In June, however, the northeast wind never blows, and the Rhine, viewed from the terrace of the Hotel Dreesen in early afternoon, looks like the legendary river of former times, the Rhine of castles and the Lorelei. In the hot, tender sun it glistens like a long braid of blond hair. On the hotel terrace, company directors from the hard, blackened towns, smoggy centers of power whose names resound like strokes on an anvil—Essen, Cologne, Bochum, Dortmund, Gelsenkirchen—sit dreaming as they gaze over the soft June countryside, their wits dulled by the capricious wines of the Rhine slopes.

The terrace of the Hotel Dreesen, the Claridge of the Rhenish bourgeoisie, is one of those quiet spots much favored by businessmen as a place of masculine retreat where serious and sometimes heated conversations can take place in an atmosphere of alcohol and cigar smoke. The waiters are perfectly trained—quiet and discreet. On weekdays, particularly at the beginning of the summer, the Dreesen is an ideal place for an important lunch or a secret meeting.

But all summers are not alike. On this particular twenty-ninth of June, 1934, the few regulars who eat at the Dreesen have been totally abandoned. Service has been suspended, while the headwaiter walks back and forth, useless and disoriented. Everyone else has left his post. The more venturesome have slipped along the hall as far as the terrace. Walter Breitmann, one of the youngest of the waiters, is among the first. He can remember the headwaiter vainly trying to call him back.

Breitmann watches with fascination as the black cars arrive—Mercedes-Benzes, two of them with open roofs—drawing to a stop beside the steps so slowly their wheels make almost no sound on the gravel. It is the Führer himself; in the burst of applause and shouts, Walter Breitmann claps his hands and then salutes, holding his arm stiff, as he sees the others doing. A large man in an SA uniform climbs down from the first car: Oberleutnant Wilhelm Brückner, combination bodyguard, orderly and aide-de-camp to Hitler. At parades and on platforms, he always stands impassive behind the Führer, looming over him with his great height.

Although he is turned toward Hitler's car, Brückner's eyes sweep the waiting crowd. Then he opens the car door, and Hitler steps out. As the cries and shouts of acclamation increase, the Chancellor raises his arm. Then he quickly climbs the steps to the terrace, his face stern and unsmiling.

The proprietor of the hotel follows him. There is a sound of slamming doors, and the car which has brought the Führer slowly moves off to park some thirty yards farther on. Brückner stops to speak to the proprietor. The proprietor is making his excuses to forestall criticism: he had only had a few hours' notice.

The Führer has been visiting voluntary-labor camps—a sweeping inspection tour across the entire Gau (Nazi Party district) of the lower Rhine and Westphalia. He also visited the regional officers' training school at Schloss Buddenberg, near Lünen.

It is raining at Schloss Buddenberg—a pleasant summer rain, so gentle it seems closer to warm steam than rain. At ten o'clock in the morning, a crowd shouting "Sieg Heil!" surrounds the Führer's open car, and Hitler, smiling broadly, shakes hands on all sides. When the car draws up before the school's central building, Dr. Decker comes out to welcome him. The rain has almost stopped, but there are puddles everywhere, and a strong smell of wet grass and damp earth.

Hundreds of young men wait, lean and virile, necks and temples shaved, their naked, sun-bronzed legs and torsos glistening with sweat and rain, their right arms held almost horizontal in the Nazi salute. Adolf Hitler walks slowly past them, wearing a long, leather coat, holding his cap in his hand, his damp hair even blacker than usual. Colonel Konstantin Hierl walks a few paces behind Hitler, like his leader wrapped in a long coat. This costume is extraordinary, because despite the dampness the air is breathlessly heavy and hot. Brückner, Otto Dietrich and Schaub follow a few paces behind them.

Soon, these motionless young men will perform before the Führer of the Reich: some will do gymnastic exercises, others will sing in chorus, or recite poetry to the glory of Nazi Germany, while the Party leaders watch this festival of youth and vigor enlisted in their cause.

However, despite these propitious circumstances, Hitler seems anxious. He barely acknowledges Dr. Decker's salute as the official group leaves the school, with its garlanded buildings and cheering trainees.

From Schloss Buddenberg, they move on to Camp Olfen for the same ceremonies, the same young bodies taut with the joy of physical discipline and moral certitude. Standing before these groups, drawn up in perfect rectangles, Hitler speaks to his aide-de-camp in a low voice. Several men set off at a run; Brückner gives an order; the ceremony is interrupted. The Chancellor has decided not to visit Camps 210 and 211, and will not see the work which volunteers have undertaken on the Niers River. Hierl will go there instead. The Führer has suddenly decided to call a meeting at Godesberg, and Brückner has chosen the Hotel Dreesen. The dignitaries rush for their cars—among them, Dr. Robert Ley, Chief of the Labor Front, Merrenbach, his aide-de-camp, and Dr. Dietrich, the head of the Chancellor's press service.

The official procession drives on to Godesberg as quickly as possible, slowing down only to pass through towns. At every place the local Nazi chiefs have assembled the inhabitants to greet their Führer with shouts and outstretched arms, and red flags stamped with black swastikas—the hypnotic emblem of the new Reich. As journalists report later, the news of the Führer's arrival spreads like wildfire through the streets and squares of these towns; within minutes thousands upon thousands have collected along the Führer's route, and every window displays a flag or pennant.

At Godesberg, too, along the picturesque, narrow streets of that favored watering place, the windows are decorated with flags. But the Chancellor's car passes quickly by, followed by the long string of official cars: the cars of the Party leaders, and leaders of Nazi organizations, who are arriving at the Hotel Dreesen from all over Germany.

The Hotel Dreesen is well known to the middle classes of Bonn and the Ruhr as a quiet, discreet place. Once again, in 1938, Hitler will meet there with Neville Chamberlain during their final efforts to avert war. But on this Friday, June 29, 1934, the Dreesen's principal claim to distinction is the fact that Gustav Stresemann, Minister of Foreign Affairs, and supporter of the entente with France, often came there to relax before the great crisis of 1929 and the agonies which brought down the Weimar Republic.

The proprietor feels honored to receive the new Chancellor, Hitler. With a borrowed gesture, he stretches out his arm to the vast panorama opening toward Bonn some six miles away, and to the Rhine, meandering through the flat, alluvial plain on its left bank. The Führer is fond of large, natural landscapes. He steps out onto the terrace overhanging the river. It is a beautiful day, and the leaders of his Party stand near him.

A last car drives up to the hotel: it is Hierl, who has rapidly visited some of the other camps before coming on to Godesberg as quickly as he can. He gives the Chancellor a brief summary of his findings, and then everyone sits down.

Listeners can hear the rise and fall of Hitler's voice: he speaks loudly, almost shouting, in sharp, brutal bursts, falling silent only after several hours, exhausted as he always is after an address to which he has given all his passion. Toward the end of the afternoon as the leaders of the SS and the SA salute and make their farewells, and their cars drive up to the steps to collect them, he is able to relax. He walks to the edge of the terrace. There the Gauleiter of the district of Cologne–Aix-la-Chappelle presents the region's important dignitaries, and lesser officials. The crowd of curiosity seekers is still there, saluting, shouting and waving flags. Maneuvering with the martial precision of ancient Prussian units, a detachment of the RAD (Youth Labor Corps) takes up its position in front of the hotel.

Hitler walks out onto the steps, saluting with pleased satisfaction the young men drawn up in the perfect immobility of statues, before reviewing them. Then, while the military band plays Nazi airs, six hundred volunteers of the Labor Corps light their torches and form up at the foot of the terrace in an enormous, fiery swastika. Hitler leans over the terrace wall. The musicians are playing the "Zapfenstreich."

The flames of burning torches leap and fall in the damp breeze rising from the river, scented with the sweet smell of vineyards and wet grass. Black barges passing each other in the growing darkness have already lit their navigation lights.

Across the river, opposite the hotel, the rounded peaks of the Siebengebirge (Seven Mountains) stand out against the sky: isolated volcanic remains: Drachenfels, Olberg, Petersberg, and

Loewenberg, the largest. From Godesberg, the eye travels first to these massive protuberances, and then down the majestic sweep of the Rhine Valley, which suggests the essence of power and peace.

All day it has been hot and humid in the Rhine Valley, without a trace of wind. In the morning it rained, and the afternoon sky is still hidden behind massed gray-white clouds, darkened over the Ruhr by the black fumes of the steel works. Perhaps the heavy dampness of the German summer is responsible for Hitler's ashen color, his vague, shifting stare. One senses that he is sweating. But gradually, on the terrace overlooking the Rhine, that much-sung, much-disputed artery of German history, he has seemed to grow calmer and more relaxed. The young waiter, Walter Breitmann, has returned to his post, passing through the terrace from time to time, or managing to look out at it. Many people are clustered about the table where the Führer is sitting. Now and then he throws back his head and seems to stare at the sky. The darkness of night has brought with it a tactile and visual sense of coolness. The river has become a more intense band of darkness winding through the dark.

Hitler smiles as he speaks to one of the waitresses with the kindly but distant tone of authority which he assumes when he speaks to the ordinary people who accepted him as Chancellor of the Reich over a year earlier, on January 30, 1933. The waitress, who appears to be much moved, answers in monosyllables, smiling somewhat foolishly. The Führer himself seems genuinely interested in his interrogation—her family and daily life, the future—but the expression on his face is distant. Words and questions follow each other in rapid succession—but is he listening to the answers?

On the banks of the Rhine, while the summer night stretches across Germany—a short interval between spells of intense heat—Hitler is aware that every minute is important. Perhaps he is talking to the waitress to cover the progress of his private thoughts. Perhaps he has come to this place, far from the agitation of the

Ruhr towns, and from the formal heaviness of official Berlin, because he knows that he must arrive at a decision as weighted and sharp as a blow from a cleaver, as burning as a hot iron against living flesh—unless, of course, the orders have already been given, and this intermission beside the river is a final respite allowed the victims, already selected, in order to dull their suspicions.

Brückner orders supper, then rises and asks for the telephone. The Chancellor follows him with his eyes, his face once again strained and tense. He huddles into the depths of the armchair which faces the view, his head lowered, his shoulders hunched, like a sick man who feels suddenly cold. He seems quiet and thoughtful. An occasional spectator, impelled by curiosity, moves up to the edge of the terrace to look at the Führer, but the detectives and SS standing guard give them second thoughts, and they drift away again. The frail man who sits in the open air of the summer night is the center of all eyes, the heart of Germany, yet his thoughts seem to be elsewhere. Motionless, resting his chin on his hands, his face slightly puffy, his black hair slicked flat, he looks like any thoughtful man. Neither Walter Breitmann nor any of the other employees at the Dreesen can possibly guess that truckloads of SS are ready at that moment to leave Berlin, and that the night which has already begun beside the peaceful, majestic river will be a night of executions and violent crime. The exhausted Chancellor seems to be dreaming, halfway between wakefulness and sleep. He has the power to unleash violence at any moment, however, or hold it back, throughout all Germany— from Hamburg to Munich, from Bremen to Breslau, from Berlin to Cologne. Perhaps it has already begun.

The silence, calm and softness of the Rhenish night are broken only by conversations in lowered voices, occasional polite laughter, the even purr of an engine rising from the valley, and the footsteps of Oberleutnant Wilhelm Brückner returning from the phone.

Young Walter Breitmann watches the Oberleutnant walk slowly across the room toward Hitler, who turns his head to greet him. They speak quickly, in lowered voices, before Brückner goes back to the telephone. Dinner has been served, and as usual the Chancellor eats very little. When Brückner reappears on the terrace, Hitler asks him for news of Viktor Lutze, whom he has summoned to Godesberg. Brückner thinks that he will be able to join them, and Hitler relaxes somewhat. Obergruppenführer Lutze is a faithful member of the Sturmabteilung. As leader of the Gau of Hannover, he is one of the ten men who head the SA military districts controlling Germany. He is a quiet, self-effacing man, with the look of a well-disciplined student. According to his superior, Ernst Roehm, Viktor Lutze is little more than "a capable and conscientious executive, without any special abilities."

Brückner reassures the Führer that Lutze is coming as quickly as he can cover the distance between Hannover and Godesberg—about two hundred miles along good roads. He should arrive within a few hours, and with Lutze an order is as good as the accomplished act. Once again the Chancellor falls silent. When the Obergruppenführer SA arrives, the choice will have to be made, and the SA units of Captain Roehm will have to accept it. How many Brown Shirts are there, in their visored caps and black armbands stamped with the swastika? Two and a half million? Three million? Or barely a hundred thousand? These men make up the core of Roehm's power. In addition to the SA, he has under his command, directly or indirectly, the SS, which has grown from 280 in 1929 to perhaps 50,000 when the Nazis seized power in January, 1933, to 300,000 in June, 1934; the NSKK (National Socialist Automobile Corps); and the Hitler Youth—some one million young men. Altogether, Generaloberst Werner von Blomberg, the Minister of War, has only 300,000. The essential element in all this is the SA. They are the core of Roehm's strength.

While the Chancellor waits on the terrace for Lutze, and news from Berlin, for the moment when he will have to make his fateful decision, he cannot help but think of all those men in uniform whose law is instant obedience to his person even unto death, and of the SA, whom Roehm, in his last speech to the foreign press

corps, on April 18, 1934, characterized as "not just a band of intrepid men bound by oath, but an army of believers, martyrs,
agitators and soldiers. The Führer has given us the red flag with
its swastika, the new symbol of our German future, and he has
given us the brown shirt, clothing the SA in combat, honors and
death. By its color, the brown shirt makes it easy to distinguish
the SA, and this is its justification: it is the distinctive sign of the
SA, which allows both friend and foe alike to recognize at a glance
those who believe in the National Socialist conception of the
world."

This evening, the fate of these Brown Shirts, these "political"
soldiers who, as Roehm said, "have opened for National Socialism
with their fists the road to the future, the road to victory"—the
fate of these men is in question, is being decided on the terrace of
the Hotel Dreesen, overlooking the Rhine.

But one has to strike with determination. As Roehm often
repeated, "The SA is not an institution for the moral education of
young girls; it is an association of hardened fighting men."

As the hours pass and the moment of decision draws closer,
the Chancellor can reflect on the tiny police force organized on
the initiative of Roehm when, on August 3, 1921, he and the
original members of the SA had to protect Party meetings and
prevent Party enemies from holding any of their own. The SA
was recruited from the hardened veterans of the Freikorps, the
marine brigade of Captain Löwenfeld; from the Jägerkorps, commanded by General Maercker; and from the Escherich organization. Before they came to the SA they had been the fighting
strength of the bands of mercenaries and freebooters who con-
fronted the Poles on the heaths and marshes along the Baltic
coast, or fought in the towns against the sailors and workers who
supported the Revolution. Their heavy machine guns supplied by
the Army, these bands of youthful but hardened veterans fought a
clandestine, dubious battle. Looking like gangs of bandits in their
motley uniforms, nervous and wiry, they were like damned souls
cast out by society to wander through the northern fogs and

the anarchy of a Germany in defeat, as through an empire ripe for conquest.

The first head of the SA, H. Klintzsch, was a veteran of the Ehrhardt Brigade. Soon after its founding, von Killinger, the murderer of Erzberger (who had signed the armistice), and Edmund Heines, who killed Rathenau, joined the organization. Then, in March, 1923, Hermann Goering took the oath of membership—the war hero and fighter ace, whose dazzling good looks were as yet unaffected by drugs and obesity. In the cold, gray streets of Munich, when the first Nazi putsch took place, in November, 1923, the SA were there, massed behind their leaders. Outlawed, like the Party itself, after the failure of the putsch, the SA were reconstituted by Roehm, always ready to build up a fighting force. First known as the Frontbann, they became the SA again in 1925.

In 1925 the Nazi Party seemed to be tearing itself apart. Goebbels was demanding the expulsion of the "petit bourgeois," Hitler, while Gregor Strasser, thanks to whom the Party controlled the north of Germany, spoke of socialism and national Bolshevism, moving away from the caution of Hitler, who had decided to look to the Right for support. Ernst Roehm, with his exclusively military outlook, wished to subordinate the Party to the SA and transform it into a new Freikorps. Hitler had decided the other way, and Roehm, the soldier and adventurer, a disappointed but disciplined loser, left Germany to organize and train the Bolivian Army.

It was then that the SS began to grow: shock troops in the exclusive service of Hitler, a personal guard whose fidelity and discipline were absolute. On January 6, 1929, the SS got Heinrich Himmler as its leader, a man with an expressionless face, his eyes hidden behind steel-rimmed glasses. "I was never able to catch his eyes," Alfred Rosenberg said of him. "He was always hidden, always elusive behind his pince-nez." But this middle-class Catholic who became Chief of the SS was able to build an organization, the Black Guard, which step by step, combining fanatical mysticism with terror, steadily increased its power.

In 1931, however, the Führer was obliged to recall Roehm to reorganize the Sturmabteilung, whose growth had accelerated with each Nazi electoral success: from 100,000 men in 1930, to 300,000 in 1933, to nearly 3,000,000 in 1934.

Now they are everywhere, the Führer's private army, with their own motorized units and squadrons of planes. Its organization into Gruppen, Standarten (regiments), and Stürme (companies) is highly efficient, clutching the country with iron talons of violence and terror.

Their principal aim is to deny the enemies of the Nazis the use of streets and meeting halls. As early as November, 1921, after only a few months of existence, they intervened at the Munich Hofbräuhaus (Beer Hall).

Hitler himself, in *Mein Kampf,* tells the story of this meeting which gave birth to the tactics of direct action by the SA: "When I entered the lobby of the Hofbräuhaus at quarter to eight, I no longer had any doubts as to the question of sabotage. . . . The hall was very crowded. . . . The small Assault Section was waiting for me in the lobby. . . . I had the doors to the hall shut, and ordered my men—some forty-five or -six—to stand at attention. I told them that this was their first opportunity to test their loyalty to the movement, and that whatever happened, none of us must leave the hall. Their reply was to shout 'Heil!' three times, their voices harsher and more bitter than usual." Hitler spoke, and then the word was given and the brawl began. "The dance hadn't started yet," *Mein Kampf* continues, "when my men from the Assault Section—from that day known as the SA—launched their attack. Like wolves, in packs of eight or ten, they threw themselves on their adversaries, overwhelming them with blows, chasing them from the room. In five minutes everyone was covered with blood. These were real men, whom I learned to appreciate on that occasion. They were led by my courageous Maurice. Hess, my private secretary, and many others who were badly hurt pressed the attack as long as they were able to stand on their feet." The Führer considered this the baptismal act of the SA.

The men were not recruited from the soft or timid segments

of society, the stiffly proper lower middle class. The economic crisis of 1929 became the breeding ground from which the SA drew its malcontents: the unemployed and workers from the "Lumpenproletariat," who were given a uniform and pay, and who found in the SA an organization which welcomed them and promised "the Revolution."

As the risks increase, they must fight the Socialists, organized as the Banner of the Empire, and the Communists, who belong to the Red League of Front-Line Fighters. The groups watch each other, parade with trumpets and banners, and throw stones. The police, who usually favor the SA, sometimes try to separate the hostile groups, but are easily overwhelmed, or are already committed. Incident follows incident in rapid succession, and the atmosphere of violence and revenge intensifies. At Essen, the Communists are burying one of their members. When the funeral procession passes the Brown House where an SA is standing guard, the marchers threaten him with summary execution. Shots are exchanged, an SA is captured, and narrowly escapes being shot. Bodies of trade unionists are found in swamps; the frequency of tavern brawls increases. When a "Red" is killed, the SA always have an excuse. At Essen, an SA, Kiewski, falls while drunk, involuntarily firing his revolver; a Communist, Ney, lies dead.

In the euphoria of January, 1933, when thousands of partisans of the new Reich march past the Chancellery windows shouting with triumph to their new Chancellor, the SA realize that the last obstacle to their violence has fallen. The courts now condemn their adversaries without hesitation. If an SA center is attacked by stones, the SA reply by shooting, and the alleged aggressors—these attacks are rarely proved—are condemned to death or life imprisonment. SA membership grows rapidly: when one wears a brown shirt, violence becomes heroism. Juvenile delinquents, sexual deviants, the dregs of society which rise to the surface in periods of profound dislocation, are mixed in with the ordinary SA troops, moving them toward sadism and violence.

Their uniformed bands patrol the streets, which ring with

their shouts. They station guards in front of Jewish stores to discourage customers, and collect funds for the benefit of the Nazis, or perhaps simply for themselves. Who can refuse them? Furthermore, on February 22, 1933, by the decision of Goering, Minister of the Interior, and soon to be President of the Prussian Council, 25,000 SA and 15,000 SS are designated auxiliary police. As Goering wrote on February 17, giving instructions to the forces of law and order: "Those police who use their weapons while performing their duties will be covered by me, regardless of the consequence. Those who avoid shooting, out of a misconceived sense of delicacy, on the other hand, must expect severe disciplinary reprisal." The road has been cleared. The SA can sing their "Horst Wessel Lied" —a song commemorating the death of an SA hero, killed in a brawl—loud and clear.

Power is in their hands, the advantage of position and strength. From all over Germany, new members join up. Sometimes these are former Socialists or Communists who wish to obliterate their earlier views. Roehm, in his usual provocative manner, has not hesitated to suggest this: "I am sure that there are many excellent soldiers in the Communist ranks, especially among 'Red Veterans.'" According to some opponents of the SA, there are sections of the SA which might properly be labeled "Beefsteak Stürme"—brown outside, Red inside.

For the unyielding opposition, the SA has prepared camps and torture. They are among the first to interrogate their prisoners. Rudolf Diels, a monarchist who for a time was chief of the Prussian Secret Police by Goering's choice, manages to visit the cellars where the SA imprison their victims. What he sees is a scene of electrifying horror: the prisoners are dying of hunger, their bones broken, their faces bruised and swollen, their bodies covered with infected wounds. He manages to rescue some of them, driving them off in police cars. "Like a mass of inanimate clay, absurd puppets with lifeless eyes, burning with fever, their bodies sagging, they sat slumped against each other on the bench of the police car. The policemen with me fell silent at this confrontation with hell." Sometimes the SA force their prisoners up into trees and make them sing like birds.

Rudolph Diels is appalled. "I was seized with horror," he writes, "as if I were watching the apparition of specters." The prisoners, "their faces discolored by yellow, green, and blue bruises, no longer have anything human about them." Suddenly, as Diels stands beside a prisoner, "Ernst, one of the SA leaders of the Berlin district, and his entourage, dressed in immaculate uniforms, with old and recent decorations hanging from their necks, burst into the room, laughing and talking."

As Roehm has said, the SA is not an organization for young girls.

Without paying much heed to Goering, the SA are active throughout Prussia. In Berlin alone there are some fifty improvised prisons—cellars, warehouses, sheds, garages—where prisoners are beaten and killed. In the provinces—in Sonnenburg, Barnim, Königswusterhausen, Wuppertal, Kemma—SA prisons echo with screams of agony. In most cases, Rudolph Diels manages to liberate the prisoners, and to close the prisons of the Sturmabteilung. But this is not done without difficulty, without arousing solid and lasting hostility between the Prussian political police, of which he is the head, and the SA, and also between Goering and Roehm. Whatever the SA engage in—whether they are torturing a prisoner, cutting the throat of an adversary or pillaging an apartment —they behave as if they are within their rights, as artisans of the Nazi victory. They can break teeth or windows, kidnap a man or kill him in a cellar or in the woods, or, as at a Berlin parade, systematically prevent young girls from watching the youth groups go by, standing in front of them, laughing and telling them: "Put your heads between our legs if you want to see."

They are the SA, beyond criticism. As Roehm himself said many times: "The battalions of Brown Shirts were the training school of National Socialism."

However, on July 31, 1933, Roehm himself, under pressure from law-abiding segments of the Party, is obliged to recommend to the SA the observation of certain elementary rules. "I am try-ing," he writes,

> to preserve and guarantee fully the rights of the SA as soldiers in the vanguard of the National Socialist Rev-olution. . . . I assume responsibility for all actions taken by the SA which may not necessarily conform to current legal provisions, but which serve the exclusive interests of the SA. In this context it is proper to re-member that the leader of an SA organization has the right to execute up to twelve members of a hostile or-ganization in reprisal for the execution of one SA member.
>
> These executions are officially ordered by the Füh-rer; they must be carried out swiftly, and with mili-tary rigor.
>
> However, I have been informed of incidents—rare, it is true—in which certain members of SA or-ganizations—I do not wish to designate these men by the name SA, which they do not deserve—have been guilty of inexcusable excesses.
>
> These excesses include the following: the satisfac-tion of personal vengeance, inadmissible cruelty, ex-tortion and pillage.

Captain Roehm expresses himself as indignant with "these profaners of SA honor and the SA uniform," and threatens with "immediate, exemplary death any responsible SA leader who, through a misconceived sense of indulgence, fails to intervene." But by the eighth of August the SA are no longer part of the auxiliary police organized by Goering: their indiscipline, strength and menacing independence have perhaps already set them apart from the central power.

That was a year ago, the summer of 1933.

2

Friday, June 29, 1934
Bad Godesberg: Hotel Dreesen

9:00—9:30 P.M.

Braking violently, a car has just pulled up in front of the Hotel Dreesen. Policemen move forward even before the doorman has had time to come out onto the steps. When the passenger emerges from the car, everyone recognizes Joseph Goebbels. High-strung, looking even paler and thinner than usual, he salutes quickly and walks toward Brückner, who has come out to meet him. The two men shake hands, and Oberleutnant Brückner points to the terrace where Goebbels will find the Führer. Goebbels smooths back his hair and limps up the steps. Walter Breitmann recognizes the bony face with its hollow cheeks and tightly stretched skin, his gleaming eyes testifying to the anxious will of a sickly cripple. Thanks to his quick intelligence, sharpened by his sense of physical inferiority, Goebbels has moved upward from his position as Gregor Strasser's secretary to become the undisputed grand master of Nazi Party propaganda. He supplanted his former boss by betraying him, joining Hitler when the two came into conflict.

Goebbels climbs the steps, dragging his weak leg, a fixed smile baring teeth which seem too large for his chiseled face. Breitmann steps back to let Goebbels pass: the party intellectual, small, dark, and highly-strung—not at all an Aryan type. When he became Propaganda Minister, the Alte Kämpfer, "the old fighters," Nazis who admired strength, smiled ironically. As the SA sang:

> Mein lieber Gott, mach mich blind
> Dass ich Goebbels arisch find.
>
> (Dear God, make me blind
> That I may Goebbels Aryan find.)

It is because of the SA that Goebbels has come to Godesberg this evening. Goebbels salutes Hitler, sits down beside him and begins to speak, gesturing as he talks. The Chancellor seems distant and suspicious. He listens in silence, watching that face, whose long chin and overwide mouth seem to be in constant, almost spasmodic motion. The flow of words is rapid, and each word produces a facial contraction, a grimace which is almost a wince, marked by deep, wide lines around the mouth. Adolf Hitler watches and listens. Later, Joseph Goebbels remembered that evening: "As I watched him weighing his painful choice, I was filled with admiration for the man, bearing on his shoulders responsibility for the fate of millions. On the one hand, there was the tranquillity and peace of Germany, and on the other, the men who, until that moment, had been his trusted familiars."

Joseph Goebbels is one of those familiars, and Hitler watches him. The "lame duck" of the Party is not a director, like the others. He has no troops at his command, no SA or SS—simply a tactician's brilliance, which enables him to sense the winning side. And he is also an intellectual—with Rosenberg, one of the few Nazi leaders to have a university degree: he is a Doctor of Literature. But after the university, his professional life quickly met with failure. He failed to obtain the post of literary critic on the *Berliner Tageblatt*—the Jews' paper, as he called it. Embittered and cynical, he turned to the Nazis. In this new party, still short of assets, his cynicism and his gifts were, and are, highly valued. Goebbels is a talented propagandist and organizer, but above all knows how to exploit the "social" and "radical" aspects of the Party—the formulae which Hitler established with Anton Drexler in 1920, in a program of twenty-five points declaring that the new party was not simply Nationalist, but Socialist. These points stated that "revenues which are not the product of labor and effort must be abolished. The slavery of interest rates must be broken . . . employees must share in the profits of big business." Together with Gregor Strasser, Goebbels popularized this aspect of the first Nazi program.

Now, on June 29, 1934, Hitler carefully watches this "Nazi of the Left," this intimate whom he had played against Strasser, with whom he had won, who has now come to him at the precise moment when it has become necessary to break those—notably in the SA—who still naïvely insist on "the Revolution."

The Revolution: more often than not this means jobs; quite simply jobs other people already have. At Danzig, soon after the Nazi takeover, Hermann Rauschning, President of the Senate of the Free City, received one of the Alte Kämpfer, one of the veterans of Nazism's first successes, who demanded, now that Hitler was Chancellor, positions of substantial advantage. The man shouted at Rauschning: "I won't go back down the hill again! You can wait if you like; you're not sitting on hot coals! I've got no job, and I'm staying here at the top whatever it costs me because I know I won't be back. Someone like me never reaches the top twice."

These SA, who were promised a national and a socialist revolution, wanted everything at once. They wanted what they were promised because among them there were also businessmen, the last of the great merchants, who wanted power and riches, who wanted the Revolution turned to their own profit. Furthermore, the Nazi Party, now the official party of the government, is filling up with "respectable" people, Hitler wears a tail coat, and the rough, proletarian veterans wonder if they haven't become the dupes of the victory they won. The misfits and the discontented, all hoping to benefit by the change of regime, joined these Alte Kämpfer. They are given a physical examination, administered the oath and incorporated into the SA. Sometimes the new recruits are used right away: if a man can be killed or arrested, that means an apartment to be occupied or a job to be taken over, or goods to distribute to the SA membership: but this is clearly not enough.

Hitler watches Goebbels as he talks, bringing his leader up to the minute on the situation in Berlin, which he has just left in such a hurry that he had no time to see Goering first. He flew straight to Bonn, where he was told that the Führer had left for an inspection tour of RAD camps. At Essen he was told that Hitler was at the Hotel Dreesen in Godesberg, for a political meeting that afternoon. So he had decided to come to Godesberg immediately.

Across the river from the hotel the band of the RAD is playing, alternating the "Horst Wessel Lied" and the "Saar Lied" ("Comrades, our men killed by the 'Reaction' and the Reds, are with us in spirit, and march in our ranks") with military marches, including Hitler's favorite, the "Badenweilermarsch."

It is cool now, and even in the darkness one can sense that the sky has clouded over, that at any moment a summer storm may break. Goebbels is still talking. He had, of course, dropped Gregor Strasser after 1926, when the latter had refused to align the Nazi Party with the traditional Right. And he had reattached himself to the forces of Hitler, who, after the failure of the putsch of November, 1923, understood that he must attain power with the help of conservative elements, and that therefore his social and revolutionary program must be limited to anti-Semitism. But can one ever be sure? Had Goebbels kept in touch with Roehm for too long? Was he, perhaps, suspect? Hitler remains silent.

Goebbels keeps on talking. He no longer has anything in common with Ernst Roehm—the Roehm who, in June, 1933, pro-

claimed: "We have won a great victory, but it is not a victory"—
and who is still a menace: "If the middle class think it is enough
for the State to change its emblem, they are wrong. It is not
enough. Whether it suits them or not, we shall continue our struggle. When they finally understand what is at stake, we shall fight
together. But if that is not what they want, we shall fight without
them—and if necessary, against them."

Roehm is incorrigibly provocative. When Goering announced
the licensing of the SA auxiliary police, for instance, the Chief of
Staff assembled his troops. Nearly one year ago, on August 6,
1933, in the summer heat, at least eighty thousand members of the
SA, wearing brown uniforms, collected near the airfield in
Tempelhof, a district of Berlin. The sky was cloudy, and the air
seemed heavy with heat and passion. Roehm did not mince his
words, which were received with shouts of passionate approbation.
"Those who think that the work of the SA is done," he cried,
"must accept the idea that we are here, and that we shall stay here,
whatever happens."

The SA themselves were more precise. "We must clean up the
pigsty," they said, gesturing with thick hands accustomed to dealing blows. "Some pigs want too much; we'll have to shove them
back from the trough."

Roehm does not back down. Is he simply following his troops;
is he pushing them forward so that he will not be overwhelmed
by them, so that he can channel their anger; or is he sustaining
their disaffection and their hopes of plunder so that he can count
on their support in his personal struggle for power?

In November, 1933, he repeats his offense. In a Berlin veiled
by icy fog, groups of SA take up positions in front of the massive
Sportpalast. The hall is already full: fifteen thousand NCOs of the
Sturmabteilung are there, massively impressive in their brown
uniforms. They salute Captain Roehm when he appears on the
platform and launches into a blunt speech: "Many voices have
been raised among the middle classes claiming that the SA has
outlived its usefulness. . . . These gentlemen are very much mis-

taken." The audience rises to its feet and cheers. "We will extirpate the old bureaucratic spirit of the petite bourgeoisie, with gentleness if possible, if not, without it." Further shouts of acclamation.

Afterward the SA scatter through the neighboring streets and cafés. Soon, they say, the second Revolution, the real Revolution, will come—the Night of Long Knives—and they wait for it, not alone but with all those who fear a prolongation of troubled times. During this Night of Long Knives, what throats will be cut? And when will it come, this night so ardently longed for by the SA, for which they have spontaneously found a name? In the early months of 1934 people are afraid. Hitler's assumption of power barely a year earlier now seems like a moment of calm compared to what the Brown Shirts are preparing. "We are not a bourgeois club," Roehm reminds them. "I do not wish to lead men who are acceptable to shopkeepers, but revolutionaries who will drag their country after them."

However, the shopkeepers and the rest of the country long for civil order; isn't that why Hitler was brought to power?

As Hitler listens to Goebbels, a torchlight parade of the RAD, shouting and singing rhythmically, marches along the river bank. The storm has drawn closer: in the valley between the hills one can hear the roll of thunder, and toward Bonn, blue flashes of lightning break the darkness on the horizon, lighting up the dark clouds bearing down on Godesberg. The parade, with its uniforms, half-visible in the torchlight, and its songs and slogans shouted into the Rhenish night, seems to exemplify order and discipline. But Captain Roehm has not yielded.

He has continued to defend his SA. As a young captain, in the mud of the trenches, he had already made himself the spokesman of the ordinary soldier, interpreting his men to the distant and lordly officers of the General Staff. Now his men are the Brown Shirts, who repeat these words, which infuriate the Alte Kämpfer:

"Today, now that we have won the fight, now that victory is ours, and the anti-German scum is at our feet, you, too, are here, shouting even louder than we, 'Heil Hitler!'—as if you also had fought. Slimy, disgusting, you insinuate yourselves into our ranks . . . trying to profit by what we have won with our blood."

Opportunists rushing to join the victorious Nazis are described by a word especially coined for them: *Märzgefallene* (Johnny-come-latelies). Aligning themselves with the Nazi victory, they arouse the ire of the SA:

> Listen well, you men of the past,
> You shall no longer insult the Alte Kämpfer. . . .

Soon the Night of Long Knives will come, the night in which accounts will be settled with the "guardians of reaction," as the SA call them. And Roehm has aligned himself with his men. On April 16, 1934, he defends their claim to the common rights from which the Ministry of the Interior tried to exclude them:

"During the years of struggle before our assumption of power, when we needed strong men, citizens who had deviated from the acceptable norms of daily life in their pasts came and joined our ranks. These men, burdened with police records, came to us because they thought that service in the SA would obliterate their pasts. Now, however, many 'old fighters' of the SA have had to retire because of their records . . . this in the Third Reich, for which they risked their lives. . . . The bourgeois mentality will never understand that it is entirely possible to keep such elements in the Sturmabteilung."

So Roehm spoke, in defense of his organization. During the spring, Hitler's old comrade senses that the Führer is slowly changing, growing more aloof toward the "old fighters," and with his imprudent, arrogant, bullying frankness, does not hesitate to say what he thinks.

When he runs into Rauschning, he blazes up: "How decadent Adolf's become! He's just bought himself a black suit. . . . He is betraying all of us now; he sees only reactionaries and mistrusts all his old friends."

This is the voice of disappointed friendship, an almost amorous disappointment, from one of Hitler's comrades of longest standing. Roehm, a homosexual, is linked beyond the range of normal sentiment to the man in whom he places his confidence. He surrounds himself with young sons of the nobility, who form a brilliant staff with the faces of perverse angels: Baron von Falkenhausen, Count von Spreti, the Prince von Waldeck: all aides-de-camp to Captain Roehm, who knows how to look after faithful supporters and who talks too much.

Every morning, Roehm goes riding in the Tiergarten. With one or two companions he trots through the fresh April air, down the Siegesallee, bordered by the statues of thirty-two Prussian sovereigns, cutting the park from north to south. Then Roehm slows down his horse and, leaning into his stirrups, his torso bulging outward, begins a harangue. His group passes the Wrangel Fountain, the monuments to Goethe and to Lessing, and turning down one of the paths toward Potsdam, which strollers avoid after dark, crosses the little brook that runs through the park.

"One April morning," a habitual companion of the Captain remembers, "we met a group of high Party functionaries. Roehm watched them as they went by, and then said, in a voice full of scorn and mistrust. 'Look at those people over there. The Party isn't a political force any more; it's turning into an old-age home. People like that might have been useful before the decision was made in our favor; now they're just dead weight. We've got to get rid of them quickly; only after that can the real Revolution begin."

Roehm's voice rings with determination as he presses his horse into a trot.

"How will that be possible?" one of Roehm's companions asks.

"I have my SA."

An April morning in the Tiergarten, 1934.

Hitler's supporters—those who fear the killers' long knives, who are reassured by big business and the Chancellor as a partisan of law and order—know what Roehm and his SA hope for. Roehm does not dissimulate. On April 18, 1934, the man whom Hitler addresses as "du," who commands the largest force in the Third Reich, Minister of State and Chief of Staff of the Sturmabteilung, decides to strike a public blow. He calls an official press conference in Berlin for the diplomatic corps and foreign journalists. Every correspondent and every ambassador is present. When Roehm stands up, thick-set and squat in his brown uniform, the room falls silent. Everyone understands that Roehm is really speaking to Germany, to his comrades in power and to Adolf Hitler.

Roehm speaks first of the principles of National Socialism.

"National Socialism," he cries, "signifies a spiritual rupture with the thinking of the French Revolution of 1789." This is banal, and a repetition of what Rosenberg, the Party ideologue, has been saying for years. The general tone of expectation diminishes; perhaps everyone has been mistaken in Roehm.

The Captain pauses for a moment. In the large, brilliantly lit room the air is heavy and hot; people cough, chairs creak. Through the large windows, one can see the garden, bathed in the fresh, April light.

"I am going to talk to you about the Sturmabteilung, its essence and nature." Immediately everyone in the room is silent and alert. "The SA is the heroic incarnation of the will and thought of the German Revolution." Roehm then launches into the history of the organization he commands. "The law of the SA," he continues, "is very clear: obedience unto death to the supreme leader of the SA, Adolf Hitler. My possessions and my blood, my strength and my life, everything for Germany."

So far, Roehm's talk has been a simple repetition of well-known formulae; his audience realizes it will have to wait. Roehm's Bavarian-accented voice continues, flat but powerful, the voice of an officer accustomed to giving orders. "The struggle of these long years, toward the realization of the German Revolution—the stage we have now reached—has taught us vigilance.

Long, bitter experience has taught us how to recognize both the declared and the secret enemies of the new Germany in whatever disguise."

Could this mean that the enemies of the new Germany hide behind Nazi masks? Might anyone be considered an enemy of the SA? Roehm's phrase is aggressive and maladroit, alarming to anyone not behind him and his SA.

"What we have made is not simply a nationalist Revolution," he goes on, "but a National Socialist Revolution, with the emphasis on the word 'Socialist.'" The tone of his speech rises to a pitch of dramatic intensity unusual before an audience of diplomats and foreign journalists. "Reactionaries, bourgeois conformists," he shouts, "we feel like vomiting when we think of them." The room is silent, an intense and embarrassed silence, as if the words just uttered, and their tone, are not fitting, as if Roehm has mistaken his public and setting, imagining himself at the Sportpalast. "The SA," he concludes, "is the National Socialist Revolution!" Applause rings out from the back and sides of the room where the NCOs of the Sturmabteilung stand listening. Roehm sits down; his aides-de-camp, especially Count von Spreti, congratulate him warmly.

Now, two months later, on the terrace of the Dreesen, Goebbels and Hitler are thinking of that occasion, even though they do not refer to the exact terms of Roehm's speech. There is no need to; Hitler remembers Roehm's words exactly.

Suddenly, the storm breaks. A few enormous drops splatter on the terrace, as a fresh wind springs up, swirling along with it a light flurry of dust. A thunderclap bursts nearby, and rain, quickly violent, sweeps across the garden in front of the terrace, making the trees and hedges double over. Everyone rushes for shelter, except Hitler and Goebbels. The Führer slowly stands up, shaking his head and laughing as he pushes back his wet hair. Goebbels laughs with him, and walks along beside him, gesturing largely.

Outside, in front of the hotel, the singing goes on, with even greater gusto than before, as if the rain is testing the energy of each young man, allowing him to demonstrate his personal resilience. Then the wind drops, as suddenly as it began; the last drops fall, and everything is calm again. An unexpected, reviving freshness rises from the damp ground.

Dry chairs are brought out onto the terrace for the Führer and for Goebbels. When Hitler reappears, the crowd shouts in recognition. Hitler responds with an almost mechanical salute. The crowd cheers again. Later, looking back on that evening, Goebbels remembers: "The Führer seemed in a thoughtful, serious mood. He stared out at the clear darkness of the night, which after the purification of the storm stretched peacefully across a vast, harmonious landscape."

The conversation between Hitler and Goebbels begins again. Brückner appears from time to time with messages. Who is loyal to the Chancellor, and who is not? Had not Roehm himself, on the twentieth of April, barely two days after his speech to the diplomatic corps, renewed his vow of fidelity? That was on the occasion of Hitler's forty-fifth birthday. Throughout Germany there were speeches and celebrations; youth clubs organized parades, and at Party meetings, beneath huge portraits of the Führer, orators exhorted the crowds to shouts of "Heil Hitler!" Goebbels had orchestrated all these ceremonies from the Propaganda Ministry. Roehm eulogized Hitler in an order of the day. "Adolf Hitler, Supreme Leader of the SA . . . It has been, is and always will be our happiness and pride to be the most loyal of his followers, on whom he can depend in good and, even more, in bad times. . . . Long live Adolf Hitler, the Führer of all the Germans, the Supreme Leader of the SA." Is Roehm a dissimulator, a plotter, or is he the adversary not so much of Hitler as of those whom the SA refer to as the "Reaction"?

Hitler has to make a choice, and Goebbels is there to see that he hesitates no longer. Further, he is there so that he will know from the first instant what the choice is.

An SS comes up to Oberleutnant Wilhelm Brückner and speaks to him in a low voice. Hitler's aide-de-camp quickly gets up and goes inside. Goebbels falls silent: like the Chancellor, he will wait. Then Brückner comes back with a message.

The message is from Reichsminister Goering. The Chancellor reads it and hands it to Goebbels. In Berlin, Karl Ernst, Obergruppenführer of the Sturmabteilung, has placed his SA in a state of alert, beginning the afternoon of Friday, June 29. Goebbels confirms this: he had been about to give the Führer the same information. It is serious news. Does it mean that the Sturmabteilung has decided to move into a phase of direct action in the capital? Is this the beginning of the SA's Night of Long Knives? Karl Ernst is a determined man, one of the SA leaders who has risen from nothing by acting as general thug for the Nazi Party, with scruples diminishing as the opportunities for power and wealth increased. Now the thugs have achieved success.

Karl Ernst is not yet thirty-five; he commands 250,000 men. Formerly a hotel doorman and café waiter, he now favors flamboyant uniforms, overloaded with medals and insignia. The cap of an SA Obergruppenführer (Lieutenant General) sits at a casual angle on his large, vulgar head, the head of a delinquent boy, whose fleshy mouth suggests gross appetites. He likes to seduce heiresses whose families belong to Berlin's high society. He is also said to be a homosexual. His cynical laugh breaks out and his eyes light up when he visits the abandoned warehouses or cellars transformed into bunkers where the SA "corrects" recalcitrant Germans. Ernst's men are themselves exempt from punishment: theft, murder, rape—all are "political," and Ernst guarantees protection to the perpetrators. In Berlin, people are afraid of him; for some, he is simply a sadist, a common thug, transformed into a responsible official, representing order and the State. Nonetheless, he is received in good society; he is constantly seen with August Wilhelm of Prussia, the fourth son of the Kaiser. This is the man who has just placed his men in a state of alert. Has the discontent of the Brown Shirts hatched a conspiracy?

As early as the end of April, Ernst had discussed his problems confidentially in an unexpected quarter. He had received the

French Military Attaché, General Renondeau—in itself a considerable satisfaction for a successful adventurer, and a considerable gauge of success. For the General's benefit, Ernst boasted of his past exploits and his new responsibilities. The private conversation lasted for almost two hours. "He recited for me," the General recorded, "many episodes of a career which was still at its beginning, but which, until Hitler seized power, was one of great risk and audacity." As one of the "old fighters," Ernst was indefatigable.

"I said to him," General Renondeau continued, "that his present duties must be easy for him to fulfill in comparison with what he had done in the past. He replied: 'You are mistaken. We have promised a lot—promises which are exceedingly difficult to keep. We must pacify many who are impatient and unreasonable. First, I took care of my old comrades who fought their way up with me. They have all been settled into jobs. But now there are others, and dealing with them isn't easy.'" General Renondeau added: "This admission by one of the most ardent of the SA I had yet met seemed to me significant."

If Goebbels and Goering can be believed, these dissatisfied Berlin SA are now in a state of alert, ready to fight.

Once again, the roar of a motorcycle disturbs the quiet of the Hotel Dreesen: another message from Goering about the situation in Berlin and Munich. In Munich, too, the SA are in a state of alert. The Chancellor rereads the communiqué, but says nothing. Goebbels, sitting opposite him, recalls later: "The Führer, as in other serious and dangerous situations, acted once again according to his old principle—say only what absolutely must be said, and say it only to those who absolutely must hear it." Hitler says nothing; Goebbels is not yet a party to his private decisions. Instead, Hitler dictates a reply to Goering.

Throughout that day of Friday, June 29, Hitler has exchanged messages with Hermann Wilhelm Goering, each time by air. Planes have taken off for Tempelhof either from the airport at Essen or from Hangelar, near Bonn, to be met by a messenger. Goering has replied in the same manner, combining secrecy and speed, which is very much Goering's style, a style appropriate to his combined duties as Minister Without Portfolio in Hitler's cabinet, Minister of the Interior in the Prussian government, and Air Commissioner of the Reich. The Chancellor knows that he need have no fear of a plot between Reichsminister Goering and Chief of Staff Roehm of the Sturmabteilung.

In high Nazi circles it is known, as the Chancellor is well aware, that on September 15, 1933, the two men discreetly clashed. Hermann Goering had wished to preside at a large parade of Nazi forces on the day of the opening session of the new Council of State; he wanted the combined forces of the SS and SA to march past himself alone. But Roehm and Karl Ernst, who were to be ignored, let Goering know that if the ceremony took place without them there would be general indiscipline in the ranks of the Brown Shirts, making Goering look ridiculous. Goering was obliged to yield. A hundred thousand men in brown and black took part in the parade, but they marched past three Nazi leaders. Ernst and Roehm had made Goering step down, but Goering was not a man to admit this—all the more so as his opposition to Roehm was profound, dating back for many years, based on far more than rivalry over a parade.

With Karl Ernst, too, Goering has old scores to settle, old ties, and shared guilt.

On September 21, 1933, the day on which the trial of Marinus van der Lubbe and the Communists, accused of setting the Reichstag fire of February, 1933, opened before the Supreme Court of Leipzig, an SA celebration was at its height in a large Berlin hotel. There were heavy drinking and singing; men clasped each other's shoulders, swaying to the rhythms of Nazi war songs. In one corner of the room, Obergruppenführer Karl Ernst stood talking and drinking, surrounded by admiring toadies. Someone mentioned the opening of the Leipzig trial of the Communist, Dimitrov; the possible causes of the Reichstag fire were discussed. No one mentioned Goering's involvement, or Roehm's. Roehm had been ready to place a group of SA at the disposal of the Reichs-minister—ready to set the building on fire as a pretext for the repression the Nazis wished to introduce a month after taking power.

Obergruppenführer Ernst let out a great laugh: people looked at him and fell silent. "If I said, 'Yes, I set the fire,' I'd be a bloody fool," he shouted. "And if I said, 'No, I didn't,' I'd be a bloody liar." He laughed again. Such complicities between an executor and an organizer are always dangerous. Ernst and Goering have reason to mistrust each other. Ernst above all has reason, for Goering is not a man to tolerate obstacles.

As early as the First World War, the brilliant flight officer with hard eyes in a handsome, even-featured face was known to his comrades as a man who attained his goal no matter what the price. He was a strict, authoritarian officer, as Lieutenant Karl Bodenschatz said of him later: "It was evident in his gestures, and in his way of talking." As a pilot credited with many kills, Goering had collected decorations: the Iron Cross, the Lion of Zähringen with Swords, and above all, the Order of Merit, the highest decoration of the German Army. As Commander of the Richthofen Escadrille, he was ready to shoot down revolutionaries.

When the Armistice fell over Germany, Goering, the brilliant hero, belonged to the group of dissident officers who proclaimed the necessity of disobedience to the new regime. He stated his beliefs one evening at the Opera in Berlin, interrupting General Wilhelm Reinhard, the Minister of War. "Comrades," he shouted, "I beg you to maintain your hatred, the profound and tenacious hatred which is no more than the brutes who have dishonored the German people deserve. . . . The day will come when we shall chase these enemies from our beloved Germany. Ready yourselves for that day. Arm yourselves for that day. Work for that day."

Shortly after, Goering left the Army, refusing to work for a republican government. He entered the aeronautics industry, traveled and, by chance, met Karin von Kantzow in Sweden. A classical beauty with a fascinating sweetness and grace of manner, she was married to a Swedish aristocrat. Goering fell in love with her; it was a passionate romance. They married and returned to Germany, in love, passionately patriotic. Shortly after their return, Goering met Hitler in the Bavarian capital. "For a long time," Goering wrote, "he had been looking for a leader who had distinguished himself during the war . . . and who would thus possess the necessary authority. The fact that I placed myself at his disposal—I, who had been the Commander of the Richthofen Escadrille—seemed to him a stroke of luck."

Rapidly, Hermann Goering became responsible for the Sturmabteilung, created by Ernst Roehm. Thus, for the first time, the paths of these two men crossed. But Goering, the former national hero, touched with the glory which surrounds surviving pilots; Goering, linked to the traditional circles of the Army and the aristocracy, married to a wealthy Swedish Countess; Goering was a very different personality from Roehm, the former combat officer. From the beginning, Goering had been a link between Hitler and conventional society, as well as a force the Führer could set against Roehm, playing them against each other so that he need not depend absolutely on either.

Goering was to pay dearly for his entry into the Nazi Party, and for the responsibilities he assumed. During the unsuccessful putsch of November 9, 1923, as the SA paraded through the streets, and Hitler's bodyguard shouted to the police, massing their fire power, "Don't shoot! General Ludendorff is coming!" when the first sinister shots rang out, Hermann Goering fell, seriously wounded in the groin. He was pulled into the shelter of a doorway and given rough first-aid. He lost a lot of blood but somehow was saved from arrest. Under clandestine conditions, however, the wound was poorly treated, and to ease his pain it became necessary to give him increasingly large doses of morphine. He grew fat, his face sagged, his steely eyes dimmed. The once slim, authoritarian officer of 1918 became an obese drug addict, suffering from epileptic fits, who had to be confined to a hospital.

However, he pulled himself together, took several detoxification cures and, above all, flung himself into political action: Reichstag deputy, Nazi agent in high financial and military circles, he soon became President of the Reichstag, and Minister of the Interior in the Prussian government.

Now active, rejoicing in his own strength, he wishes to assure his hold on power. For a man like Goering, not satisfied with fine words alone, who has seen the Nazi domination rise from violence in the streets, power means, first of all, fighting men: especially since Roehm is now Chief of Staff of the SA.

But Goering is extremely adroit. He knows it would be unwise to clash directly with a rival who commands millions of men. So Reichsminister Goering moves obliquely against Roehm, as well as toward the destruction of the Nazis' adversaries. "German brothers," he shouts in Frankfurt on May 3, 1933, "no bureaucracy will ever paralyze me. Today, I am concerned primarily with justice. My mission is to destroy and exterminate. . . . I will not be able to lead such a struggle—a fight to the death—with only the police at my disposal. I shall lead our struggle with those who stand here before me—the Brown Shirts." All the 25,000 SA and 15,000 SS have to do to become police is to slip white armbands over their brown and black sleeves. Nevertheless, the power of Ernst Roehm has to be reduced; Roehm, who speaks of liquidating the reactionaries, while Goering is most at ease with Ruhr magnates, Prussian landowners and officers of the German Staff.

There is also the fact that within his Prussian fiefdom Goering clashes daily with the power of the Sturmabteilung. SA advisers are attached to every administrative department; Prussian police prefects even wear SA uniforms: all of these are men of power, and are quite outside Goering's control.

So the Reichsminister maneuvers. Upon his assumption of power in Prussia he organizes a special branch of the police under the command of Rudolf Diels based on an existing function (Section 1A) of the Berlin prefecture. Diels is a capable and active man. He has collected experts in intelligence work and young, effective criminologists to create a political bureau of information which will become the State Secret Police. The service grows; specialists are drawn to it, and are given complete freedom of action. They may proceed, if they wish, in total disregard of the Constitution. Soon, Diels' men leave the police headquarters in the Alexanderplatz and install themselves in the Karl-Liebknecht Haus, the former offices of the Communist Party, and in 8 Prinz-Albrecht Strasse, near Goering's home. Henceforth, Diels' service will be known by its official name, which will resound throughout the world for years like a knell: Geheime Staatspolizei or Gestapo. The leader is Hermann Goering.

HIMMLER, HEYDRICH AND THE SS

Goering and the Gestapo are immediately obliged to defend their authority against the SA, whose prisons Diels is cleaning out, and against the SS, whose leader is the shadowy Reichsführer SS Heinrich Himmler. Goering quickly understands that he cannot fight Roehm and Himmler at the same time, that he will have to choose between them. One day in October, 1933, Diels walks into his office to find Herbert Packebusch, one of Gruppenführer SS Karl Daluege's confidential agents, going through his papers. He has the man arrested, but next morning, after talking to Daluege, Goering orders the man set free. Rudolf Diels understands immediately: his chief has decided on an alliance with Himmler.

Reichsführer SS Himmler is, theoretically, a subordinate of Roehm's. Every year, without fail, he swears an oath of allegiance to him.

"As a soldier and friend, I wish you all you could desire in obedience and loyalty," Himmler writes to Roehm. "It has been and always will be my greatest pride to be counted among your most faithful followers."

But this allegiance is also a guarantee of jealousy and ambition.

Himmler has risen swiftly. His SS in their black uniforms with their death's-head emblem are hand-picked troops. Acceptance into the SS is not automatic, and discipline is strict. In Berlin, popular wisdom has it that the SS does not talk, it acts. They leave street displays and flourishes to the SA. They are the hard, impenetrable shield which really protects the Party. Each Nazi leader has his personal SS guard, who wears embroidered on his sleeve in white letters the name of the man he protects. These black militiamen are in fact the elite, shadowy overlords whose real power, discreet and effective, continually grows. Reichsführer Himmler himself makes the comparison with the SA. "The SA," he says, "are the common soldiers; the SS is the Elite Guard. There is always an elite guard. The Persians had one, the Greeks, Caesar, Napoleon and old Fritz. For the New Germany, the SS is the Elite Guard."

Himmler is a cold realist who understands the role of the police, and adds to the directorship of the SS the presidency of the political police of Bavaria (Bay Po Po). For this job he has found an accomplice—a former naval officer who was dismissed from the service: Reinhardt Tristan Eugen Heydrich. This icy seducer, with his athlete's body and hawk-nosed face that suggests a bird of prey, has seen his career shattered over an affair with a woman. Called before a jury of naval officers by Admiral Erich Raeder, Heydrich's testimony, involving a former mistress, was so signally lacking in any sense of honor that the jury decided on a penalty without appeal: "Immediate separation from the service for scandalous behavior." The only course left open to Heydrich was to join the SS. On June 14, 1931, he met Reichsführer SS Himmler. By October 5, Heydrich had joined the staff of the SS, as a Sturmführer in charge of organizing the intelligence section. In this capacity Heydrich will perform marvels: a calculating and dissimulating perfectionist, he organizes the Sicherheitsdienst (SD—the Security Service of the SS). As Himmler says, Heydrich is "a born intelligence agent, with a mind which knows how to unravel every thread, and tie it up again at precisely the necessary point." Heydrich wants to watch, control and spy on everything. His ambition is to make the SD the all-powerful intelligence service of the Nazi Party. He succeeds.

Throughout the German states, Himmler, the ideologue, and Heydrich, the technician, spin a web of secret police in the service of Hitler, and themselves, duplicating official organizations and functionaries. Soon, except for Prussia, Himmler and Heydrich control the Secret Police throughout Germany.

And Goering has decided to ally himself with them. Rudolf Diels becomes alarmed: he has clashed openly with the SS, and he has, in effect, been repudiated. Well aware of their methods, he flees to England. However, this is not yet the end of Goering's police powers: he is ready for hand-to-hand combat. Diels is allowed to return to Berlin and by a decree dated November 9, 1933, is authorized to wear the uniform of an SS Standartenführer —proof that an agreement has been reached, that the past has been forgotten.

But the hidden struggle continues. Heydrich goes on with his work of undermining and organizing. He has the support of the Minister of the Interior, Wilhelm Frick, who wishes to unify the police of all the German states. Goering is obliged to give ground, inch by inch, because he needs Heydrich and Himmler and the SS to combat Roehm and his growing SA, who are increasingly restless and restive, parading through the towns and cities in dark columns preceded by drums and trumpets, shouting loudly for the Revolution.

In April, 1934, Himmler achieves his goal: on the tenth of the month, accompanied by Heydrich and Goering, he visits the headquarters of the Gestapo at No. 8 Prinz-Albrecht Strasse. He has just gained control of the Prussian Secret Police. Rudolf Diels has been dismissed, and named Regierungspräsident of Cologne. By April 20, Himmler and Heydrich between them control the entire Secret Police apparatus of Germany.

Himmler and Heydrich divide their roles and functions: the Reichsführer is head and inspector of the Secret State Police

(Gestapo), while Heydrich, as representative of the Führer, directs the Geheime Staatspoliseiamt—the Gestapa (or Gestapo administration). Heydrich remains leader of the SD, which becomes the official Party intelligence service. Henceforth, Himmler and Heydrich direct the police forces which control Germany and the Party.

"From now on, the repression will be more severe," reports the *National Zeitung*. And to indicate that the SA will be watched too, the paper continues: "The term 'enemy of the State' is not confined solely to Bolshevik agents and agitators. It also includes all those who, by word or deed, whatever their intentions, compromise the existence of the Reich."

The writer adds, criticizing the supposed leniency of the preceding few months:

> Since the Revolution, our political enemies have not run any risks. During the first weeks there was some brutality, but today agitators, denigrators, saboteurs and calumniators of all kinds are exposed to worse than preventive detention, of varying duration, in a concentration camp. This kind of imprisonment has not been especially frightening, but all of this will now change. We shall not torture anyone; we shall shoot them—beginning with the Communists.

Every agitator is thus threatened with the firing squad. The SA has been given fair warning; Goering can congratulate himself for having chosen an alliance with the Reichsführer SS.

At Nuremberg, facing the Allied judges with his arrogant intelligence, Georing will explain how he reacted in April, 1934, when Hitler decided to entrust the direction of the Gestapo to Himmler and Heydrich.

"At that time," he explained, "I had not expressly opposed that arrangement. It was an unpleasant idea to me because I wished to direct the Secret Police myself. But when the Führer asked me to accept it on the grounds that it was correct and necessary so that our struggle against the enemies of the State could be waged uniformly throughout the Reich, I handed the police over to Himmler, who placed Heydrich at its head."

Thus Himmler has achieved his ends, and Roehm must include in his calculations this subordinate whose vast power will henceforth be secret, his net spreading over all Germany. Goering, who has given way, and who knows that he has in Himmler an ally against Roehm, is no less mistrustful. He swiftly creates a new, personal police, a new praetorian guard, the Landspolizeigruppe, which settles into quarters at Lichterfelde, near Berlin.

Now Goering feels more at ease. In his luxurious apartment on the Kaiserdamm, he receives royalty, assuming a light-footed manner, although he weighs close to 280 pounds, and shows everyone the portrait of his wife Karin, dead of exhaustion and emotional strain during the course of his struggle for power, and whose memory he honors with histrionic sincerity.

Hitler has rewarded him well for his services. In addition to his ministerial duties, Goering, as the Reich's Grand Master of the Wolf Hunt and Grand Master of Waters and Forests, is responsible for the protection of wildlife, drawing up precisely worded laws, and putting them into practice on the property he has conferred on himself in the district of Schorfheide, near the Wackersee. He builds a vast structure there—hunting box and seigneurial residence, sanctuary and mausoleum (his dream is to install his wife's body in the building)—which he names Karinhall. On the rough heath, where cold winds blow the fog through stands of dark trees, he uses his baroque residence to entertain in megalomaniac style, as a powerful and able master of the Reich. But the man whom Hjalmar Schacht, the financial wizard of the Reich, described as "a person whose knowledge concerning anything relevant to his position as a statesman was null" knows very well who his enemies are.

Roehm is one. Goering will have to get rid of him before he can enjoy his power, fortune and titles with any sense of ease. Goering collects titles: he has also just been made a general. In

Schacht's view, it was all ridiculous. "His behavior was so theatrical one had to compare him to Nero. A lady who had tea with Goering's second wife can remember the Field Marshal dressed in a kind of Roman toga with jeweled sandals. His fingers were covered with rings, and from head to foot his body glittered with precious stones. His face was made up, and he wore lipstick."

Ridiculous? Schacht added: "I have called Hitler amoral. Goering can only be called immoral and criminal." One of Hermann Goering's close relatives is very precise: "With his lack of scruple, he would have trampled on a corpse."

Hermann Goering, Heinrich Himmler, Reinhardt Heydrich: Roehm, Ernst and the SA have good reason for their distrust.

And it is Goering who is in communication with Hitler throughout the day, Friday, June 29, 1934, and who has just sent him another message, by air, to the Hotel Dreesen.

3

Friday, June 29, 1934
Bad Godesberg: Hotel Dreesen

9:30–10:00 P.M.

Goebbels watches the Chancellor as he reads the latest message. Later he remembers he was able to see from the Führer's face that the news from Berlin and Munich was serious. Goering's and Himmler's messages report on the state of tension of the SA, and their preparations. "The Führer was deeply wounded in spirit," Goebbels adds. "But he was also absolutely firm in his resolution to act without mercy, to put down the reactionary rebels who, hiding behind slogans of a second Revolution, planned to break the law and the bonds of fidelity which united them to the Führer and the Party, plunging the country into a turmoil whose end could not be foreseen."

Does Goebbels really believe in this menace, as he examines and confirms the messages Goering has sent the Führer from Berlin? He is sufficiently perceptive to understand that no matter what he thinks, that night, the twenty-ninth of June, he must accept the reality of the plot if he wishes to remain the Nazi leader and Minister he has become. He can congratulate himself for being where he is, in Hitler's shadow, the protégé of Goering, Himmler and Heydrich; for having chosen the right side in time.

For several months there have been signs, and Goebbels has always known how to interpret them. As an expert juggler of truth, he understands the value of words. The first warning signals were sounded almost a year earlier, on July 6, 1933.

On that day, Hitler himself received the Reichsstatthalter (governors of the Party districts) at the Chancellory. As the Führer walked into the large marble hall, all the Nazis of power and position were on their feet, saluting. It was one of those military-style meetings which Adolf Hitler loved above all things. His voice was loud and brutal, as if speaking past the walls of the room to all those millions of Brown Shirts whom the Nazi rise to power has not appeased.

"The Revolution," the Führer says, "is not a permanent condition; we cannot allow it to become so. The unleashed stream of revolution must be guided into the sure channel of evolution." This is tantamount to saying that the Revolution is over, that there will never be a second one.

On the sixteenth of July, in Leipzig, in a new speech, Hitler was even more outspoken: "Revolutions with successful beginnings are much more common than those which, having succeeded, have been stopped at the appropriate moment."

Undoubtedly, Goebbels' understanding that his relations with Roehm and the SA must henceforth be prudent dates from that time during the summer of 1933.

However, is an immediate choice necessary? Roehm is still powerful, and Hitler himself is still moving with extreme caution. A personal letter, the use of "du," and the promulgation in December, 1933, of the law of union between the Party and the State, the entry of Roehm into the government with his title of Chief of Staff of the SA—the game has not yet been played out.

Along with Roehm, Hess—that curious figure with the assymetrical face who acted as Hitler's secretary while he was writing *Mein Kampf,* imprisoned in the Landsberg fortress—entered the government as Hitler's first private secretary. As the Führer's personal representative, enjoying his total confidence, Rudolf Hess, with the look of a fanatic visionary, has now become the second man in the Party after Hitler himself.

Rudolf Hess takes a stand against the methods dear to the SA: "Each National Socialist should understand that the brutalization of adversaries is proof of a Judeo-Bolshevik mentality and represents an attitude unworthy of National Socialism." What must men like Karl Ernst, the Obergruppenführer who laughs in the tortured faces of his prisoners, think of such an attitude?

Naturally, one should not take Hess' insistence on "correct" methods of punishment literally. Goebbels understands perfectly that this insistence is simply the most effective means by which Hess can separate himself from the SA, forcing them to yield to the discipline of the Nazi government, and requiring from them, even in brutality, the order and methodical organization which are already the hallmarks of the Gestapo and the SS.

The warnings directed toward the SA grow more frequent and more pointed, but Goebbels does not join the chorus of the partisans of order. He waits, observing the positions taken by the contending parties, and understands. Goering licenses an auxiliary SA police and proclaims: "The moment the Führer and Chancellor of the National Socialist State judges the Revolution has ended and National Socialist reconstruction begun, every act not in conformity with penal law, no matter who initiates it, will be mercilessly suppressed."

Frick, the Minister of the Interior, is even more precise. "The most important task of the Reich government now," he writes, "is to consolidate, ideologically and economically, the absolute power concentrated in our hands. The success of this undertaking will be seriously compromised if we continue to speak of 'the next phase of the Revolution' or a 'second Revolution.'" This is once again a direct thrust at the SA. Frick concludes on a note of menace: "Anyone who continues to speak in these terms should get it into his head that by such talk he is in rebellion against the Führer himself, and will be dealt with accordingly." This was on July 11, 1933.

As the months pass, pointed complaints continue. Goebbels follows the progress of the assaults in the name of order—both subtle and direct—which the old German bureaucracy, rallying to National Socialism, or to the Party and its powerful leaders (Goering and Hess), directs at the SA and its leader.

On the sixth of October, Frick discloses that charges against the SA for offenses against the common law have been dismissed. The Minister of the Interior continues: "The administrative functions of the National Socialist State and of the police must no longer be disturbed by the inadmissible intervention of the SA. Any reprehensible acts committed by a member of the SA must be the object of energetic pursuit."

Goebbels knows how to read a communiqué: this means that the SA has to get back into line. Some months later, on February 24, 1934, after Roehm has become a minister, Hess throws out a new warning in the *Völkischer Beobachter*: "Every member of the SA is a Party combatant, like every political leader, or leader of the Hitler Youth. . . . There is not, and in the future will not be, any reason for an independent existence."

Roehm and the SA have to give way. They can chant, as they have previously:

> Listen well, men of the past,
> You shall no longer insult the Alte Kämpfer,

but their margin for maneuver has shrunk. Goebbels watches them flounder, and keeps his peace. He is well placed in Berlin, in the Party and in the government to keep his eyes on any intrigues or plots. Moreover, he is in touch with Ernst Roehm, and listens to him attentively, hoping to catch in the words of the Chief of Staff something that will reveal his intentions: "We must make

Germany completely ours, ein totaler S.A.-Staat." Roehm is extremely stubborn.

Goebbels also follows Himmler's progress toward secret power. He knows that Roehm is self-confident, optimistic, trusting; Himmler is an old friend of his from the heroic days of Munich in 1922–1923. At that time, Himmler belonged to the Reichskriegsflagge. At the time of the putsch he was at the barricades, holding the Party flag. Roehm likes his old friend Himmler. The growth of the SS doesn't worry him. He thinks it perfectly normal that some of the SA should become SS, especially as the strength of the SS cannot exceed 10 percent of that of the SA. Moreover, in the spring of 1934, Goebbels learns through his informers that Roehm and Himmler have met.

ROEHM AND HIMMLER

During the last days of February, several official cars drive into Rathenow from Berlin, forty-eight miles away. They drive rapidly through the little town at the moment when workers from the optical instruments factory are leaving the gray buildings on their bicycles for the midday break. The cars stop at the entrance to the Gross-Wudicke estate, which belongs to Herr von Gontard.

SA Standartenführer Count von Spreti, the aide-de-camp with the girlish face who is Roehm's latest passion, SS Gruppenführer Bergmann, Roehm's ADC with the title of Chief Adjutant, and finally, Rolf Reiner, Roehm's private secretary, step from Roehm's car.

From a second car step Himmler and his aide-de-camp, SS Obersturmbannführer (Lieutenant Colonel) Karl Wolff. Slowly the group, a mixture of black and brown uniforms, walk toward the estate buildings. They plan to eat there; the conversation is amicable. Roehm has even taken Himmler familiarly by the arm.

At the table, the tone of the conversation sharpens. Roehm,

who has eaten and drunk a great deal, speaks peremptorily to Himmler, informing him that the SS is conservative, that they are protecting the "Reaction" and the lower middle class. Himmler remains silent: he is not accustomed to public challenge. It is his ADC, Karl Wolff, who—as he remembers years later—comes to the defense of his superior and the SS.

Goebbels and the other Party leaders—above all, Goering— had known of the meeting and its object. Himmler is as always the apparently faithful supporter of Roehm, but his police network is growing. Goering communicates with him through intermediaries, especially through Pili Körner, who is the chief liaison man between "the mad aviator," as Goering is known to some professional officers, and the leader of the Black Shirts. Goering is looking for guarantees for himself, and is trying to push Himmler and Heydrich into opposition to Roehm.

Joseph Goebbels watches these preparations. He knows that in Berlin Himmler and Heydrich are collecting a group of "reliable" collaborators whom they have brought from Munich: Müller, Heisinger, Huber, and Flesch. The ring around Roehm draws tighter.

The Gestapo and Army intelligence agents in Berlin have found a former orderly from the officers' mess at Himmelstadt, a small town where Roehm was once garrisoned. He now runs a restaurant in the capital. Gentlemen whom there is no question of refusing come and put certain questions to him, precise questions about the remote past of Captain Roehm, and the private life of that past. The former orderly begins by saying that at Himmelstadt Roehm was involved in an affair with a young girl. Of course, the restaurant owner adds, all the orderlies knew about Roehm's private peculiarities.

"He was always trying to involve us orderlies in activities that were not moral."

The interrogators take down his deposition. When the police manifest an interest in the private life of a minister, that means, at the very least, that his private life is not beyond discussion, that someone is interested in building up a dossier toward an accusation.

April, 1934: Roehm proclaims to all that the Revolution must be continued, and carried to a successful conclusion. "Don't unbuckle your belts yet," he shouts to the SA; and, as always, the SA talk of "cleaning up the pigsties."

Toward the end of the month, Himmler asks Bergmann and Rolf Reiner to arrange another meeting between Roehm and himself. This interview is still shrouded in mystery, but it may well have been Roehm's final opportunity to be given a last chance. Goebbels knows nothing of it until after it has occurred. Apparently Himmler warned Roehm: "Homosexuality represents a danger to the movement." He doesn't implicate Roehm himself, but denounces SA Obergruppenführer Heines, Koch, Ernst and several others who are openly deviant. "Does it not constitute a grave danger to the Nazi movement," Himmler asks, "if it can be said that Nazi leaders are chosen for sexual reasons?"

Roehm doesn't answer; he simply nods and drinks. Himmler speaks of the rumors current in Berlin: that the SA leaders have organized a recruiting network that spreads throughout Germany, that draws young and handsome SA members to Berlin to participate in orgies arranged by Roehm and his ADCs. At this point Himmler contents himself with recalling the interests of the State, which override everything else. Roehm suddenly bursts into sobs, and taking Himmler by the shoulders vehemently thanks him for his advice. It seems as though, with the help of alcohol, Roehm has recognized the error of his ways and is promising to make amends, taking the advice of his old friend Himmler.

The leaders of the SS and the SA leave the secluded inn where the meeting was held. But the next morning, Himmler's agents report that one of the most fantastic orgies they have ever seen took place the night before at Roehm's headquarters. Bottles thrown from the windows smashed on the pavements below, and the sound of raucous laughter echoed in the street. Roehm himself had been an all-night participant, with his *Lustknaben,* his male prostitutes. Himmler is furious. Later, when he hears that Roehm had also journeyed through Germany, visiting SA units, he realizes that a confrontation cannot be postponed much longer. A few days after Roehm's trip, he takes one of his own to several towns and cities, giving his orders to the SS.

Joseph Goebbels, who has his own informers in every group, also senses that a showdown is near. He learns that Heydrich has begun to draw up lists of enemies, to which Himmler and Goering are adding names. Himmler is already talking of Viktor Lutze as a possible successor to Roehm.

Goebbels is clearly not the only one who knows about the dissension between Roehm and the other Nazi leaders. Toward the end of March, an Associated Press correspondent in Berlin asks some probing questions, but the Chancellory press service indignantly dismisses them as unfounded rumor. As is often the case in political circles, denial tends only to confirm. Hitler understands so well that he has convinced no one that a few days later he personally receives Louis P. Lochner, an American journalist. With the audacity and bluntness of American reporters, Lochner puts the pertinent question at once:

"Mr. Chancellor, it is said that among your close associates there are men who wish to replace you. It is further said that among the most eminent of these is a man who is trying to frustrate your measures."

Hitler is not outraged by this; on the contrary, he smiles. "He seemed to be passing in review the men who were closest to him in his struggle," Lochner notes, "and to be pleased with what he saw in them." Then the Chancellor states that within his entourage there is not the slightest rivalry with him. "Of course," he continues, "I am not surrounded by nullities but by real men. A zero is round, and rolls away when things go badly. The men close to me are straight and upright. Each has his own personality, each is ambitious. If they were not ambitious, they would not have arrived at their present positions. I admire ambition." The Chancellor strikes an attitude. "In such a group, composed of such personalities, friction is inevitable. But never has one of these men tried to impose his will on mine. On the contrary, they have all yielded absolutely to my wishes."

Is this duplicity on Hitler's part, or rather an expression of hope that in the factions around him everything can still be resolved by compromise? In any case, Goebbels is well aware of the Chancellor's hesitations. He keeps in touch with Roehm, and acts as intermediary between Hitler and the Chief of Staff. At the same time, he is ready to abandon Roehm if Hitler should give a clear sign that he has decided to liquidate him. Further, Goebbels is careful about his contacts with Roehm: the two men meet in discreet, secluded inns, without witnesses. Goebbels knows very well that Heydrich's lists are growing rapidly, with each name identified by a serial number. He knows also that Hess, Martin Bormann, and Major Walter Buch, president of the Uschla (the supreme tribunal of the Party), are collecting evidence of corruption and debauchery among the SA leaders; that entries on Heines, who took part in the assassination of Rathenau, are accumulating.

This round-faced SA Obergruppenführer—despite all the surface manifestations of a calm, discreet civil servant, well groomed and dignified—is a notorious homosexual. He is also one of Roehm's closest collaborators, and a participant in Roehm's orgies. In 1926 Hitler had excluded him from the Sturmabteilung; on Roehm's insistence, he was reinstated and given a command position.

In 1934 he became Chief of Police of Breslau. His staff resembles Roehm's—they are the objects of its chief's amorous passion. The homosexual Engels is Obersturmbannführer (Lieutenant Colonel), and the young Schmidt is aide-de-camp. This twenty-one-year-old is Heines' latest folly. Whatever that handsome young blond does, he is protected by his lover. Once, in a moment of drunkenness, he publicly kills a drinking companion with his sword, but the Chief of Police forbids the public prosecutor to intervene. In fact, Schmidt is motivated more by avid ambition than by homosexuality: as a Hitler youth of seventeen, he yielded to Heines because he needed the money. Beside this couple, the depraved Engels, a watchful intriguer, plays the part of Heines' evil genius. He is one of those who use the SA organization and the Hitler Youth to recruit participants for his erotic games. Moreover, one Peter Granninger, in whom the SA leaders have complete confidence, draws a monthly salary of some two hundred marks for the job of finding "friends" and organizing the festivals of debauchery which Roehm and his friends enjoy.

Goebbels knows all this. He knows also that a great deal of hatred has built up against Roehm and his close associates; that Major Walter Buch, and his son-in-law, Martin Bormann, have scores to settle with Roehm that go back over years; that in the name of morality they have been trying to strike him down ever since he returned from Bolivia to take over the SA. Roehm makes no effort to hide his proclivities. "I do not consider myself a 'good' man," he once said. "I have no such pretensions."

In 1932 Buch set in motion a plan to liquidate Roehm and his staff: Counts von Spreti and du Moulin Eckart and SA intelligence agent Georg Bell were pointed out to a group of killers led by the former Standartenführer Emil Traugott Danzeisen and a certain Karl Horn.

But Horn panicked, and revealed the plan to the SA. When the assassins fail one morning in an attempt to liquidate him, Roehm and von Spreti and du Moulin Eckart realize that Horn had not been lying.

Alarmed, they report the affair to the police, and in October, 1932, Emil Danzeisen is tried and sentenced to six months in prison for attempted murder. To protect himself, Roehm has even been in touch with the enemies of the Nazi Party, the Democrats.

In the Buch-Bormann group there is a sense of general outrage. They do not drop their pursuit of Roehm, and in the spring of 1934 are hard at work, compiling their dossiers and drawing up their lists. The principal difference from 1932 is that the Nazi

Party is now in power. Reichsführer SS Himmler, Heydrich, chief of the Gestapa and the SD, and Reichsminister Goering are at the root of the new operation. In 1932 Himmler did not openly move against Roehm, but acted, instead, as intermediary between Major Buch and Roehm. Perhaps he still remembered his first meeting with Roehm in May, 1922, at the Arzberger Keller in Munich, when Roehm persuaded him to join the Nationalist organization, the Reichskriegsflagge.

Twelve years have passed since then, and the situation has changed. Henceforth, Himmler is Roehm's adversary.

4

Friday, June 29, 1934
Bad Godesberg: Hotel Dreesen

10:00–10:30 P.M.

Suddenly the Führer stands up, and Goebbels realizes that an SS man he knows well is hurrying toward them: Gruppenführer SS Sepp Dietrich. Dietrich is of average height, with a square, powerful jaw and dazzling teeth, frequently bared by his large, calm smile. His smile is disturbing precisely because of those teeth, which are firm, white and clenched, like the teeth of a wild animal. The gilded oak leaves of his rank gleam against his black uniform. The Führer must have called him at the end of the afternoon, and Dietrich must have left for Godesberg immediately, first by plane from Berlin to Bonn-Hangelar, and then by road. Goebbels stands a few feet behind Hitler. The presence of Sepp Dietrich proves that the Führer is moving toward a decision, arming himself for action.

Dietrich is a faithful executor of orders, whose daily life takes place entirely within Hitler's entourage. He commands Hitler's personal guard—an SS unit of some two hundred hand-picked men. Members of the guard are characterized by absolute loyalty to the Führer; they must also be highly skilled in the military arts. Each man is a first-class marksman, and an accomplished athlete, chosen after a rigorous series of trials. Hitler is sure of Sepp Dietrich, and Dietrich is sure of his men—an essential, since Hitler lives in fear of assassination, and the guard is responsible for his life. At each of Hitler's public appearances, 120 men of the guard surround him with a triple security cordon. It was at Nuremberg, in September, 1933, at one of the first public ceremonies of the new regime, the Reichsparteitag, under the glow of thousands of burning torches held by the Nazis, that the Führer gave his guard its name: Leibstandarte SS Adolf Hitler. The Führer knows he can rely on this unit and its leader: their eyes are the eyes of fanatics, ready to kill or be killed.

The Gruppenführer SS salutes the Chancellor of the Reich. The Chancellor gives a brief order: "You will take a plane to Munich. As soon as you have arrived, telephone me here at Godesberg."

Dietrich salutes, clicks his heels and walks away. A few seconds later, one can hear the engine of his car, and its swift acceleration. Sepp Dietrich is a reliable officer. He will soon be in the Bavarian capital. From there, if necessity dictates, he can easily reach the little town of Wiessee.

Bad Wiessee lies on the west bank of the Tegernsee. The lake mirrors the wooden houses and hotels, built in the style of 1900. Rounded peaks ring the lake, their slopes alternating pasture and woodland. The peaceful, undulating green of Bavaria is interrupted here by the narrow, tapered lake, shaped like an oversized raindrop, reflecting its surroundings and replenished by mountain streams.

Couples stroll along the promenade at Wiessee before returning to their hotels and their cures. Wiessee has the soothing air of a watering place: springs of sulphurous, iodized, iron-rich waters, gush up in fountains. It is claimed the waters cure everything from rheumatism to cardiac difficulties, from gout to nervous complaints. Families hurry past: it is the hour for the baths, or for massage.

It is cool during these last days of June, 1934. The neighboring peaks of Wallberg, Baumgartenberg and Risserkogel—favored settings for scenic walks—are often shrouded by clouds. It is raining in the mountains, so the visitors stay in town, looking at the lake, or setting out in the small boats which travel between Egern, Rottach and Wiessee. Then there is the castle at Tegernsee, and the vast Abbey Park. One can also climb to the Giant Umbrella, the rotunda which affords a view over the whole panorama, of the lake and valley of Wiessach. On this Friday, June 29, many people have come from Munich, fleeing the Bavarian capital and its humidity and heat. Some are camping out; tents can be seen dotting the pastures. Perhaps these campers are Hitler Youth.

During their walks around the lake, tourists and persons taking the cure avoid the Pension Hanselbauer, which is set back from the road. During the day it is guarded by soldiers, and official cars often wait in its park. It is said that many SA leaders are staying there, including the Chief of Staff of the Sturmabteilung himself, Reichsminister Ernst Roehm, who suffers from rheumatism.

The white boats on the lake sway rhythmically. As on every evening, a cool breeze blows down from the mountains through the valley of Wiessach, raising little waves on the Tegernsee, rustling the leaves of the trees around the Pension Hanselbauer, where Ernst Roehm sleeps—less than an hour by road from Munich, where Gruppenführer SS Sepp Dietrich will soon be arriving.

After Dietrich's departure from Godesberg, it is quiet again. The birds have fallen silent, as if to catch their breath, and the band has stopped playing. Adolf Hitler restlessly paces the terrace. The arrival of Sepp Dietrich had momentarily eased his tension with an action to take, an order to give. But now he must wait again, and hesitate, and face the contradictory rush of his thoughts.

Every witness to that night mentions the Führer's face—deeply
lined and at the same time swollen and pale. His eyes are brilliant,
like the eyes of a sick man burning with fever. With a mechanical
gesture, he frequently brushes back the glossy lock of hair which
falls across his forehead. And he goes on waiting. Suddenly
trumpets ring out, shattering the quiet of the night, while the
silence of the Rhine Valley amplifies the sound, which fills the
night with its prolonged echo.

Brückner stands up: a man wearing a brown uniform has
just appeared on the terrace. It is Viktor Lutze, Obergruppenführer SA of the district of Hannover. Hitler walks toward Lutze
as the latter salutes. He takes Lutze by the hand and congratulates
him for having answered his call and arrived at Godesberg so
quickly. Lutze bows and clicks his heels. He says that he was
about to leave for Wiessee, where Roehm has called together the
leaders of the SA and where, so he had believed, Hitler himself
was supposed to arrive the next day for a discussion between
friends. Hitler makes a sweeping gesture, as if to brush these
considerations aside, and asks Lutze if he can count on his absolute
fidelity should any serious complications arise. Lutze replies that
he has sworn fidelity to the Führer, and that all he possesses,
including his life, lies in the Führer's hands. He is at his leader's
disposal. "Mein Führer," he concludes.

Hitler smiles and relaxes. He has picked the right man.
Himmler had also spoken to him of this Obergruppenführer SA,
but in the end the Chancellor made the decision alone, barking
out Lutze's name today as if it had suddenly come into his mind,
when for weeks he has known exactly how much he valued Lutze's
absolute reliability.

One day in the beginning of March, 1934, Hitler had spent
several hours at Berchtesgaden. Dressed in Tyrolean lederhosen
despite the sharply cold air, he stood outside on his terrace for
several minutes in the noonday sun, gazing at the panorama of
snowy peaks, in that still and silent altitude which seems to lend
every word and gesture special weight and symbolic grandeur.

Hitler loves this countryside, and by choice receives his intimates here. On that particular day, Obergruppenführer Viktor Lutze had asked to see him, and had come to the chalet terrace to drink tea, while Hitler's wolfhound slept beside his master, his head on his paws.

In the gleaming light of the Alpine spring while the snow-fields glittered like sheets of polished metal, Lutze spoke of Ernst Roehm in the timid voice of a good, reliable pupil.

Some of the SA were discontented, he said, and on the twenty-eighth of February Chief of Staff Ernst Roehm had taken an intolerable position. He had openly criticized the Führer: "What that ridiculous Corporal said doesn't concern us," Roehm had cried. "If we can't work with Hitler, we shall get on without him." Lutze whispered Roehm's final remark: "Hitler is a traitor. We'll have to send him on a long vacation." Then Viktor Lutze fell silent.

Hitler did not allow his feelings to show, but asked for details. Had Lutze said anything to Hess, Hitler's second-in-command? Lutze had already confided in him. Hitler merely murmured: "We must let this matter ripen."

Lutze went away anxious and disappointed. Had he shown his hand to no end? He then decided to speak to a man with growing influence, General Walther von Reichenau, to tell him about Roehm. In an affair of this kind the protection of an officer in the Reichswehr could be indispensable.

Walther von Reichenau has the grand manner of a Prussian officer: the stiff bearing, the athletic body, the monocle. He is a young general in the artillery, with a penetrating and intimidating eye. However, he does not resemble the other officers of the German Army, molded by tradition and trained in cadet school to unconditional obedience and arrogant authority.

Reichenau is not arrogant and distant. He knows the soldiers under his command. He joins them in foot races and other competitions and speaks to them as if they were human beings. He is said to favor a popular army.

The Nazi leaders had quickly singled out this ambitious general, a member of the German committee for the Olympic Games and an unequaled student of military science and strategy. He had been one of the most brilliant pupils of Max Hoffmann, said to be responsible for the spectacular operations of Hindenburg and Ludendorff during the Great War. Walther von Reichenau seems to represent the possibility of a living link between the traditional Army and National Socialism.

THE REICHSWEHR

The Army has long represented a serious problem for Hitler and the other Nazi leaders. In the Germany of 1933 it is the only organized force outside the Party. The members of the Freikorps and the original Nazis had come from the Army, but for most officers the Army remains their first and only allegiance, almost a religious organization, entered in a religious spirit. More than 20 percent of the officers are aristocrats, and since there has been no Emperor since 1918, they have become the trustees of the traditions of the German State. They wait, leading the tiny army of 100,000 men imposed on them by that shameful decree, the Treaty of Versailles. They have already crushed the Spartacists, the soldiers' councils which betwen 1918 and 1920 had wished, as Hindenburg put it, to bring "terrorist Bolshevism into Germany." The officers invent ways of circumventing the Treaty's restrictive provisions—testing new weapons for instance, in Bolshevik Russia, far from possible inspection. They are obsessed with revenge, with the desire to wipe out the insult of defeat, which they want to believe was the result of a "stab in the back." They fear a French invasion, which would destroy Germany. They fought against the French forces which occupied the Ruhr in 1923. Members of the Officers' Corps were involved in assassinations: the murderers of Rathenau came from the Army. Tense, thin, stiff and stern, the officers of the Reichswehr yearn to embody the austere, unfaltering spirit of a Germany whose heart is the Army, over which they watch.

Clustered around the Army are the veterans' associations; such as the Stahlhelm (Steel Helmet). Each year the Reichsfront-soldatentag (Front-Line Soldiers' Day) brings together tens of thousands of men—survivors of Germany's great wars: 1866, 1870, 1914—around the Crown Prince, to parade to martial music in their helmets and field-gray uniforms, bearing heavy sticks instead of guns. General Hans von Seeckt defined the spirit of the Officers' Corps when he said to Chancellor Stresemann on September 7, 1923: "Herr Chancellor, the Reichswehr will be with you if you take the German way." Who is to define this "deutscher Weg," if not the leaders of the Army?

Everything was simplified after April 26, 1925, when the re-sults of the run-off election were announced and von Hindenburg, former Chief of the General Staff, was elected President of the Reich. As imposing as a bronze statue, Paul von Beneckendorff und von Hindenburg is himself the son of a Prussian officer. A former pupil of the Kriegsakademie (War College), a veteran of the wars of 1866 and 1870, von Hindenburg reached the maxi-mum age for active duty in 1911. When he appears in his gray military cape with its lining, his pointed helmet with its gilded tip, carrying a field marshal's baton, he seems the embodiment of the old, undying Prussia, the indestructible Junker; all German tradition seems to move with him, at his regular, solemn pace.

The Army is not simply a matter of memories; it also has arms, men and power. The War Ministry is a powerful place— the most powerful in the government; the massive buildings on the Bendlerstrasse, with high, columned rooms and marbled walls, guarded by soldiers pacing back and forth in parade step, had seemed, before Hitler became Chancellor, like the true center of power.

Generals Seeckt, Heye and Groener, all former members of the General Staff, have defined "the German way," making and unmaking ministers. Their collaborators, the Bendlerstrasse officers, who are seen arriving punctually each morning at the Ministry, are, for the most part, elitist. In their persons and attitudes the old Imperial General Staff survives, although officially replaced by the Truppenamt (Office of Troops). The top commanders of the Army are respected and powerful figures.

But the Nazi storm is now battering against the barracks walls and the walls of the Ministry on the Bendlerstrasse; every officer must define his attitude toward the Austrian Corporal. To ignore him is no answer, for often, within the units, the younger officers have already been won over by Nazi ideas. Even the general officers, once reticent, are now beginning to express considerable interest in the Nazi paramilitary groups: perhaps these constitute a useful and usable reserve of men; perhaps Nazism is a means by which the German people can be forever welded to its Army, the guardian of Germanic tradition.

Many officers have spent some time in the U.S.S.R. as advisers to the Red Army, in exchange for the use of camps for training with modern weapons. Bolshevism has furnished the Red Army with considerable power, and popular prestige of the kind the younger officers of the Reichswehr dream about. Might not Nazism play a similar part in Germany?

KURT VON SCHLEICHER AND WERNER VON BLOMBERG

The last chief of the Reichswehr Ministry, Kurt von Schleicher, an able and intelligent general, and former member of the German General Staff, shares these notions. Born in 1882, he is personally ambitious and thinks of himself as a Machiavellian politician. He wishes to lean on the Nazis, to use them, to play a subtle and devious game with Hitler, whom he met in October, 1931, and whom he hopes to "domesticate," since he hopes to split the Nazi Party and govern with Gregor Strasser—against Hitler, if necessary.

To attain his ends, Schleicher continues his predecessor's practice of toppling Chancellors. A visit to Hindenburg, a meeting, a judicious amount of pressure, and Heinrich Brüning is finished. Schleicher pushes forward a former officer who is loyal to Hindenburg, an Army man—Franz von Papen. Then Papen falls, and on December 2, 1932, Kurt von Schleicher becomes the last Chancellor of the Republic.

However, he is Chancellor for only a short time. Hitler turns the situation to his own advantage, using Army divisions which place Papen and Schleicher in opposition to Hindenburg. Papen puts pressure on the President, and Hitler becomes Chancellor, with Papen as Vice Chancellor. Schleicher has lost, but is the Reichswehr losing too?

Hindenburg is still President. The Minister of War is still a general, Werner von Blomberg, a tall, smiling aristocrat, blond and monocled, an officer in the traditional style. He has made the trip to Russia. "It was a very close thing," he confided to friends one day. "I could easily have come back from Russia completely Bolshevik." That is his way of saying that he can no longer support a parliamentary regime like the Weimar government, a regime of disorder which the Presidency of Hindenburg will be unable to save. He thinks Germany needs a strong national government, founded on a broad base of popular support. Blomberg is fascinated by Hitler, and is well thought of by Hindenburg. He is the perfect War Minister for Hitler's cabinet.

His first concern is to get Schleicher's men out of the Bendlerstrasse. General von Bredow, the head of the Ministry, is replaced by Walther von Reichenau, who has also come to think that with Hitler's help the Army can once again become an immense power, the basic framework and support of German society.

However, there is some resistance: the Blomberg-Reichenau line is not universally accepted among the Officers' Corps. There are those who think of Blomberg as a Gummilöwe, a rubber lion; others who fear the demagogy of Corporal Hitler; and, above all, the doubts of those who do not wish to see the Reichswehr lose its prerogatives for the benefit of Captain Roehm's Nazi army. The Army wishes to use Hitler for its own ends, not to disappear. Officers of the General Staff, charged with the highest responsibilities, like Blomberg or Reichenau, and commanding officers in individual units feel an instinctive revulsion toward the leaders of the SA, who call themselves officers, but who are, in fact, former hotel doormen, notorious debauchers and fomenters of scandal. The Officers' Corp will never bow down to the SA.

Also, in January, 1934, when Kurt von Hammerstein, the last of Schleicher's men, resigns his post as Commander in Chief of the Army, Hindenburg yields to those officers who urge him to reject the candidacy of Reichenau, who is supported by Blomberg and Hitler. General Werner von Fritsch, a more traditionally minded officer, whose sympathies for the Nazis are less marked, is named instead. Hindenburg and the Reichswehr are defending their prerogatives, and Hitler understands very well that in the eyes of the public the forces commanded by these men represent the national tradition.

Therefore, it is necessary to take their feelings into account, to shift and maneuver. However, there is also the SA, with its following of several million, and the tempestuous Captain Roehm, with his own ideas about the Army and national defense.

THE FÜHRER AND THE ARMY

In 1933, shortly after the Nazi takeover, Roehm meets Hermann Rauschning. With his round, bald head, laughing eyes and attentive silence, the President of the Senate of Danzig inspires confidence. Roehm speaks frankly to him, telling him that the leaders of the SA, including himself, are officers, but never desk officers. "We fought in the Freikorps and in the Ruhr." Roehm expresses the discontent of the lower officers and the noncoms chafing against the strict hierarchy of the regular Army. The Nazis have seized power—why haven't they rewarded the

SA with promotions and titles and money? Why are they so so-
licitous of the feelings of the Reichswehr officers, who never lifted
a finger during any of the street fighting, or the battles in the
smoke-filled halls?

Roehm grows more and more excited as he speaks: "The
foundation of the new Army must be revolutionary. We can't
wait until later; we won't have more than one chance to make
something big enough to shake the world on its foundations. But
Hitler puts me off with fine words. . . . He wants to inherit a ready-
made Army, ready to march."

Roehm pauses for a minute, his face a study in disappointment
and distrust. He bangs his fist on the table—a veteran of the Western front, of the Munich putsch of 1923, who had pitted himself
against Generals von Lossow and von Kahr. He remembers all
of that, but Hitler has forgotten. "Hitler claims that later on he'll
turn all the soldiers into National Socialists. But he's begun by
abandoning them to the Prussian generals. He won't find any
revolutionary spirit in that bunch. Their wits are as dull as ever,
and they're certainly going to lose the next war."

In fact, Hitler sees the situation perfectly. On the one hand,
there are the generals, both powerful and respected; on the other,
there is the SA, often feared and despised. There is Hindenburg,
still President, and Vice Chancellor Papen, linked to the Reichswehr and to Hindenburg; there are the monarchists, and the conservatives. Then there is himself—Hitler—who is only Chancellor.
He has only just seized power, he must not lose it.

On the morning of January 31, 1933, less than twenty-four hours
after his nomination to the post of Chancellor, Hitler goes to the
barracks of the Berlin garrison. He harangues the troops assembled
in the courtyard, motionless in the icy air, speaking to them of the
future of National Socialist Germany. Their officers react instantly
and negatively to this procedure, which shatters tradition and
disregards the hierarchy.

To efface the memory of this incident, and to facilitate normal relations, von Hammerstein invites the new Chancellor to
dinner on February 2. It is a serious occasion: the generals and

admirals are in full uniform, but Hitler is not in the least intimidated. He speaks for two hours, and with that sense of political timing which has led him to success, he pledges that the Army and Navy will remain sovereign, that he will not involve himself in their affairs. He promises to do all he can to further rearmament; he also says he will remove the military from the jurisdiction of the civil courts. Hitler flatters his audience, emphasizing their privileges; during the course of the evening he wins over almost everyone present. Admiral Raeder remarks: "No Chancellor has ever spoken so firmly on behalf of the defense of the Reich."

With his customary prudence, the new Chancellor multiplies his acts of seduction. When he has to deal with powerful figures, Hitler knows how to wait out whatever time is required. On March 21, 1933, Goebbels and Hitler organize the ceremony of opening the new Reichstag in the church of the Potsdam garrison. All the marshals are there, along with von Mackensen and the Crown Prince, in the uniform of the Death's-Head Hussars, and Hindenburg, who remembers coming to this church as a pilgrim in 1866, after taking part in the Austro-Prussian War. In this church the Hohenzollern had knelt to pray, and Wilhelm II had taken his seat. Hindenburg salutes the Emperor's empty chair, then Hitler turns and addresses him: "Sir, the union between our new strength and the symbols of ancient grandeur has now been celebrated. We render homage to you. God, our Protector, has placed you at the head of the new forces of our nation."

It is the Army who is receiving Hitler's homage in the person of Hindenburg. The Chancellor goes on to add signs of good will to those of respect. Hitler needs the Army. Its officers are professionals, and if there is to be a war of revenge, their loyalty will be indispensable. The SA counts for very little compared to professional soldiers. The Army must be reckoned with in any calculations concerning the maintenance of power. It has weapons, the support of conservative circles and the respect of the major part of the country. Hitler needs the officers behind him in any attempt to enlarge his power. If Hindenburg dies, he will have to be replaced. Any replacement will need the Army's backing.

Since his accession to the Chancellory, even while with lowered eyes he respectfully takes the Marshal's hand, Hitler has been thinking of that death, which will allow him to considerably enlarge his scope. But for that he will need the agreement of Generals von Blomberg, von Reichenau, von Fritsch and Ludwig Beck, the new Chief of the Army General Staff—plus the agreement of the military caste which constitutes the Officers' Corps. The Führer handles the Army with caution and respect.

On the first of July he speaks to the leaders of the SA, meeting at Bad Reichenhall. The SA men listen, and applaud their Führer, who is saying, in their name, things they do not believe. "The political soldiers of the Revolution in no way wish to replace the Army, or to enter into competition with it," Hitler shouts. The officers of the Reichswehr take all this in with satisfaction. Better still, on Stahlhelm Day Hitler makes a speech in praise of the Army. To the SA this Association of Steel Helmets seems a haven for all the forces of hierarchy and tradition, of an aristocracy stiffened by antiquated privilege. However, Hitler understands that he has assumed obligations toward the Stahlhelm and toward the German Army. "We can assure the Army," he says, "that we will never forget, that for us the Army is the heir to all the traditions of the glorious German Imperial Army, and that we shall support this Army with all our heart and strength."

The Army is charmed by this kind of talk, and Hitler does not limit himself to words. The promotion of younger officers is accelerated. Young Colonel Erwin von Witzleben is promoted to the rank of major general, commanding the 3rd Infantry Division of Berlin—even though he is said to be anti-Nazi. General Renondeau, the French Military Attaché, grows anxious, writing to Paris at the beginning of 1934: "In this way, the Party has won over the Reichswehr, conquering both the summit and the base. The Army is losing its neutrality." In September, 1933, General Blomberg issues an order confirming this analysis: from that date, in certain situations, officers and troops are required to salute in the stiff-armed Hitler style.

All would have gone well had there been no SA. However, without the SA Hitler would probably never have come to power. The SA grow more and more aggressive, constantly finding fault with the Army. At every level of contact there is hostility and mistrust.

When General Fritsch invites Roehm to take part in Army maneuvers at Bad Liebenstein, in Thuringia, Roehm, with a gesture of lordly arrogance, sends his aide-de-camp, a notorious homosexual, to attend in his place. The officers are outraged. Roehm does not appear until the final day, for the official dinner. Throughout Germany there are an increasing number of incidents, and direct clashes.

Ratzeburg is a small, tranquil town in East Prussia, clinging to the shores of a lake whose blue waters are almost black. Sunday is a day of rest, during which families attend services in the twelfth-century cathedral, the pride of the town. However, on the second Sunday in January, a column of Brown Shirts parades through the streets, arrogant and provocative. An SA platoon moves along the sidewalk, knocking off the hats of passers-by who do not instantly freeze or salute, frequently showering them with blows. Two soldiers in the crowd seem to be jeering; immediately the SA fling themselves on the two men. One of the soldiers defends himself with his bayonet, the other yields, and later lodges a complaint with his commanding officer. The soldier who did not fight is punished by several days of arrest. The other is congratulated, and the SA is forbidden the use of the Reichswehr training ground until they have apologized.

At the Jüteborg camp, where the German artillery is on maneuvers, there are daily clashes between members of the SA and the Reichswehr, ranging from verbal insults to physical blows. An SA is even arrested by the Army, and sentenced by an Army court.

The SA leaders are furious: as they see it, Nazi power is their power, but its rewards are escaping them. They have both men and arms; their adversaries of the Left are in concentration camps, Hitler is in power, and Roehm is a cabinet minister. The next step is to take over control of the German Army, unite it with the SA, and make the Sturmabteilung into a revolutionary army. Then they can assure themselves good positions and high rank, and the era of cavalry officers and Junker nobility, landed titles and hereditary position, which accepts outsiders only as inferiors, and only after strict preliminary examinations—that era will be over. They, the SA, have already proved their worth—in the streets, before January, 1933.

"The SA," Roehm shouts to his excited audience, "are soldiers who have continued to do their duty while many others are resting on the laurels of the Great War."

But Roehm doesn't limit himself to shouting. He deliberately frustrates the scheme of General Reichenau, who in May, 1933, proposed the fusion of the Stahlhelm and the SA, hoping by that maneuver to ensure that all command positions went to officers of the Reichswehr. Roehm counterattacks, relying on the strength of the SA—in effect, the Party army, with its five Obergruppen (armies), and its eighteen Gruppen (corps). "There are no links of any kind between the Reichswehr and the SA," he proclaims. A few days later, in a speech which shakes the establishment on the Bendlerstrasse, he claims for the members of the SA "a position of privilege within the Third Reich, even in relation to the Reichswehr, because the SA alone are responsible for the victory of National Socialism."

The war between the SA and the Reichswehr is now out in the open. Bendlerstrasse is in a state of turmoil. "Unanticipated steps are being taken," a General Staff officer confides: "One project is followed by another contradicting it, and from all this officers are suffering a certain breakdown in morale." Contradictory rumors circulate throughout the Reichswehr; from unit to unit differing assessments of Roehm's plans are discussed: he wishes to build up an elite praetorian guard recruited on the basis of attachment to the Party and, with it, a popular militia modeled on the SA.

The regular officers, who have sweated their way through military school, are outraged by the SA officers' demands for equality. In the various staff offices the name Heines produces knowing grins—Heines, whose network of procurers of young boys stretches across all Germany. An officer returning from Breslau, where Heines still reigns as prefect of police, gives an outraged account of what he witnessed. The SA leaders had organized a meeting at the Savoy, one of Breslau's most elegant hotels. The Chief of Staff for the SA of Silesia, Count Pückler, had tried in vain to calm the SA group, who were firing into the air and shouting, and who finally bombarded their chauffeurs and their official cars with full bottles of champagne. If Roehm has his way, men like these will be integrated into the Reichswehr—even with the rank of general!

Another officer reports that the SA leaders have forbidden their men to take part in a training course organized by the Grenzschutz (Border Patrol), making it impossible to carry out the contingency plans drawn up against the event of mobilization. Heines in particular has promised that he would correct this situation, but von Rabenau has been obliged to make several futile trips to Breslau. Each time Heines swears that it will be attended to, but nothing is ever done. Regular officers curse the irresponsible "amateurs" who are compromising the defense of the Reich. General Walther von Brauchitsch summarizes the feelings of many of his fellow officers, whose motives are utterly sincere, when he confides to intimates: "Rearmament is too serious and militarily essential; that gang of homosexuals, thugs and drunks should be allowed no part in it."

Tension mounts. The frequency of Roehm's intervention in Army affairs increases, and the generals unite against him. Hitler, torn between the SA, with its millions of men, and the powerful Reichswehr, which holds the key to the legitimate succession to Hindenburg—Hitler hesitates, hoping for a compromise. But with each day his margin for maneuver shrinks.

"The gray rock will be drowned in a sea of brown," sing the SA in front of regular soldiers. By this they mean that they, the SA, will drown the Reichswehr.

They slap an officer who did not bow to the SA flag. A cadet who fails to salute the SA Sports Commissioner when he walks into a garrison bar is roughed up, while the Commissioner shouts at him: "Stand up, you young hooligan, when the Sports Commissioner of the Reich enters."

In the Bendlerstrasse, at one of the regular meetings scheduled by the Minister of War, the generals listen, motionless and grim, to a recitation of these grievances. Their conclusions are pointed: those who have not defended themselves against SA provocations should be dismissed from the Army. The cadet should have slapped the Sports Commissioner of the Reich. Instructions are sent out from the Bendlerstrasse to all garrison commanders: "A sense of personal worth must be strengthened in every officer and every member of the Army."

But Roehm yields no ground. On the contrary, he presses on toward his goal—a new Army. He knows that he is backed by considerable strength; he intends to force Hitler to take his side.

On February 2 all corps commanders of the Reichswehr meet at the Bendlerstrasse to discuss the relationship between the Army and the SA. The atmosphere is icy. Blomberg announces that Roehm has issued a memorandum proposing no less than the creation of a large new Ministry which will regroup and combine all the armed forces of the Party and the State. This would mean an end of the organization at the Bendlerstrasse, the end of the organization patiently put together by Seeckt, the end of the Office of Troops, the end of the Reichswehr. Refusal is stamped on every face. General Liebmann, who annotates the text of the declarations, points out that von Fritsch has declared that he will oppose the demands put forward by the SA with all his strength. Fritsch has the backing of the entire Army: there is not a single officer who will admit Roehm to the succession of Bendlerstrasse generals, heirs of the Imperial General Staff. And there is no doubt that President Hindenburg could not even begin to imagine such a thing. If Roehm wishes to have his way, he will have to make a second Revolution—with, without or against the Führer.

After briefly considering the question, von Blomberg leaves

the room, and Fritsch, a brilliant technician, begins to speak on questions of military instruction. Suddenly an orderly enters the room and leans over General Reichenau. As Fritsch continues his talk, Reichenau stands up, requesting that his interruption be excused: an urgent message has just arrived. In the vast hall, as austere and solemn as a Lutheran church, there is silence. Von Reichenau reads, in his clear voice: "I recognize the Reichswehr solely as the school of the nation. Henceforth, the conduct of operations, and therefore mobilization, shall be the province of the Sturmabteilung. Heil Hitler. Roehm."

The telegram serves as another provocation, to fuse the members of the Reichswehr into a bloc. Blomberg, Fritsch, Reichenau and the commandants of the seven Wehrkreise (military districts) unanimously reject its message. Von Blomberg demands an appointment with Hitler; he plans to submit his resignation. The thrust of this gesture will be perfectly clear to Hitler: it will mean the hostility of the entire Reichswehr, and the impossibility of succeeding Hindenburg without affronting the large number of Germans—conservatives, Christians, oppositionists and those who are simply indifferent—who are not Nazis. The Führer has no choice but to refuse von Blomberg's resignation, to placate the Army.

But there is the SA and Roehm, who refuses to yield. He has just asked that two thousand SA officers and twenty thousand NCOs be incorporated into the Reichswehr. The Führer decides to meet with his old comrade. The Chief of Staff comes to the Chancellory. It is the end of February; the weather in Berlin is implacably cold and clear. Roehm arrives, striding into the Chancellory with an air of purposeful confidence. He knows Hitler well, knows that he hates opposition and that if resistance is firm, he will yield. Roehm is tenaciously firm. In the office waiting room, he notices Count Fritz-Gunther von Tschirschky, one of the closest collaborators of Franz von Papen, that link with Hindenburg and the Reichswehr whom Hitler has accepted as Vice Chancellor. A consummate intriguer, von Papen hopes to exploit the split between the SA and the Reichswehr for the benefit of the conservatives and his own military circle. It is rumored that there is a plan to push the SA into action. Inspired by Papen, Hindenburg will then declare a state of emergency—to the advantage of the Reichswehr. Hitler's reaction, as Roehm suspects, cannot be relied upon. The Chancellor knows that his strength is drawn from both forces—the SA and the Reichswehr.

In the anteroom, Tschirschky has been waiting for a considerable time. He hears voices which grow louder and louder, and recognizes Hitler's, harsh and violent. Brückner sits motionless at his desk.

Tschirschky turns to him. "My God," he says ironically, "do you suppose they're cutting each other's throats?" Then he picks out Roehm's voice, speaking of the integration of two thousand officers into the Army, and Hitler's, which is even louder: "The President of the Reich would never agree to it, and I would risk losing his confidence."

Shortly thereafter, the two men leave the Chancellor's office. Tschirschky stands up, but Hitler, exhausted, doesn't see him. He walks past, seeing Roehm out, and then returns and secludes himself in his office.

The next day is Volkstrauertag (Day of National Mourning); the National Socialist Chancellor is received by President Hindenburg. After reciprocal exchanges of compliments, Hitler presents Roehm's proposals to the Marshal. Hindenburg rejects them with a single word; Hitler holds his peace, accepting the slap in the face for which Roehm is responsible. He knew it was coming, as he knew that von Papen was probing military opinion. Will Generals Beck, Rundstedt and Witzleben intervene to clear out the SA and their Nazi rabble? But the officers hesitate, sometimes refusing even to consider the possibility. After all, the Minister of War and the men who occupy key positions at the Bendlerstrasse are from their circle. Furthermore, their obedience is to Hindenburg only, and Hindenburg is still there, receiving homage from the National Socialist Chancellor, and refusing Roehm's proposals. Naturally, if Roehm's proposals should be accepted, if the SA should revolt . . . But Hitler will put a stop to that.

A few days later, Hitler moves in favor of the Reichswehr. But he also wants reconciliation between the Army and the SA—he needs them both. On the twenty-eighth of February he calls a large meeting at the Bendlerstrasse—a parade of uniformed dignitaries from the SS and the SA. Roehm is present, and so are the Reichswehr generals.

Hitler stands up, staring straight ahead. He is the point of contact among all the men in the room, between the two camps; and he wishes to convince them all. He speaks slowly, with many pauses, separating his phrases, forcing his audience to listen closely.

"The German people are moving toward a period of intense misery." These are Hitler's opening words, and despite the absolute silence, one can sense the surprise they produce. This thesis is in complete contradiction to the vision of a dazzling future which the Führer promises the enthusiastic crowds at his mass rallies. "Nazism has eliminated unemployment," Hitler goes on, "but when the State orders have been filled—in, say, eight years' time—there will be an economic recession. There is only one remedy for this: the creation of more living space for our surplus population." The officers listen, astonishment clearly visible on faces which have been trained to perfect impassivity. "The Western powers will never yield this vital space to us," Hitler goes on. "That is why a series of decisive blows may become necessary—first in the West, and then in the East."

The date of that speech is February 28, 1934. Hitler is already conjuring up the specter of war. However, none of the officers present grasps the importance of these omens. No one speaks of them. For that day, anyway, Hitler's projects remain secret. Some suspect he is painting an apocalyptic picture to persuade the SA to yield to the Army. It is not until much later, in 1945, that an officer who remembers that meeting speaks of it to von Blomberg. They are then aged men, greatly affected by the turbulence of the times. They stand watching the American sentries who guard the camp in which they are prisoners and remember that day when, for the first time, Hitler enunciated to the SA and the Reichswehr his vision of a lightning war, a blitzkrieg, to gain living space. But who then could have imagined the tenacity of that visionary, who had just barely assumed power? In February, 1934, the Führer's audience was not expecting a declaration of war, but a solution to the SA-Reichswehr conflict which threatened the New Reich.

Hitler falls silent. For the moment he has spoken only of a dark and warlike future, while he is obliged to attempt a settlement of immediate difficulties. He begins to speak again, in a low voice, summarizing the military past—which seems a rather long detour. Suddenly he turns to Roehm and observes in a strong voice: "A militia is not called up simply to defend a small piece of ground." Roehm seems to dissociate himself from what Hitler has just said. His flushed face is set in an expression of affected indifference, and he stares at the ceiling. Hitler raises his voice. He is still speaking to Roehm, and what he has just said seems a repudiation of Roehm's ambitions: "The SA must limit itself to its political task." Hitler's voice is very firm. "The Minister of War," he continues, "may call upon the SA for border control, and for premilitary instruction."

There is a pause. Roehm says nothing; the generals sit in stiff and silent immobility. "I expect from the SA loyal execution of the work entrusted to it." Hitler has made a decisive move: the Reichswehr will be the sole foundation of the future national army. There is no applause. Everyone rises, Roehm, Blomberg—each man near his leader. Hitler is in the middle, smiling and relaxed—or apparently relaxed. He speaks rapidly, taking Roehm by the arm; it is the grand moment of public reconciliation. Facing each other on either side of Hitler stand Blomberg, his monocle deeply set beneath the blond eyebrows which stamp his round, distinguished face, and Roehm, smaller and squat in his brown uniform. The two men shake hands, and the Chief of Staff of the Sturmabteilung invites the generals to a lunch of reconciliation in his quarters. When the doors are opened, an immense table is revealed, laid with the ostentatious display of the nouveau riche. The places are marked: Roehm and Blomberg sit at each end. Servants hurry forward; the menu is excellent, champagne flows in abundance; but the atmosphere is icy and no one speaks. The reconciliation seems more like a funeral ceremony. At the end of the long, dreary meal, at a signal from Roehm, the SA stand up. After the obligatory salutes, handshakes and clickings of heels, the heavy Reichswehr cars drive slowly away.

Roehm has asked the SA leaders to stay with him. They return to the table and wait. Roehm pours himself another glass of champagne. Some of the others follow his example. "That was a new Versailles Treaty," Roehm remarks suddenly. The SA officers are silent, sensing the rising anger of their leader, an anger which had been contained and repressed during the long hours of the "reconciliation."

Suddenly it all explodes. From a corner of the room, Viktor Lutze is watching and listening. "Everything that ridiculous Corporal said," Roehm begins. Lutze becomes wary, reluctant to understand, keeping his face impassive to hide his dismay. "Hitler? If only we could get rid of that limp rag," Roehm concludes.

The room breaks up into groups. Talk is bitter, punctuated with curses. Obergruppenführer Lutze says nothing. He argues with nothing Roehm says, he mixes silently with the others, the most ineffectual of the SA leaders. However, a few days later he gives a full account to Rudolf Hess, the number two man in the Party. On Hess' advice he goes to see Hitler in his chalet at Berchtesgaden. The Führer, on that occasion, contents himself with saying: "We must let this matter ripen." The Obergruppenführer, astonished by such moderation, asks General von Reichenau's advice.

The Führer forgets nothing of what has been said, or who has said it. On June 29, 1934, he calls Lutze to Godesberg. When Lutze arrives, Hitler nervously asks him if he can be absolutely trusted.

5

Friday, June 29, 1934
Bad Godesberg: Hotel Dreesen

Approaching 11:00 P.M.

Hitler has been talking to Lutze for a long time now. He questions him about the meeting at Wiessee, assuring himself that nothing has been planned beyond a meeting between himself and the SA leaders. As he has already done several times, Viktor Lutze repeats his protestations of loyalty. Goebbels draws closer to the two men. He approves of Lutze, and is trying to demonstrate that he, too, has never been motivated by anything other than devotion to Hitler's cause. Otto Dietrich, the chief of Hitler's press service, strides up and down the terrace with Brückner. One or the other takes care of telephone calls, and watches the stairs leading down from the terrace, beside which motorcycles and cars from the airport at Hangelar pull to a stop.

Shortly after eleven o'clock, while the RAD band plays another military march, Brückner and Dietrich approach Hitler with a new message which has just arrived by air from Berlin;

the band's music covered the sound of the arriving motorcycle. The message—from Goering—is brief. Hitler reads it, and hands it to Goebbels. A few hours ago, Goering was informed that Dr. Sauerbruch, one of Berlin's most celebrated physicians, has been called to the bedside of President Hindenburg at Neudeck. Hitler says nothing, but places the message on the table, stroking it with the tips of his fingers. He stands absolutely still, staring straight ahead, one of his cheeks and an eyelid twitching uncontrollably, as often happens in periods of great tension. Following Hitler's lead, Goebbels, too, is silent. Perhaps this is the moment they have been waiting for, the moment which will offer Hitler a new opportunity to exploit his luck, the moment which will see the bronze figure of Hindenburg crumble, struck down by death.

Death has hovered around the old Reich President all through the spring. The veteran of Sadowa and Sedan, who seemed to defy time, began to lose his memory, and his absences from official life were frequent. At the beginning of April, doctors attending him warned his relatives. In the shadow of the Marshal are his son, Colonel Oskar von Hindenburg, a mediocre and ambitious man in his fifties, who has been stifled by his father's glory and authority, and various cynical and worldly advisers, such as the old Chamberlain, von Oldenburg, who is given to quoting a favorite maxim: "The mangers never change, just the cattle who use them." There is also Otto von Meissner, secretary general to the President, fat and round-faced, whose gentle, myopic expression masks his firm intention of keeping his position even after Hindenburg's death. These men, who will survive Hindenburg, are intent on assuring their futures. They can use their influence to their own advantage as long as Hindenburg is alive, but after his death what will happen to them?

As soon as the younger Hindenburg and Meissner learn that the Marshal is failing, they inform General von Blomberg and Chancellor Hitler—the two men who represent the most powerful forces at the moment—a move dictated by both duty and self-interest.

April, 1934: The General and the Chancellor alone know

the secret which could shake the future of Germany. Blomberg and Hitler decide to meet.

On the morning of April 4 the pocket cruiser *Deutschland* is gripped by the rush of presailing preparations. Sailors in their black berets, with two streamers floating behind in the salt air, run about on the bridge to the blasts of a whistle. The anchor is slowly raised, and the *Deutschland*, a large gray mass flying the Navy flag, leaves Wilhelmshaven and moves slowly toward the North Sea, passing Brunsbüttel and Holtenau. Young girls from a boarding school wave their scarves while a military band on the shore plays martial airs. The ship is moving to Kiel, to take aboard the leaders of the Third Reich, who will watch the large-scale spring maneuvers. Throughout the trip the crew is subjected to a frantic whirl of activity. A section of the superstructure is being repainted, to a continuous series of alerts and simulated combat. On April 9 the *Deutschland* enters the port of Kiel, greeted by the sirens of destroyers and the small, dark, wide-bellied fishing boats which ply the waters of this famous naval port. The crew is confined to the ship, and on the following day Hitler arrives at Kiel in his usual three-engined plane. When he has inspected the honor guard provided by the Navy, the Führer boards the *Deutschland*, accompanied by Admiral Raeder and Generals von Blomberg and von Fritsch.

Hitler is radiant; when he appears at the gangway, the boatswains modulate their strident whistles. Gulls wheel overhead as the Chancellor learns the fascinating order and efficiency of a large warship. The *Deutschland* sails on April 11; Hitler remains on board to observe the world of perfected military technique in action. Here the naval professionals are absolute rulers, men formed at the most exacting naval academies, who have mastered the mechanized instruments of warfare. There is no question of yielding to the authority of a turbulent, undisciplined, drunken and debauched SA. Here war is a matter of scientific precision. Hitler watches, striding the bridge with Raeder, Blomberg and von Fritsch. Since February he has been saying to the officers of the Reichswehr: "It is my firm decision that the German Army of the future shall be motorized. Whoever attempts to put obstacles in the way of this historic task of giving the German nation the means of self-defense shall be crushed." He cannot help but be affected by the smooth-running mechanical perfection of the *Deutschland*.

The cruiser moves at medium speed through the Grand Baelt, and then along the coast of Lolland. At six in the morning it passes Skagen; in the lifting fog, one can glimpse the lightship in the distance. Then the cruiser turns north and sails up the Norwegian coast. Snow falls into the gray sea.

Hitler and Blomberg have conferred and have decided to tell Raeder and Fritsch, who are, practically speaking, the heads of the Navy and Army, what they know about the President's health. Hitler and Blomberg then retire alone to the Commandant's large cabin. Outside, snow continues to fall, and the distant coast is only a high, dark bar, like a long, breaking wave. Hitler and Blomberg talk together for a long time. Perhaps it is then that they agree on the "*Deutschland* Pact," which will be referred to so often in the future: Hitler promises to curb the ambitions of Roehm and the SA in exchange for the support of Blomberg and the Army in his succession to the Presidency. The Sturmabteilung will never agree that the Reichswehr alone is responsible for the defense of the Reich.

No one actually knows what Hitler and Blomberg said to each other, but everything supports the thesis that the two men agreed, at least in principle, on the means to be employed in reducing the SA and in making Hitler Hindenburg's successor. For the Führer, this is of first priority.

On April 12 the *Deutschland* enters the Sogne Fjord. The blackish walls of the fjord are streaked with long trails of snow. The Admiralty, together with the Führer, has chosen this fjord as the setting for a salute to the Fridtjof Monument built by Kaiser Wilhelm II—further homage from the Nazi regime to historic Germany. Suddenly the Führer appears on the bridge, surrounded by the crew, in a moment of relaxation from its steel-hard discipline. The sailors cheer, and the officers smile, albeit somewhat uneasily. The Führer even allows the sailors to photograph him. Then the ship rounds the point. On the thirteenth it enters the Hardanger Fjord, and turns south again. Hitler has climbed to the bridge several times, obviously enchanted by the voyage, and by the conversations he has had with General von Blomberg, far from indiscreet ears. On the fourteenth the lightship of Skagen appears, and some hours later the ship arrives at Wilhelmshaven. There has been only one unpleasant incident: during one of the maneuvers on the final day, a man fell into the sea.

Hitler returns to Berlin by air and goes directly to the Chancellory. His personal flag is raised, informing Berliners of his presence. Groups of people wait patiently in front of the heavy doors for the changing of the guard or the departure of some official car, for during this month of April the comings and goings at the Chancellory are almost continuous.

In fact, since the cruise of the *Deutschland* there has been a steady series of political meetings and decisions. Where before he hesitated for weeks, Hitler now acts, as if his conversations with Blomberg have led him to a definitive choice; as if the *"Deutschland* Pact"* were not hypothetical but real. On April 20 Himmler and Heydrich become the masters of the Gestapo; at the same time, Joachim von Ribbentrop, that former champagne dealer and friend of Himmler, with a finely drawn, regular face, is named Hitler's Ambassador Extraordinary on questions of disarmament. The police apparatus has by now been thoroughly infiltrated by Party members; the Ministry of Foreign Affairs is next on the list. One of the first disarmament moves which Hitler and Ribbentrop propose to France and England is a large reduction in SA membership.

On April 20, without comment, and in small print, like any harmless news item, the *National Zeitung* publishes a bulletin

from the General Staff of the SA announcing that the Sturmabteilung will be given a month's leave in July. Under the circumstances, however, this demobilization of the entire SA for thirty
days is not a routine decision, but an unexpected, indeed exceptional, measure. However, no one in authority makes any comment, and the news is absorbed into the constantly changing
situation in which new elements are daily added to the puzzle.

On April 27 the front pages of the German press carry a bulletin set in wide, black lines: the physical condition of the Reich
President is causing his doctors considerable anxiety. There are
photographs of Hitler bowing to the old Marshal, and many
people understand that Hindenburg's successor will be none other
than the Chancellor of the Third Reich. Some officers express
irritation. There are other candidates: General Ritter von Epp,
who, despite being a Nazi and Governor of Bavaria, is nonetheless
a distinguished member of the Officers' Corps. There is also the
Crown Prince, who could be declared Regent if he became President—many officers remain loyal to the old dynasty. But von
Blomberg makes it clear that there is no longer any place for
monarchical dreams. In mid-April an order is sent out from the
War Ministry to every unit: from the first of May, officers and
men must wear the eagle and swastika, the emblems of the Nazi
Party and the Third Reich, on their caps and uniforms. A few
of the older officers protest, but they speak softly: everywhere,
young officers and the mass of troops accept the order with enthusiasm. Furthermore, how is it possible to protest an order issued by the head of the officer caste, and the dignitaries of the
Officers' Corps, who, it must be assumed, know what they are
doing? When these officers made their decision, they must have
thought solely of the interests of the Reichswehr, and, as the two
interests are intertwined, of the Reich.

On May 1, 1934, companies from every barracks march for
the first time beneath Nazi colors, and there are large rallies in
every German town to honor National Labor Day.

Stripped to the waist, with spades on their shoulders, labor volunteers march in regiments—on those shoulders, a spade becomes a weapon. At Tempelhof on the outskirts of Berlin, Hitler speaks to a crowd of 100,000 people, who shout out the "Heil Hitlers" which have become traditional. Elsewhere, on platforms, or in grassy woodland glades, thousands of young men meet to engage in a curious kind of duel, in which swords are replaced with wooden staves some six feet long. Everywhere the Nazi government demonstrates the strength of its hold on the young. The Nazi State seems well established.

However, during the days immediately preceding the May Day demonstrations, SA Obergruppenführer Lasch speaks to the SA parading at Jena, declaring that "The National Socialist Revolution has not been completed, and will be completed only when the SA state has been formed." On the platform, beside Gauleiter Sauckel, sits Maximilian von Weichs, a Reichswehr officer who is very hostile to the Sturmabteilung. Von Weichs leans toward Sauckel: "What is this SA state?" The Gauleiter simply shrugs. On the following day, an SA Brigadeführer (Brigadier General) shouting drunkenly in the streets of Jena is arrested, and Sauckel refuses to release him. Although Gauleiter Sauckel belongs to the SA, his functions have turned him into a man of the government, of order. When Roehm convokes a Sturmabteilung Court of Honor, and calls Sauckel to appear before it, Sauckel refuses on the grounds that he had acted according to orders.

Once again, opposing forces have clashed. When Goebbels speaks to the German nation on May 4, he is perhaps thinking of the SA. "The Party propagandists," he shouts, "have decided to lead an energetic campaign against professional critics, spreaders of rumors, provocateurs and saboteurs, who, it seems, have not abandoned their hope of destroying the constructive work of National Socialism." In his hard, nasal voice, Goebbels announces a program of action. "From the first of May until the end of June, there will be daily meetings and demonstrations, with a particular purpose. These demonstrations will put the German people on guard against this denigration, which is a real scourge for our country. This scourge must be banished once and for all. It must disappear forever." Not surprisingly, this is followed by a threat: "We shall use methods which have proved successful."

HINDENBURG AND FRANZ VON PAPEN

Some days later, a procession of official cars draws up in front of Berlin's central railway station. An honor guard is waiting to greet it. Leaning on von Papen, Field Marshal Hindenburg is leaving for his country estate at Neudeck.

He loves the ancient countryside of East Prussia, whose horizons seem to melt into gray skies. Neudeck is his seigneurial property, his link with the soil, across which numberless Teutonic legions have marched. But from generation to generation the family property has shrunk, because impoverished officers have been obliged to sell. Throughout the region, other Junkers— also servants of the Reichswehr—have seen their properties melt away under the pressure of their needs. When Hindenburg became President, they hoped to change all that. In 1927 the property of Neudeck was bought back by national subscription, and offered to Hindenburg on his eightieth birthday. The old Marshal accepted this gift without realizing that the group of Junkers who surrounded him hoped, in this way, to capture him, to align him with their projects. Actually, the so-called "Eastern Relief" (Osthilfe) Law loaded them with benefits. They were to be given various special favors, including large subsidies and tax relief. The property of Neudeck itself was given to Oskar von Hindenburg, so that at the Marshal's death there would be no death duties to pay.

Von Papen, who accompanies Hindenburg to the departure platform of the Berlin station, often plays on the Field Marshal's passion for Neudeck. It is rumored that he blackened his rival, General von Schleicher, in the Field Marshal's eyes by alleging that Schleicher was planning to reveal the secret arrangements concerning Neudeck. It may have been on Papen's advice that in August, 1933, Hitler added eight hundred acres, tax-free, to the Neudeck estate.

Franz von Papen, cavalry officer, military attaché to the United States during the Great War, organizer of sabotage, member of the exclusive Herrenklub, conservative and Catholic, is highly esteemed by the old Marshal. Hindenburg leans toward him before boarding the train. "It's all going very badly, Papen," he says. "Do your best to straighten things out." Later, giving an account of what was said that day, Papen added: "Even today, I can still remember that last remark, uttered in his deep, impressive voice."

Papen remains on the platform with the other officials while the train pulls out, the soldiers of the honor guard motionless beside them. Vice Chancellor Papen is left face to face with responsibility. An able man, with his smiling face, pepper-and-salt mustache, his carefully groomed, graying hair and bourgeois appearance, he is a member of the officer caste. He attended the Cadet School, where he managed to survive the implacable discipline imposed by the authorities on children of eleven, and the equally inflexible code which the cadets imposed on themselves: children trained to a high standard of honor, and ready to be killed for it. Like his fellow pupils, Franz von Papen was marked forever. Later he was to explain how, in the spring of 1897, he had received "magnificent news." "I was one of the ninety pupils, out of six hundred candidates, who were chosen to form the class 'Selecta.' This honor meant that I would remain under the rigid discipline of the Cadet Corps NCOs for an additional year, and that I would also be placed on the list of candidates for the much-sought-after honor of page to the Emperor."

Now von Papen must act: this former page to Wilhelm II, former country gentleman and member of the Herrenklub, Fränzchen (little Franz)—as he is called by Hindenburg, who feels for him the paternal attachment which often links certain powerful old men to their close collaborators—must decide. But the developing circumstances make him uneasy. Can it be that by introducing the Nazis into the Chancellory he has unloosed the devil? Papen believes in the strong excercise of power, but he is shocked and horrified by the unlimited use of terror. Certainly, without taking too many personal risks, he wishes to come to terms with the dictatorship, but he also hopes to affect its course. Later, always adept at finding excuses, he would write: "Until 1933 German history had not dealt with the phenomenon of an anti-Christian dictatorship, or with a head of government without faith or morals. Consequently, we didn't know how to fight him."

In this situation, Papen makes several speeches. In December, 1933, the city of Bremen is celebrating the 150th anniversary of the founding of the Hanseatic Club. Everyone of importance in the city is invited to a meeting, to hear the Vice Chancellor. Papen pays tribute to the new regime without singling out anyone in particular, and takes issue with those who deny "the personal value of the individual." His words produce frenetic applause, and represent, for his audience, an attack against the Nazis.

Some months later, he addresses a much more important audience: the Dortmund Industrial Association. Outside, the streets of the industrial town are empty. People are either working or sleeping. Inside, in the brilliantly lit clubroom, the leaders of local industry, sunk into deep leather armchairs, are listening to the Vice Chancellor all the more attentively because he is one of the men who introduced Hitler to the industrial magnates. On that evening, April 26, 1934, Papen touches on themes to which they are all sensitive. "The part played by industrial leaders," Papen says, "is essential. In relation to the State, they must maintain the broadest possible degree of liberty." The applause is vigorous but well mannered—the applause of influential and responsible people who do not indulge in extravagant display. The sense of approval is even stronger when Papen discusses plans for economic autarchy. "Autarchy makes the existence of a world economy illusory," he concludes, "and carries with it the more or less distant danger of war."

After his talk, Papen is congratulated. He has expressed the point of view of a large segment of the business world, which is equally disturbed by the inflammatory speeches of the SA and by certain tendencies of members of the government, like Walther Darré, Minister of Food and Agriculture, with his dreams of a pure and vigorous peasant race, of a Germany regaining her strength through blood and the land. If such attitudes prevail, what will happen to industry? There is also Kurt Schmitt, Minister of Economics, of whom it is rumored that he wishes to limit the rearmament program, and reorganize German industry to weaken the power of the Krupps.

Conversely, in the Ruhr Papen is trusted. Nevertheless, the Vice Chancellor does not conceal his uneasiness from the members of the powerful Dortmund Industrial Association. "Each time," he says, "I draw Hitler's attention to the dangerous consequences of any concession to Roehm, he ridicules the demands made by the leader of the Brown Shirts, and treats them as aberrations of no importance."

Naturally, Hitler has his informers: he sees himself caught in the meshes of a web which stretches from the Reichswehr to Papen to industrial circles. He also knows the Vice Chancellor's immediate circle. He knows that men like Herbert von Bose, Papen's chief private secretary, and von Tschirschky, the former monarchist who has rallied to Papen for want of anything better, and Dr. Erich Klausener, the Director of Catholic Action and a high functionary in the Ministry of Communications, are, in varying degrees, adversaries of Nazism. Above all, there is Papen's private secretary, Edgar Jung, Christian, conservative and monarchist, who has been widening his range of contacts for months now, with a view to overturning the new regime. These men are all the more dangerous in that they could have the support of the Reichswehr: the Army recognizes them as kindred spirits.

The Führer, therefore, is on guard against this nest of vipers in the Vice Chancellor's office. But nothing is simple; Hitler hesitates, and lies awake at night, torn by anxiety and doubt. Often, in the company of a somnolent Brückner, he immerses himself in long sessions of listening to music. The choice open to Hitler is extremely difficult. To stop the conservatives from seducing the Reichswehr, it is certainly necessary to put an end to the violence, and, above all, the pretensions of the Sturmabteilung. But if there were no longer any SA, would not the Army also abandon Hitler, since he would no longer have anything to bargain with in exchange for its support?

The situation is delicate and ambiguous. Hitler watches, waits and reads reports.

HIMMLER'S AND HEYDRICH'S TRAP

Reports on the Vice Chancellor multiply rapidly. Himmler and Heydrich also fear Papen and his collaborators, and to prepare themselves for defense or attack, they introduce one of their own men into his entourage.

In April, 1934, Otto Betz is called to Munich by Heydrich, SD leader of the Gestapo. Betz is a counterespionage agent who has been working for Heydrich in the Saar. A seemingly modest and colorless man, he was involved in the successful assassination of a Rhenish separatist on the night of January 8–9, 1923. He had met Dr. Edgar Jung on that occasion. Heydrich puts forward his proposal: Betz can collaborate with Papen quite naturally because the Vice Chancellor is Commissioner for the Saar. But Heydrich, always impassive and efficient, limiting himself to exactly the number of words required, adds: "You are to keep under surveillance: (1) Franz von Papen; (2) Herbert von Bose; and (3) Dr. Edgar Jung. Your reports will be delivered to me personally."

On May 4, 1934, Heydrich's agent assumes his duties in Berlin, in two rooms only a few steps from the head office of the Gestapo, the fief of Himmler and Heydrich, at 8 Prinz-Albrecht Strasse. Heydrich has arranged things very well: Otto Betz has two secretaries and four police inspectors at his disposal. The next day, he presents himself at the Vice Chancellory, where von Bose receives him with suspicion. Men from the SD and the Gestapo are not liked at the Vice Chancellory. But Betz renews his acquaintance with Jung, recalling 1923, the year of their struggle against the French and the separatists, and the wound Jung received. Betz makes headway; relations between himself and members of von Papen's staff gradually relax. He even warns them about their telephone conversations, which he says are monitored by the SD. This friendly warning, however, does not prevent him from sending detailed reports to Heydrich and Himmler, the nearly omnipotent chiefs of the Nazi secret services, from whom only the Abwehr (Army Intelligence Service) is safe. Himmler and Heydrich, in turn, modify these reports to suit their own purposes before sending them on to Hitler.

The reports confirm Hitler's fears, detailing rumors and actual preparations. In conservative circles Roehm's projects give rise to anxiety; in others, consideration is given to alliance with the Sturmabteilung. Heydrich's men can prove that certain conservatives are in touch with Prince August Wilhelm of Prussia, a Nazi deputy and SA Major General who is the son of the last Emperor, brother of the Crown Prince. For the monarchists, the Prince is a natural candidate to succeed Field Marshal Hindenburg. Thus the fate of the SA is linked to the death of the old Reich President. Reports from the SD and the Gestapo pile up on Hitler's desk. Hindenburg has made his political testament, they say, and von Papen has drawn it up. Fränzchen, according to confidences collected by SD agents, has had little trouble convincing Hindenburg to express his desire to see the monarchy restored after his death. A Gestapo report indicates that Hindenburg's will was signed on May 11.

The Chancellor is more disturbed by other rumors which

reach him through Heydrich and Himmler. Lists for a new cabinet have already been prepared. The English historian, Sir John W. Wheeler-Bennett, who is living in Berlin, frequents the political cafés of the capital, where he meets many prominent German figures. One day, in one of those bars, a man he is talking to produces a sheet of paper bearing the names of future cabinet members. Ignoring the waiters moving back and forth past the table, he comments on these names for Wheeler-Bennett's benefit. It is well known that the waiters at this bar work for the Gestapo. Heydrich can thus recite specific names to Hitler: Roehm would be allied with General von Schleicher, who wishes to get rid of Papen. Gregor Strasser would be Minister of Economics, Roehm Minister of Defense. The SA would be incorporated into the Reichswehr, and Brüning would have the Foreign Ministry. Hitler would remain Chancellor: the victims of the change would be Papen and Goering. Wheeler-Bennett remembers that "all these rumors circulated through Berlin at that time; typed lists purporting to give the composition of the new cabinet were passed from hand to hand with a lack of caution which made more than one foreign observer shudder."

Heydrich and Himmler are able to collect information without difficulty. They even announce that Schleicher and his assistant, General von Bredow, are in contact with French emissaries.

In fact, General Schleicher—formerly the political head of the Reichswehr, on confidential terms with Hindenburg, with the power to make or break chancellors and himself the last Chancellor before Hitler—is bored. He has been living in retirement in his villa at Neubabelsberg beside Lake Wannsee since January, 1933. His young wife and daughter seem to fill his life. However, he is in touch with Generals Bredow and Hammerstein, and through them keeps informed of the rivalries which are tearing apart the Nazi Party, and the uncertainty about the future. He hopes once again to play a major role in public affairs, and in the spring he re-enters the world of dinners, meetings and plans. Has he seen Strasser and Roehm? At a reception given by the Ru-

manian Minister, he talked at length with the French Ambassador
—a talk which was the subject of several reports by Heydrich's
agents, and whose significance would be increased when André
François-Poncet and the General met again.

"I knew Schleicher quite well," François-Poncet wrote later.

> I had last seen him on Easter Monday (April 2); we
> spent the day together in the country. It was his habit
> to speak quite freely to me, and he had never misled
> or deceived me. On that occasion, as before, he made
> no secret of his opposition to the regime, but he never
> said anything which might lead me to suppose he en-
> tertained any subversive plans or was involved in any
> kind of conspiracy. He never spoke like a traitor to his
> country, and each time he mentioned Roehm it was
> in terms of disdain and disgust.

But the agents of the SD care little about Schleicher's real
intentions. They watch him as they watch von Bredow, who lives
near the French border. On a trip to Paris, Bredow is even asked
to get off the train at the frontier. A letter to a prominent French-
man is found in his bags. A telephone call to Blomberg begging
for his intervention would have been fruitless: Blomberg, Minister of the Reichswehr, would have refused to intervene.

For a man like Hitler, alert to the possibilities of trouble,
these signs—which Heydrich is at pains to multiply—must all be
taken into consideration. The Führer knows that power is vulnerable, and can be overthrown. Might not his opponents be
looking for French support? What did Schleicher and François-
Poncet say to each other? Did not the German Ambassador to
Paris report that on May 9 the Foreign Minister, Louis Barthou,
made some "sensational declarations about the internal situation
in Germany" before the Foreign Affairs Commission of the Chamber of Deputies? What did the French hope for? Who was keeping them informed? Was Schleicher their man?

Himmler and Heydrich use and interpret every detail in support of their thesis that Roehm and the SA are a threat to the power of the Reich. But gradually around this central kernel, a conglomeration of other dangers is developed by the masters of the Gestapo and the SS—dangers embodied in a few men: Papen's advisers, Jung and Bose, and Generals Schleicher and Bredow. In complicity with Goering, both Himmler and Heydrich add new names to the list—whether those of Catholics like Dr. Klausener, a potentially embarrassing witness or an SA officer.

It has now reached the point of lists, drawn up by the confidential agents of Himmler and Heydrich. One of these fills a position new to the Third Reich: he is commandant of a concentration camp at Dachau—one of those camps first conceived of by the Reichsführer SS, which will be so greatly expanded. Theodor Eicke is the SS Oberführer: in his presence, Dachau prisoners must stand at attention, military style, holding their caps in their hands. The prisoners are for the most part Communists and members of the Left-wing opposition; but when Heydrich meets with Eicke and asks him to prepare the SS for an eventual swift action against the SA, the Oberführer asks no questions. He immediately begins making such plans. Together with SD agents, he draws up lists. These grim papers circulate between the offices of the Gestapo and Goering: names are added or crossed out according to the sympathies or fears of the moment. Goering erases the name of Rudolf Diels, the former head of the Gestapo, which either Heydrich or Himmler had placed on one of the lists. Betz tries to protect Obergruppenführer Schneidhuber, but Betz is only an SD agent without Goering's authority: Schneidhuber remains on the list.

What should be done with these lists? Heydrich has convinced Himmler that there is only one solution: the liquidation of Roehm and his clique, of all opposition. Then he wins the support he needs for this definitive solution: from Goering, who has already decided on an alliance with the SS and the Gestapo, and from General von Reichenau.

Von Reichenau, the Reichswehr chief, is seen with increasing frequency at the Prinz-Albrecht Strasse offices of the Gestapo. In his key position, von Reichenau could be extremely useful. It would be easy for him to place arms, transport and barracks at the disposition of the SS. And reports from the Abwehr which reach the Chancellor's desk could "be arranged" to confirm those of the SD and the Gestapo. For Heydrich's plan has won over Reichenau: if any action is taken against the SA, the SS will take it. The Reichswehr will lend covert assistance, and enjoy the fruits of the operation. If the SA is liquidated, the Reichswehr will become the real strength of the Third Reich, and Hitler will have to accept the wishes of the Officers' Corps.

THE REICHSWEHR'S CHOICE

On May 16 the little town of Bad Nauheim is filled with official vehicles. The Reichswehr inspectors and the ranking officers from the Bendlerstrasse have chosen the town, surrounded by the fields and forests of Wetterau, and protected from the wind by the slopes of the Taunus, as the site for their meeting. General von Fritsch presides with the imperious authority of an officer of the General Staff, and everyone of any position in the Reichswehr has come to take part. Any decision taken here at Bad Nauheim will become the decision of the entire Officers' Corps. Blomberg and Reichenau are present.

General von Fritsch launches immediately into the central theme of the forthcoming discussion: whom does the Reichswehr wish to see as successor to Field Marshal Hindenburg? The officers suggest several names which have already been in circulation for some time: Ritter von Epp or the Crown Prince. Reichenau speaks, then Blomberg. Both are partisans of Hitler. Reichenau stresses the dangers represented by the SA, and observes that Hitler would rid Germany of the Sturmabteilung in exchange for the Presidency. Blomberg is even more blunt: a pact was drawn up on the cruiser *Deutschland,* trading the SA for the Presidency.

From that moment, further discussion is pointless because everyone agrees: the Reichswehr, heart and soul of the Reich, is ready to rally behind Hitler.

When the official cars carrying the pennants of Generals Blomberg, Fritsch and Reichenau drive off through the soft spring air along the little country road from Bad Nauheim toward Frankfurt, an important stage has been passed. None of the patients taking the cure, who watch from the tree-lined walks as the cars pass, have any idea that once again the Reichswehr has made a decision for Germany.

On May 25 von Fritsch publishes a new version of *The Duties of a German Soldier,* intended for the use of every member of the Reichswehr. It is the Army's breviary, its code of honor, which young conscripts have to swear to respect.

"Military service is a service of honor to the German people [Volk]," says the new text, in place of the traditional affirmation that the Reichswehr serves the State. "Volk"—another reference to Nazi concepts introduced into the Reichswehr, following the eagles and swastikas worn by the soldiers. The meeting at Bad Nauheim has borne fruit in less than two weeks.

At about the same time—toward the end of May, 1934—during the course of meetings, walks through the Berlin countryside and small dinners, two men, former Chancellors Brüning and Schleicher, are warned to be extremely careful. Their informers claim to have received information from members of Goering's entourage, who have let it be understood that Goering himself is not unaware of the leak. In a subtle manner, Brüning and Schleicher are given to understand that lists have been drawn up in preparation for a purge, whose form is not yet entirely clear. They are told that their names are on these lists of future victims, and that they must leave Berlin. Brüning, who has recognized Nazism for what it is, does not hesitate. In disguise, he leaves Germany without any difficulty. General Schleicher simply shrugs. At his friends' insistence, he agrees to take a holiday by the lake of Starnberg. However, he absolutely rules out the idea of an officer of the Reichswehr's abandoning his country. Furthermore, he doesn't really believe in the seriousness of the danger. He still has faith in his own ability and in the protection afforded him by his position as a general of the Reichswehr. He fails to understand that the Army now has a single obsession: to rid itself of the threat posed by the SA.

Via Heydrich's reports, Hitler learns that the SA is procuring arms abroad—especially machine guns. The Führer is inclined to be skeptical, but Himmler and Heydrich insist: one of their SS men, Major General Friedrich Wilhelm Krüger, a former pupil of the Cadet School, works in the SA.

Krüger left the Army in 1920 and entered the SS in 1931. He is now liaison officer between the Reichswehr and the SA. At the SA he is responsible for the instruction of young recruits—a way in which the Reichswehr, despite the Versailles Treaty, can insure itself of adequate military preparation on a national scale. Krüger very quickly becomes more military than the military, denigrating the SA and agreeing that the SA General Staff at Munich is a "pigsty," and that "the stables must be swept clean." He is also Himmler's spy, and his work on Himmler's behalf is undoubtedly to poison the relationship between the SA and the Reichswehr. His reports, which Heydrich shows to the Führer, mention SA arms depots in Berlin, Munich and Silesia. As Hitler remains skeptical, Heydrich supplies some details: the arms come from Liège, and were registered as freight for Arabia. The head of the SD is even better informed because the SA, when it buys arms, often does so on behalf of the Reichswehr, with money and means supplied by the Abwehr, the Army Intelligence Service. Provocations, traps, ingeniously false information—it is essential that the SA be doomed, that Hitler be persuaded to act. A special operation is organized. An agent dressed in civilian clothes bumps into a crate on the platform of Berlin's freight station. The box falls over and breaks, revealing dismantled machine guns. The crate is addressed to the SA leader Ernst. A further revelation: the Commandant of the Stettin military region, Field Marshal

Fedor von Bock, has also—by chance—seized one of these deliveries: this one of Belgian guns and machine guns. Reports from the SD and the Abwehr converge in Hitler's office. The proofs seem irrefutable. But everything has to await the Führer's verdict.

The SA themselves are watching the Führer hopefully, for inside the Sturmabteilung Adolf Hitler is still trusted. However, the SA has heard rumors; they know that lists are being circulated. The attitude of the military—arrogant, often mistrustful, and whenever possible unhesitatingly severe toward the SA—has enlightened them. But how can Hitler break with Minister Roehm, his oldest friend and supporter? It would be an act against nature. As long as Roehm is alive, the Sturmabteilung has nothing to fear. Danger comes from men like Goering and Papen. The NCOs of the Sturmabteilung hate these top Nazis, who rallied to the cause at the eleventh hour. Unlike them, Hitler, like Roehm, wants a second Revolution. Only the "Reaction"— Goering and the Reichswehr—stand in the way.

The duty of the Sturmabteilung has been to protect Hitler —Hitler, who sees the reports from Heydrich and Himmler denouncing the SA piling up on his desk; Hitler, for whose verdict everyone is obliged to wait.

6

Saturday, June 30, 1934
Bad Godesberg: Hotel Dreesen

Approaching Zero Hour

The stillness of midnight hangs over the valley of the Rhine and the town of Godesberg. The light breeze which usually rises from the river, carrying with it faint, distant sounds, has died down, and a gentle stillness has moved gradually up from the valley to the surrounding peaks, covering the countryside and stretching to the invisible horizon. Halfway to the summit gleams an island of white light: the Hotel Dreesen, surrounded by the silence and density of a quiet country night. The RAD volunteers, after a long series of "Sieg Heils," the bandsmen and the torchbearers have just left. Only the police remain, in their long leather coats, taking their hundred paces along the edge of the illuminated zone, disappearing into the darkness, emerging again into the light. The upper stories of the hotel are marked by an irregular checkerboard of lighted windows. The terrace is dimly lit by small spotlights, buried in mounds of flowers; the zones of light do not quite meet. In this semidarkness, in which the light dissolves and hangs in the air like a trail of dust reluctant to settle, a group of men silently wait for the Führer.

Hitler's face looks gray; there are seamed pouches under his eyes, and his stare is fixed, turned out to the night, seeing nothing: the look of a man who waits and hesitates. Goebbels sits beside him, watching him, making no effort to hide his anxiety. When Oberleutnant Brückner appears, Hitler stands up. Brückner tells him that Gruppenführer SS Sepp Dietrich has arrived in Munich, that he has called from there as the Führer ordered, and is on the line now, awaiting further instructions. Hitler does not hesitate, and as he harshly, somewhat hoarsely, barks out his orders, he seems to gain assurance, as if the sound of his own voice feeds his confidence. The men of his special guard, the Leibstandarte SS Adolf Hitler, should have arrived at Kaufering. Gruppenführer Sepp Dietrich should go directly to Kaufering, take command of the two companies, and proceed with these men to Bad Wiessee. Brückner repeats these orders before running back to the telephone: Leibstandarte, Bad Wiessee—Hitler's words return amplified, like an echo. They ring out once again at the telephone, close to the terrace: Brückner is obliged to shout into the mouthpiece. Then silence falls once more; the same silence that enfolds Bad Wiessee and the Pension Hanselbauer, where Ernst Roehm and the leaders of the Sturmabteilung are sleeping.

No one comments on the order Hitler has just given. Goebbels sits straight in his chair and smiles nervously; the deep lines in his face frame his mouth. Hitler remains standing. He asks someone to bring him his leather coat, and throwing it over his shoulders, begins to pace up and down.

By now Sepp Dietrich has left Munich. The car put at his disposal by the SS headquarters of Munich, the fief of Heydrich and Himmler, is rolling through the damp fields, its headlights picking out the flowering apple trees. The road to Kaufering is deserted. The chauffeur is told to dim the lights, which he does instantly. An SS officer has accompanied Sepp Dietrich; both men are silent. In their quarters, the SS of the Leibstandarte are lying fully dressed on beds lent them by the Reichswehr.

These men do not ask questions: they simply obey. Everything about this operation seems well organized, and must have been planned long in advance. They have been ready for action for several days now, instructed that the mission they are to carry out will require their utmost loyalty to the Führer. First they waited in Berlin. A supply unit attached to the Reichswehr and stationed at Ludwigsburg moved them from the capital. They lie now, half-sleeping, ready to carry out their orders, as Gruppenführer Sepp Dietrich drives toward them through the soft night.

In the hall of the Hotel Dreesen, Adolf Hitler has just received a call from Berlin. It is Reichsführer SS Himmler, telephoning from Gestapo headquarters. As he listens to Himmler, Hitler seems to be less and less able to control his nervousness. He answers in monosyllables, and then, almost dropping the telephone, begins to shout, his eyes suddenly brilliant. Using Goebbels as his sounding board, he pours out his grievances. It is almost 12:30 A.M. He explains that Himmler has just told him that the SA General Staff in Berlin has ordered a general alert for today, Saturday, at 4 P.M. At 5 the SA is to occupy the government buildings. "It's a putsch!" Hitler shouts, cursing, and repeating the word "putsch" several times. "Ernst did not go to Wiessee as he was supposed to." He must be the leader of the putsch. "They have been ordered to move into action." The violence of Hitler's language increases. Goebbels draws closer, also cursing the SA. Had not Stennes, the head of the Berlin SA, revolted against Party leadership as early as 1931? In a low voice, Goebbels recalls this, reminding the Führer of the pamphlet the SA distributed in the streets of Berlin on April 1, 1931, asserting that the Nazi Party and its leader had betrayed the SA and "National Socialism." Wasn't this the same thing all over again, only far more dangerous?

Hitler is visibly more and more nervous. Anxiety and violence are reflected in his face. He seems not to doubt for a moment the accuracy of Himmler's information. Goebbels, however, who arrived from Berlin late the previous evening, knows that Karl Ernst has left the capital for Bremen, to take a steamer to Teneriffe and Madeira, where he is planning to spend his honeymoon. But he says nothing of this to Hitler.

Some minutes pass, and just before 1 A.M. the telephone rings again. For the second time Hitler takes the receiver. Adolf Wagner, Gauleiter and Minister of the Interior of Bavaria, is calling from the Ministry. In Munich the Sturmabteilung have taken to the streets, shouting slogans hostile to the Führer and the Reichswehr. The Bavarian SA must have received the same orders as the Munich SA.

"It's all been planned," Hitler exclaims. The Führer curses the SA leaders, shouting that they are "vermin," traitors. The storm has broken. Goebbels looks on approvingly as Hitler speaks of retribution, pacing recklessly up and down.

At Bad Wiessee, Roehm is sleeping peacefully; in Munich the SA are in their barracks. A few SA did in fact demonstrate earlier in the evening, protesting the position of the Reichswehr, but their officers had intervened. One of the officers, standing on a car in the Königsplatz, had shouted to his men: "Retire peacefully to your barracks and wait for the Führer's decision. Whatever happens— whether Adolf Hitler dismisses us, whether he authorizes us to wear this uniform or forbids it—we are with him, and support him." The demonstration ended with shouts of "Heil Hitler!"

But Wagner has just telephoned the news of an SA insurrection, and the Führer is in the throes of one of his night rages, intensified by lack of sleep. He shrieks Roehm's name, drowning it in a stream of insults.

Suddenly Hitler shouts: "We must go to Munich immediately, and then to Bad Wiessee." After so many hours of uncertainty the moment of choice has come; Hitler has decided.

Later, on July 13, he will declare: "Only one decision was open to me. It was clear that only one man could stand up to Chief of Staff Roehm. It was I he had betrayed, and I alone could call him to account."

Hitler's verdict has been given, and the trap, so carefully prepared by so many men with such divergent interests and aims, is closing around the SA.

PART TWO

This Month Which Dies As This Day Dawns

Saturday, June 30, 1934

Hitler has made his decision. The Night of Long Knives will soon become reality. For Hitler, the time for action has come. He flies to Munich and on the way each day of the decisive month of June, 1934, will surge back to life in his memory. When he lands at Munich, June is nearly over—it will be 4 A.M. Saturday, June 30.

1

Saturday, June 30, 1934
Bad Godesberg: Hotel Dreesen

1:00 A.M.

Saturday, June 30, 1 A.M. In front of the Hotel Dreesen, men are running to the garages, or to the cars parked outdoors, some of them even in the garden itself. Oberleutnant Brückner, an imposing figure, stands motionless on the lawn, his legs wide apart. An SS NCO is receiving his orders: he must see that the road from Godesberg to the airport at Bonn is clear: a distance of about ten miles. The Führer does not wish to waste any time. Soon engines backfire, and two messengers start off, their powerful, black motorcycles leaning over until they look as if they will topple to the ground. But at the last moment, with a thrust of their spines, the drivers adjust the balance, and all that remains are two cones of white light cutting through the night, followed by dancing red taillights.

The front hall of the hotel is a scene of feverish agitation. Walter Breitmann runs to knock on the doors of the second floor bedrooms where some of the visiting Nazi leaders had already retired. He has warned them of the Führer's imminent departure, and they are now talking, their leather coats thrown over chairs. Hitler walks back and forth between the terrace and the hall with Goebbels beside him. The two men are locked in a running, sometimes whispered conversation. Goebbels rubs his hands together as he talks, watching the Führer's face for signs of approbation. But the Chancellor ignores the Minister of Propaganda. He walks, leaning slightly forward, interrupting Goebbels, his eyes gleaming, his face contorted. "A putsch!" he shouts. "Against me!" Is he playacting his surprise for Goebbels' benefit, for Goebbels, who knows that the messages sent by Himmler from Berlin are false? Is Hitler unaware of their falseness; has he really just arrived at his decision, or is he playing a part like the consummate actor he is?

He continues to talk, drawing up a balance, reordering history, already preparing the speech he will someday have to deliver. "For months," he says, "Roehm and I were engaged in extremely serious discussions." He calls the Party dignitaries to witness. Among them is Viktor Lutze, standing respectfully at attention. "During those discussions, for the first time, I began to have doubts about the man's loyalty."

Brückner appears and announces that the Führer's private plane will be ready to take off in less than an hour at the Bonn-Hangelar Airport. Hitler seems not to have heard him, wrapped up as he is in his accusations, in justifying the decision he has just made. This act has already passed beyond his control, having become at one with the plane whose motors are now being checked by mechanics in the steely light of their portable lamps—at one with Gruppenführer Sepp Dietrich's men, now standing in the courtyard of the barracks at Kaufering receiving their orders. Young boys in the black uniforms of the SS, they listen, numb with sleep, not yet wakened by the cool night air. Hitler's decision has become an act which gathers life and power with each passing minute, an act which will soon affect all Germany.

Hitler talks while Brückner and the hotel servants carry coats and black briefcases to the cars. He talks as though he is unable to stop, as if he must account for all the years he has known Roehm, for all the months since he took power, and above all for all the days of the month of June which will die with this day just beginning, this day only one hour old. Every hour of every day of this June, 1934, has seen move and countermove in a game which began months ago, moves which nevertheless now seem ineluctable.

(Friday, June 1, to Saturday, June 9)

It is dawn, Friday, June 1; at the Dachau camp, the prisoners wait, lined up between the wooden huts, staring straight ahead at the flat gray countryside beyond the barbed-wire fence. Rollcall seems to drag on much longer than usual. The mud of the walkways between the huts clings to their wooden shoes. On this particular morning, Oberführer Eicke, Commandant of the Dachau concentration camp, reviews the prisoners after they have stood without moving for several hours. Dark, sinister, Eicke is the arbiter of this curious life, regulated to run like a macabre clock. Now he no longer delays; he wishes to meet with his squad leaders as quickly as possible. He has just received an order from Heydrich involving his men in a swift action against the SA of Munich, Lechfeld and Bad Wiessee. The squad leaders of the Dachau SS ask no questions: at Dachau the SS are even more disciplined and blindly obedient than elsewhere. They are true members of the Totenkopfverbände (Death's-Head Troops), who obey, kill and sing. In calling on the men from Dachau, Heydrich has chosen wisely.

Oberführer Eicke is a man admirably suited to Heydrich's requirements, a good officer, blindly devoted to his leaders. He has drawn up lists of men to be liquidated, asking no questions. He knows how to do what is asked of him, and does it. With his group leaders he draws up plans for a swift action to seize the SA on their own ground.

In Munich, also, the SS sections receive Heydrich's orders,

and prepare for action. Although the date has not yet been set, Heydrich's orders are formal: the men who will participate in the action must be ready to start within a matter of hours. The leader of the SD and the Gestapo and Reichsführer Himmler seem to be sure of their position. On Saturday, June 2, Eicke begins preparing his men, and then waits, while the Death's-Head Troops take out their nervous irritation on the prisoners.

Who knows what is happening in the Dachau camp during these first two days of June, 1934? Dachau is a small, tranquil town whose sinister destiny is still as unknown to the Germans as to the rest of the world. Guidebooks place it five miles to the west of Schleissheim, where there are two magnificent castles of the twelfth and eighteenth centuries, the latter resembling the château at Versailles. Dachau is nothing more than a town in a privileged position, dominating the Bavarian plain. From the town one can catch glimpses of the Dachau marshes, a spot favored by painters because of its greens and grays, blues and whites, its changing mix of sky, earth and water. Who is aware of Oberführer Eicke's orders? Why be concerned for these prisoners, who, on Saturday, June 2, line up before the SS, their fingers and arms tensed by the strain of standing at attention, their caps in their hands? Blows shower down on some of the prisoners; some of them fall.

Even at Dachau, however, on Sunday, June 3, rest is respected. The prisoners lie somnolent in the smelly heat of their barracks, watching the day pass—their single day of false liberty—which is hard and without joy because their minds are constructing their own memories and torments, measuring time past and future, and listening to the world's silence and Germany's shouts of "Heil Hitler!"

The Catholic prisoners pray, unaware that on that day, at Fulda, the bishops of the Third Reich have come together in plenary session.

In the small town, as beautiful as a museum, Mass has been celebrated in the cathedral, which lifts its two baroque towers and its dome into the light-blue air of the June morning. In the distance lie the Rhön; the peak of Vogelsberg is veiled by fog. The Mass is solemn, as if the centuries had stopped at the age of triumphant faith. Beneath the choir the Chapel of St. Boniface contains the relics of the saint martyred by the pagans in 755: Boniface, the apostle to Germany. The bishops take Communion, some of them kneeling on the stone paving: how could they fail to think of the martyr, now that a Black Order has established itself in Germany? Monsignor Faulhaber, the Primate of Bavaria, is there in his priestly vestments, an old man who, beneath the gold trim of his garment, already looks like one of the statues of gilded wood which ornament the churches of South Germany.

Beside Monsignor Faulhaber is a young man with an animated face which is not aged by the gold of his habit. The young man's expression is vital and lively; he often turns his head, in a sudden movement, to look at the other worshipers. He is Monsignor Barres, the new Bishop of Berlin. Since his installation less than six months earlier, in January, the Gestapo has been watching him, and Himmler has personally been reading the reports which come in about him. Monsignor Barres has rallied militant Catholics; his pastoral letters condemn violence and excess. Often, the car of a high official of the Reich, Dr. Klausener, is seen parked in front of the Bishop's residence. Klausener, Director of Public Works, is a practicing Catholic and a man of principle. He is close to Vice Chancellor Papen, also a Catholic. For weeks, Klausener's name, along with the names of Jung, Bose and others, has been on the list of those to be kept under close watch. He may also be on the lists drawn up by Heydrich. He frequently sees Monsignor Barres, and the Gestapo does not like coincidences. Several Gestapo agents have been sent to Fulda; they watch, listen, make notes. Reichsführer Himmler, himself a born Catholic whose Black Guard apes the Jesuit Order, personally gave them their orders. However, it seems that nothing out of the ordinary is happening. The Gestapo agents wander about the old episcopal city. After Mass the bishops retire, led by Monsignor Bertram, the Cardinal Primate of Silesia and Head of the Assembly.

Everything is calm until the phrase "Beware of false prophets!" is heard.

The Bishop's pastoral letter denounces the "atheists who, with hands raised against us, consciously fight against the Christian faith." At the hour when Dachau Socialists, Communists and Jews answer the evening rollcall to the sound of barking dogs and the harsh voices of the SS, this phrase can refer only to the Nazis and the men of the Black Guard. Step by step they are re-establishing a pagan cult that revives pre-Christian Nordic mythology, to the sound of horns which ring back to remote Germanic tribes.

At No. 8 Prinz-Albrecht Strasse, Himmler and Heydrich are anxious. The switchboard of the Gestapo's central office in Berlin is also a monitoring station for all communications emanating from Fulda. Gestapo agents note that in Berlin itself many Catholic figures refer to the text of the pastoral letter. Is the Catholic Church, for so long passive, about to take a stand against the regime? Goering is informed, and there are a series of consultations. Is all this the beginning of a Papen-Hindenburg maneuver, perhaps supported by Generals Schleicher and von Bredow and certain elements in the Reichswehr? And what position will be taken by Roehm and the SA?

The Chancellory, in turn, is informed; but Hitler remains aloof, while Goering, Himmler and Heydrich join efforts. From the large, silent building where the Black Guards of the Leibstandarte SS stand like blocks of sculpted granite covered by cloth and metal, Hitler watches the movements of men. Hermann Goering, war hero, officer, Junker, linked to the worlds of high finance and the Reichswehr—could he, with the support of certain conservatives, not be a rival for the succession to Hindenburg, an aspirant to the top position in a Reich without Hitler?

As day breaks on Monday, June 4, Hitler is still uncertain as to the best method of attaching to himself the powerful men in the Army and in industry, men whom he fears and mistrusts. Should he pay for their support by sacrificing the Sturmabteilung, following through on the "*Deutschland* Pact" to its logical conclusion, or should he preserve a tamed and domesticated SA, still sufficiently strong to act as a threat, a sheathed sword, a pretext, a means of blackmail? Is it possible to avoid acting at this moment when everything seems to be accelerating?

During the morning of Monday, June 4, Otto von Meissner, secretary to von Hindenburg, calls the Chancellory. The Field Marshal is not well; he will be leaving Berlin that day for Neudeck. It is hoped that on the flat, quiet plain the President's strength will rally. But Hitler is no fool; he understands that this will be Hindenburg's last journey. The old warrior from another century is going to lay his bones in the earth at Neudeck, the center of strength and faith of his caste. From the Chancellory orders are sent out to ensure the old man a smooth journey. Then Hitler shuts himself up to think again about the future, which is drawing steadily closer. At Neudeck, beside the dying old man, will be Meissner, ambitious and devoted, in whom Hitler has confidence, and Oskar von Hindenburg, who thinks only of his lands and his rank in the Army, and who can be held by a few hundred acres and a promotion. However, these men will be reliable allies only insofar as they understand that the Führer will be able to hold onto power by himself. This brings Hitler back to the choice before him. He has been warned that Papen will accompany Hindenburg to Neudeck, and will stay there several days—Papen, a fox without courage, but who is emblematic of the whole clan of Jungs, Klauseners, Boses, Tschirschkys; Papen, who drew up Hindenburg's testament, and to whom the old man turns as a son, successor and friend, with a mind already touched by death.

At the central station in Berlin the guard performs the ritual honors for Hindenburg, who will never return. Brusquely, Hitler arrives at a decision: Brückner makes a phone call, and a motorcycle messenger leaves the Chancellory. Ernst Roehm is called to an immediate meeting with the Führer, today, Monday, June 4, 1934. At the Gestapo offices, the unexpected news passes from desk to desk until it reaches Heydrich and Himmler. Will they be obliged to recall their lists, cancel the orders given to Oberführer

Eicke, break all the arrangements arrived at with Hermann Goering and von Reichenau? What is Hitler thinking of? This Monday is a dark day at No. 8 Prinz-Albrecht Strasse: the Führer can still reverse himself and reach a new understanding with Roehm. It is necessary to wait, to avoid precipitous action. Heydrich, apparently unperturbed, sorts index cards, reads reports of monitored telephone conversations and meets with his agents planted in the heart of the Sturmabteilung. He must find out what he can.

With a clatter of boots, the guard salutes Ernst Roehm at the entrance of the Chancellory. He responds with happy assurance, walking briskly to his moment of revenge. He smiles at Oberleutnant Brückner as the Führer comes to meet him, relaxed and friendly, as in the good old days of their friendship. Then the tall black door of the Chancellor's office shuts behind the two men.

Five hours later, Brückner bows as Roehm and Hitler come back through this door. Hitler is slumped with exhaustion, fatigue the only expression on his face. Roehm, too, is marked by the hours of argument: his neck and cheeks are covered with red blotches. He walks slowly and alone through the Chancellory hall to his car.

Later, on July 13, 1934, after Roehm's death, Hitler, the only witness to this final encounter, will describe it to the deputies and to Germany, beneath the bright lights of the Kroll Opera: "At the beginning of June, I made a final effort with Roehm. I asked him to come to my office, and we talked together for nearly five hours." What was actually said on that occasion we shall never know, but perhaps some of the truth of that last meeting between the two men, one of whom contributed to the rise of the other, survives in Hitler's account.

"I told him I had the impression that certain conscienceless elements were preparing a Nationalist-Bolshevik revolution, which could lead only to miseries beyond description. I also told him that I had heard a rumor that the Army was to be involved in this action."

Perhaps Hitler actually mentioned Schleicher and Bredow, or perhaps he dwelled only on the second Revolution, the Night of

Nuremberg, 1933: Less than a year before the Night of Long Knives, Hitler reviews the SA with Chief of Staff Major Ernst Roehm. (H. Hoffmann — Zeitgeschichtliches Bildarchiv)

February 1, 1934: One of the last meetings between Roehm and Hitler. (Ullstein)

January 30, 1933: Hitler takes over. The Nazi leaders pose for a photograph, from left to right: Wilhelm Kube, Gauleiter Kurmark, Wilhelm Frick (seated), Joseph Goebbels, Hitler, Roehm, Hermann Goering, Walther Darré, Heinrich Himmler, Rudolf Hess. (H. Hoffmann — Zeitgeschichtliches Bildarchiv)

Ernst Roehm (H. Hoffmann — Zeitgeschichtliches Bildarchiv)

Daluege, Himmler and Roehm review the SS. (Keystone)

Hitler, Roehm and Brückner (far right) during an SA parade. The SS and soldiers follow. Sepp Dietrich is on the far left. (Ullstein)

The SS and SA are joined "fraternally," as Goering and Roehm attend the wedding of Karl Ernst. (Süddeutscher Verlag)

1934: The SA banners are presented to Gruppenführer Ernst. (H. Hoffmann — Zeitgeschichtliches Bildarchiv)

Roehm and SS Reichsführer Himmler. (H. Hoffmann—Zeit-geschichtliches Bildarchiv)

May 1 youth demonstration in Berlin: Franz von Papen (holding top hat), General Werner von Blomberg (second row, directly to Hitler's right), Hitler and Goebbels. (H. Hoffmann—Zeitgeschichtliches Bildarchiv)

Hitler talks with Reichswehr leaders, General Blomberg (left) and General Freiherr Werner von Fritsch. (H. Hoffmann — Zeitgeschichtliches Bildarchiv)

Roehm meets officers of the Reichswehr. To Roehm's left, Field Marshal Guenther Hans Kluge; to his right, Krüger, who effected the liaison between the SA and the Army. (H. Hoffmann—Zeitgeschichtliches Bildarchiv)

The *Deutschland* cruise: Hitler with Admiral Erich Raeder (to his right) and Captain von Fischel. (Archives of author)

June 16, 1934: Hitler meets Mussolini in Venice. (Keystone)

Several days later Hitler visits the ailing Hindenburg at his estate at Neudeck. (H. Hoffmann—Zeitgeschichtliches Bildarchiv)

Joseph Goebbels delivers his final warning to Roehm. (Bibliothèque Nationale, Paris)

Both camps make plans. (right) Roehm and his aide Count Spreti. (Keystone) (below) SS Sepp Dietrich meets often with Brückner. (H. Hoffmann — Zeitgeschichtliches Bildarchiv)

Erich Klausener, Government Minister and leader of Catholic Action. (Ringart)

Viktor Lutze, Roehm's successor. (H. Hoffmann—Zeitgeschichtliches Bildarchiv)

SA Führer Walther Stennes. (Ringart)

General Kurt von Schleicher. (Keystone)

Just before takeoff, Hitler examines the flight map. Brückner is at his side. (H. Hoffmann — Zeitgeschichtliches Bildarchiv)

Hitler descends first from the Junker.

June 28, 1934: Hitler visiting the Krupp factories at Essen. (Archives of author)

The Führer reviews a unit of the Labor Front (RAD) at Bad Godesberg, June 29, 1934. (Archives of author)

Goebbels, arriving in the Rhineland, June 29, 1934, en route
to the Führer at the Dreesen Hotel. (Archives of author)

On the road with the SS: Sepp Dietrich in the center, behind
Hitler. (H. Hoffmann—Zeitgeschichtliches Bildarchiv)

Bad Wiessee. Pension Hanselbauer is to the right at the edge of the lake. (Engel-Sonnefeld)

Hitler leaving the Brown House in Munich. (H. Hoffmann — Zeitgeschichtliches Bildarchiv)

Sunday, July 1: Hitler's tea at the Chancellery in Berlin. He salutes the crowd while the vigilant SS keep watch. (Süddeutscher Verlag)

July 13, 1934: The Reichstag meets at the Kroll Opera House to approve Hitler's action. The Führer has just delivered his famous speech. Goering is at the rostrum as President of the Reichstag. (Süddeutscher Verlag)

Long Knives, dreamed of by certain of the SA. But the essence of what passed between Roehm and himself was not reported. His real purpose appears in this part of his account:

"I said to the Chief of Staff that those who thought that the SA should be dissolved were entirely mistaken, that I myself could not prevent the spread of this falsehood, but that any attempt to spread disorder in Germany would be met by my immediate personal opposition, and that whoever attacked the State must consider me his enemy."

Hitler must have explained to Roehm the vague dangers threatening the Third Reich, the Party and himself. The violence of the SA only compromised the reputation of the Party, and weakened it.

"I also complained somewhat bitterly about the excesses of the SA and demanded sanctions against the elements responsible for these excesses so that millions of brave Party members would not have their honor tainted by the actions of a minority."

But the question was one less of honor than of prudence. Roehm defended himself against every accusation, declaring that he had already made inquiries and had punished the guilty, and that he would "do whatever was necessary to re-establish order," attacking in turn the Alte Kämpfer and all those who wished to make difficulties for the Sturmabteilung. Then, after their five-hour talk, the two men left Hitler's office.

In his speech of July 13, however, in which he justified the repression which was operating throughout Germany, Hitler failed to mention the central consideration. On Tuesday, June 5, the SD and the Gestapo were warned that an agreement on several points had been reached between Hitler and Roehm. This agreement, to be sure, did not touch on the deepest source of their differences, but did demonstrate that the two men had arrived at a truce. Heydrich and Himmler, and then von Reichenau, studied its terms. The central offices of the Gestapo and Bendlerstrasse were in constant communication. Everything seemed clear: as decided on April 20, the SA were to be sent on leave during the month of

July. Roehm had already let it be known that he was planning to take a well-earned holiday during July, and had laughingly announced that he would go to Bad Wiessee to take a cure for his rheumatism and his wounds. To the SA leaders who had been waiting for him impatiently, he simply said that Hitler had wished to dissipate their misunderstanding, and that he would meet with the entire General Staff of the SA at Bad Wiessee before the leave began, to complete discussions on the future of the movement. Roehm did not comment any further on his conversation with Hitler; instead, he turned the subject to Wiessee, which he knew well, to the lake and its thermal waters. He had already delegated his powers to Gruppenführer von Krausser, his adjutant at the General Staff of the SA. His decision and his words were known at the Gestapo offices by Wednesday, June 6. Heydrich's agents inside the SA made their report: the leaders of the Sturmabteilung had accepted all Roehm's arrangements. A few had asked somewhat anxiously if their enforced leave did not anticipate a "putsch" against Hitler by the "Reaction"; but the majority had rejoiced: a vacation is in itself one of the advantages conferred by power.

Karl Ernst, the former hotel doorman who commanded the Berlin SA, was extremely pleased by the news, and launched into a long reverie about the sun, islands and the ocean, like a contented newly rich man. He was preparing his honeymoon trip; he had just married, with Hitler as his witness, and was going to the Canaries and Madeira. He reserved passage on a steamer sailing from Bremen at the end of the month. Gruppenführer Georg von Detten, head of the SA political branch, made plans to go to Bad Wildungen, a small and charming watering place on the Wilde, a tributary of the Eder. There, some ninety miles from Cologne, he would treat his rheumatism. Others were planning foreign trips; some rented rooms and houses for their families. All these reports were received anxiously at 8 Prinz-Albrecht Strasse: it would be difficult to accuse these absent men of preparing a putsch. The trap carefully set by Heydrich, Himmler and Goering, and approved by Reichenau, might not work if the SA were allowed to leave for holidays during the month of July. To destroy the SA, they would have to strike before the end of June, and convince Hitler before Saturday, June 30.

Heydrich and Himmler studied all the possibilities of action. The evening of Thursday, June 7, the text of a bulletin from the General Staff of the Sturmabteilung was delivered to Gestapo headquarters. The bulletin was to be published in a day or so (it was, in fact, published on June 10 by the *National Zeitung*). Heydrich read it first, and immediately, his mind alert to the possibility of a chase, saw the advantages to be drawn from this declaration, so full of Roehm's pride and lack of caution.

"I hope," Roehm wrote, "that on the first of August a well-rested SA, filled with fresh strength, will be ready to undertake the glorious mission it owes the people and the Fatherland. If the enemies of the SA think that it will not return from leave, or return only in part, let them enjoy their illusions as long as they can. When the day comes, these people will receive an adequate reply, in whatever form necessity dictates. The Sturmabteilung is and will remain the destiny of Germany." The last phrase resounded like a slap: Hitler had not managed to win Roehm over. The Chief of Staff, an officer from the trenches with a rough and ready manner, had granted only a deferment. He had renounced none of his ambitions.

Thursday night, June 7, the black cars of the Gestapo stopped in front of Hermann Goering's residence. His legs planted far apart, his huge body draped in white, his fingers glittering with rings, Minister Goering received two men: Himmler, with the drab, insignificant face common among fanatics, and Heydrich, thin and icy. They brought with them Roehm's bulletin. He had revealed himself too soon as a garrulous adventurer, a rash and foolhardy soldier of fortune.

The Führer, withdrawn in a disturbing silence, said nothing. Himmler, Heydrich and Goering continued to collect proofs of their version of things: arms, troubles in Prussia provoked by the SA, ties with France, with Schleicher and Bredow. Himmler also brought up the name of Gregor Strasser: he, too, belonged to the conspiracy. Werner von Alvensleben, president of the Herrenklub, in which Papen was an eminent figure, would have been in touch with all the co-conspirators. Everything was ready. Ernst in Berlin, Heines in Silesia, Hayn in Saxony, Heydebreck in Pomerania— all these SA Lieutenant Generals were part of the plot. Colonel Julius Uhl had been chosen to kill the Führer.

Hitler was given the reports, listened to the speculations, but came to no final decision. Heydrich, Himmler and Goering were committed and ready, but Chancellor Hitler said nothing.

At the Bendlerstrasse there was a period of self-questioning. Hitler's attitude was unclear. Would the *"Deutschland* Pact" be respected? Blomberg, Fritsch and Reichenau conferred. Messengers carried letters to the Gestapo offices, and Reichenau himself, a General of the Reichswehr, did not hesitate to meet Lutze and Himmler, or to see Himmler again at 8 Prinz-Albrecht Strasse. The Gestapo's automobiles were often seen parked beside Army cars or cars of the General Staff. The night of Friday, June 8, and Saturday, June 9, a new element was added: the Bendlerstrasse building was suddenly placed in a state of alert; patrols walked the Ministry roof, and Reichswehr trucks filled with armed troops were parked along the Bendlerstrasse and on the neighboring embankments. Cars also arrived from the Gestapo. The next day the papers did not mention the incident; however, it was considered serious. The Army had feared a sudden attack by the SA. During the day there were several brawls between Army officers and men from the Sturmabteilung. The Army was uneasy: the honor of the entire caste had been tainted, for a police inquiry had just established that Fräuleins von Natzmer and von Jena and Frau von Falkenhayn, all relatives of well-known generals, were gravely compromised in an affair of Polish espionage. Sosnowski, an elegant Pole, who had at one time been a German Army officer, had, with the help of these young women employed in the Bendlerstrasse offices, managed to pass on some secret documents. The Reichswehr Captain responsible for the documents had killed himself, even though he was innocent of any crime—a Reichswehr officer has a sense of honor. The SA might use this incident to discredit the Reichswehr, to foment a Brown Shirt riot and force Hitler into a surprise action.

However, on the morning of the ninth the cordons of soldiers stationed in the Bendlerstrasse were withdrawn; the SA assault had not taken place. But Generals Blomberg and Reichenau were to remember this night.

2

Saturday, June 30, 1934
Bad Godesberg: Hotel Dreesen

1:15 A.M.

The cars are drawn up beside the steps of the Hotel Dreesen. Hitler and Goebbels get into the back seat of the first Mercedes, Brückner into the front beside the chauffeur. The Chancellor's car starts off as soon as the doors are shut. Obergruppenführer SA Viktor Lutze, Otto Dietrich, the head of Hitler's press service, and the other Nazi leaders leave in no particular order. Their destination is the airport at Bonn-Hangelar. After a few wide curves through vineyards, the road becomes a long straight line across the flat alluvial plain. The heavy cars move swiftly forward, leaving behind them the villas of Bad Godesberg, already approaching the gentle slope before Hochkreuz, splashing water from puddles on the road left by the downpour of a few hours ago, when nothing was definite, when Hitler had not yet given freedom of action to Himmler, Heydrich and Goering.

At this moment, while Hitler proceeds to Bonn, Goering has already been informed of the Führer's decision by the Gestapo.

In his presidential palace, surrounded by cordons of police since the beginning of the afternoon of June 29, guarded by nests of machine guns, Hermann Goering feels well protected. In one of the dimly lit rooms of the palace sleeps Councilor Arthur Nebe, a high official of the criminal police. Since two o'clock in the afternoon he has been responsible for the safety of Goering's person. During the afternoon he shadowed Goering and his wife, Emmy, who had innocently gone shopping in one of the big shops on Leipziger Strasse. It seemed an odd mission to Nebe, whose rank ordinarily required of him neither shadowing nor acting as a bodyguard, but such were the ways of the New Reich. Now Nebe dozes as best he can, listening to the almost nonstop ringing of the Minister's telephone, the hurrying footsteps of messengers, and the orders which begin to resound through the great hall of Hermann Goering's presidential palace.

(Sunday, June 10, to Saturday, June 16)

Goering had tried to make the heavy, pompous Karinhall truly magnificent, following the usual pattern of megalomania which left its marks on everything he touched. On Sunday, June 10, Nebe had been given the assignment of protecting Karinhall during Goering's housewarming. Goering had invited some forty people, diplomats and dignitaries of the regime, to the baroque dwelling crammed with old masters, animal skins, portraits of Frederick the Great and Napoleon.

Among the guests visiting the card room, the gold room, the silver room, the library, the cinema, the gymnasium, Sir Edgar Phipps, the Ambassador from the United Kingdom, watches Hermann Goering with the ironic eye of the British establishment. Goering, enormously fat, changes his clothes several times during the course of the evening. Dressed first as an "aviator in a rubber suit with high boots and a large hunting knife in his belt," and then in tennis clothes, Goering tries, before the eyes of his guests, to arrange the mating of a bison and an ordinary cow. "The bison," Phipps remembers, "left his stall with the greatest reluctance, and, having considered the cow with an air of intense sorrow, tried to turn away." To complete the tour, the guests were obliged to visit the vault destined for the coffin of Goering's first wife, Karin.

Arthur Nebe had been a witness to these exaggerated displays. Now the noise of the comings and goings in the Ministry wakes him, and confirms his impression that the night which has just begun will be filled with fateful events, that it is the night he and his friend H. B. Gisevius had foreseen. Nebe has promised to telephone Gisevius—a high official in the Ministry of Interior—if something happens during the night. These two young police officials have their reservations about Nazism. Aware of the fresh information steadily coming in, they both have sensed that tension between the Nazi factions is rising, and that a confrontation with Roehm and his SA is inevitable. They wait and watch: police reports from every town in Germany are daily proof that neither the individuals involved nor their organizations can tolerate each other much longer.

On June 10 the Museum of the National Socialist Revolution was inaugurated at Halle, in the heart of town, beside the university. Army veterans belonging to the Stahlhelm, the rightist group, arrive together. The SA is already stationed on the steps, aggressively denying entry to anyone wearing insignia other than the Party emblem. The veterans protest: some of them are wearing brown shirts, but the SA hold firm. The prefecture of the Halle police has decreed that any insignia other than that of the Party "would be an insult to a movement whose glories the museum celebrates, glories in which they [the Stahlhelm] do not wish to participate." When certain members of the Stahlhelm try to push past the SA, a fight breaks out, short but rough. The Stahlhelm is repulsed: if they remove their insignia, they may enter.

The veterans' protests reach Berlin on Monday, June 11. On the same day, an even graver incident occurs in Magdeburg.

Magdeburg is an austere Prussian town, its fortress of glistening greenish stone embraced by two arms of the Elbe. The Reichswehr feels at home here; the town houses the command headquarters of the IV Army Corps. On Monday, June 11, members of the Stahlhelm have assembled to welcome their former president who is now Minister of Labor of the Reich. Franz Seldte has gone over to Hitler, and has pushed his organization toward Nazism, but he and the Stahlhelm do not favor the Sturmabteilung. According to the SA, Seldte and his veterans did nothing to help the Nazis take power, and are simply running after the victors now that they have won. When Minister Seldte arrives at Magdeburg, only the Stahlhelm and representatives of the Reichswehr are on hand to welcome him. In the hall near the Domplatz, as Seldte prepares to speak, the SA intervene. Seldte is roughly manhandled and arrested. Members of the SA burst into the hall and break up the meeting; Seldte is dragged off and held for several hours by the SA. Witnesses in the Reichswehr and the Stahlhelm protest in vain, then try to get in touch with the police prefect, who is also the SA General Schragmuller. However, the general-prefect cannot be found. With ironic smiles, his office replies that he has gone on an inspection tour; when the witnesses persist, shouting that Seldte is a Minister of the Reich, the answer is that the SA knows nothing whatever of the matter. In his official comment, General Schragmuller later declares that Seldte had not been recognized, and that an inquiry has been opened.

In Berlin, at the Ministry of the Interior, Nebe, Gisevius and everyone else aware of such comments can only conclude that the complicity of the SA police prefect prevents him from pursuing the guilty parties. However, on that same Monday, June 11, the journalist Erich Seipert, who is considered well informed, and whose articles reflect the opinion of the government, publishes an article entitled "The Sturmabteilung and Disarmament." In it, Seipert implies that relations among the SA, the Reichswehr and the Party are excellent, and that Germany faces a period of internal peace. Obviously, in circles close to Hitler, there is an effort to reassure public opinion; perhaps it is also hoped that the various factions will understand that the Führer wants agreement among all those who support him.

It is therefore not surprising that on Tuesday, June 12, none of the German papers mentions the incidents at Halle or Magdeburg, or that on the same day a meeting takes place which is known to only a few people, and which indicates that nothing is yet settled.

ROEHM AND GOEBBELS

In the early morning the proprietor of the Munich restaurant Nürnberger Bratwurstglöckl am Dom, at No. 9 Frauenplatz, receives a visitor who asks him to reserve a private room for the evening, as two important personages wish to meet there.

The Bratwurstglöckl is well known in Munich, and is particularly celebrated for its grilled sausages. Situated on the beautiful Frauenplatz, where four streets converge, the restaurant faces the Church of Our Lady, the Frauenkirche, whose stiff grandeur and austere design are somewhat softened by the reddish color of the bricks and the white marble of the tombstones inserted in the façade. It is a small piece of old Munich; the Frauenkirche was built in the fifteenth century.

On Tuesday evening, June 12, within the space of a few minutes, two cars stop in the shadow of the Frauenkirche, and park at the corner of Filserstrasse, where the street runs into the square. A man gets out of each car, and walks alone into the restaurant. Both are in civilian clothes: one wears a large hat, the other is bareheaded; one is fat, dressed without elegance, and walks with a heavy tread; the other is slender and limps. In the general uproar of the main dining room where drinking songs are sung in chorus by the waiters to the rhythmic table-pounding of twenty or thirty heavy tankards, the men pass through unnoticed. The headwaiter takes them to a back room with a heavy door. Inside, the sounds from the front are muffled. As the two men meet, and shake hands, the headwaiter cannot help but recognize Ernst Roehm and Joseph Goebbels. Before he enters with their beer, the headwaiter knocks firmly, and allows a long moment to pass. Discretion is the rule. The Gestapo, who are tailing Roehm, as well as all the other important figures in the government, will probably report on this meeting. For Heydrich, Himmler and Goering, the report is serious, and will be carefully evaluated. Is Goebbels acting on his own initiative, taking Roehm's part and rediscovering his past as a Nazi of the Left, or is he, as usual, being prudent and cunning, sniffing out the lay of the land before making his move? Or—another possibility—is he a messenger from Hitler, who may not wish to lose contact with Roehm, since he has not yet decided what to choose: repression and liquidation, as the Gestapo, SS and Reichswehr want, or compromise?

During the evening of Wednesday, June 13, the SD and the Gestapo send new information to 8 Prinz-Albrecht Strasse, indicating that Goebbels has been acting for Hitler. For the Sturmabteilung's enemies this is extremely serious. The information is entirely unexpected, indeed spectacular: that afternoon the Führer met with Gregor Strasser, the pharmacist from Bavaria, former head of Nazi propaganda, who had led the Nazi faction in the Diet of Bavaria, and then in the Reichstag, and who has not exercised any official functions for more than two years. Nonetheless he remains a man with an important name in the Party and Adolf Hitler knows it. Perhaps he also remembers the day when, protesting Hitler's imprisonment in the Landsberg fortress, Gregor Strasser had cried: "The imprisonment of this just man is a stigma of infamy for Bavaria." With his large face and shaved head, Gregor Strasser still casts too long a shadow for Hitler, even though he is no longer active. Heydrich and Himmler know this very well, and have put their former comrade's name on their lists. However, Chancellor Hitler still seems disposed to a reconciliation with Strasser. Gestapo agents report that Strasser is once again allowed to wear his Party insignia of honor engraved with a number 9. Certain informers claim that Hitler has offered Strasser the Ministry of Economics, but that Strasser, sure of his strength, has demanded the elimination of Goering and Goebbels.

And who else? At Gestapo headquarters and in Goering's presidential palace, there is silence. The plotters weigh the cost of turning Hitler back. Perhaps Roehm, too, has drawn up lists; perhaps teams of SA killers are ready to strike, like the SS of Colonel Eicke, in training at Dachau. When a trap has been set, it must snap shut, seizing its prey; otherwise vengeance may strike, and the trap used against those who set it. While Hitler seems to hesitate, Himmler, Heydrich and Goering are more than ever determined to act, to bring pressure to bear on the Führer. But Hitler is no longer in Berlin.

At the Munich-Oberwiesenfeld Airport, Thursday, June 14, is a day of continuous orders. At 8:10 the Führer arrives in his black Mercedes. Shortly after, Brückner, Otto Dietrich, Schaub and Hoffmann arrive in other official cars, and then officials from the Foreign Office: Konstantin von Neurath, Hans Thomson, Hans Ulrich von Kotze, and the Director of the Bavarian Press Service. Hitler makes a few jokes, and shakes the hand of Bauer, his pilot, before going over to his personal plane, whose engines have just stopped after a test run. High on the cockpit one can read the name of the plane: the *Immelmann*; and on the gray fuselage, its registration number: 2,600. Those who know the Führer detect signs of nervousness despite his good humor: a frequent smoothing of his hair, an uneven gait. Hat in hand and wrapped in a beige raincoat, slightly stooped, he looks like a German civil servant of medium rank. Waving to various officials as he climbs the steps to the plane, this man is going to meet the most-talked-about head of government in Europe and the world, a man of vigorous appearance, with his shaved head and declamatory style: Il Duce, Benito Mussolini. In many ways he has served as a model for Hitler; the Chancellor undoubtedly remembers the day in 1923 —before the November putsch in Munich, itself an imitation of the 1922 March on Rome—when, an almost totally unknown political agitator, he asked the Duce for a signed photograph, which Mussolini haughtily refused to send. Today Hitler will meet the Duce in Venice.

At 8:20, Hitler's plane takes off, followed by a second plane piloted by Schnäbele, carrying various German experts. The discussion (the first between the two dictators since Hitler took power) will be of prime importance, touching on the future of Austria and reviewing relations between the two national parties. There have been discreet meetings in the corridors of the Wilhelmstrasse; emissaries of Vice Chancellor Papen and others acting for Goering have explained that the Duce, with his great authority, could advise the Führer on how to get rid of the anarchy within his own party. Special envoys have been sent to the German Embassy in Rome: there the diplomats listened, made appointments, saw their Italian colleagues, particularly members of the Duce's cabinet—and made discreet allusions to Roehm and the violence of the SA. Hitler would surely take the Duce's advice. Nothing had been said on that point, but the Germans had made themselves understood. Would the Duce speak out, and would Hitler listen?

The two planes slowly rise. Immediately the peaks of the Alps come into view, spotted with brilliant patches of glacial lakes that seem frozen to the valley floors. On the shores of one of these lakes, the Tegernsee, is the town of Bad Wiessee, where SA Captain Roehm has just arrived. Slowly the sky clears, and beyond the Brenner Pass one can see Brixen and the Dolomites.

As he often does, Hitler sits beside the pilot. He likes flying: he pursued his electoral campaigns flying from town to town in his personal plane. Now he flies on his tours of inspection too, moving in a couple of hours from one district to another. The pilot shows Hitler the whitish mass of the Marmolada, a kind of natural fortress, and then the Venetian Alps and, in their shadow, the long, sinuous ribbon of the Po. The German planes make two descending turns over the lagoons. Glittering points of light appear in the sky: the Italian squadrons coming to meet the

Führer. Soon the planes are flying over Murano and the Lido, and at ten o'clock they land at the San Nicolò Airport.

First the sun, then a crowd of Italian officials, and then Mussolini in dress uniform, and the diplomats, and the Fascist *Squadre*. The small group of Germans cuts a poor figure, and Hitler, in his badly made clothes, seems even more shrunken and awkward than usual. He walks over to Mussolini and respectfully shakes his hand. The Duce, his chest bulging, smiling and condescending, shows his guest Venice—radiant in its dazzling, secular beauty, which in the gentle air of spring seems more than ever a stranger to the vicissitudes of time. The German Ambassador, Ulrich von Hassel, salutes the Führer. Von Hassel is one of the men who told the Duce that he must urge Hitler to restore order in the tumultuous ranks of the Sturmabteilung.

Soon after the Germans' arrival, Hitler and Mussolini leave in a motor launch, escorted by a fleet of small boats which, to the howling sirens and the shouts of the crowd, head out into the lagoon. Torpedo boats do the honors for the two heads of government, their crews lined up on deck in white uniforms. Then, through the blackish water of the Grand Canal, past flower-decked gondolas, the Doges' Palace, the Grand Hotel, where Hitler will stay, to the Villa Pisani di Strà, where Hitler and Mussolini will meet for a private conversation of some two hours. Did the Duce mention Roehm? The Italian diplomats watch the Führer: "Physically, he looks very Teutonic," notes Baron Aloisi, "but there is something about his eyes suggesting depth of thought."

The evening of Hitler's first visit abroad, a grand concert is given at the Doges' Palace: "Marvelous decor and chandeliers," observes a diplomat, "but poor organization. The crowd cheered the Duce throughout the concert, producing a dreadful cacophony. The Duce's popularity is immense." With a tense smile, the Führer watches these disorderly demonstrations, in which he seems to be completely ignored.

On Friday, June 15, the Führer and the Duce are surrounded by delirious crowds. Seventy thousand people jam the Piazza San

Marco for a reception in honor of the German Chancellor. Departure is set for the morning of Saturday, June 16. The hangar where the Führer's plane waits is decorated with Italian and German colors, swastikas and *fasces*; bands play, and then at 8:50 A.M. the plane takes off. Two hours later, the two German planes land at the Munich-Oberwiesenfeld Airport.

Here, too, there are bands, "Deutschland über Alles," and as always, the "Badenweilermarsch," Hitler's favorite.

The Führer seems tired, nervous, somewhat disappointed. All the shouting has been for the Duce, the all-powerful leader of a country in good order. By comparison, he has seemed insignificant, ill at ease. Mussolini's advice—for the Duce has done a lot of talking—irritated him. Now, as the car rolls back toward Munich, Hitler knows that in Germany everything is still in suspense, and that people are waiting for him.

In Berlin, Heydrich is already telling Goering that, in effect, the Duce told the Führer he had to re-establish order in the Party and in the SA. The Duce had alluded to his own actions in the year 1924. He had known how to make the original *Squadristi* yield. Order is essential in a totalitarian state—order and obedience to the leader. How had Hitler taken this advice?

In barely two weeks, the SA will leave for their month's holiday. It is essential to take action before then. Will Hitler make up his mind in time?

Saturday, June 30, 1934
Between Godesberg and Bonn-Hangelar

1:30 A.M.

The car is already passing through the outskirts of Bonn. Its headlamps light up the closed shutters and throw shadows of the gently stirring tree branches against the walls of these residential villas far from the smoke and fumes of the Ruhr. The two motorcyclists have been waiting for the cars at the edge of town, and start up as soon as they appear. The sound of their engines echoes through the suburban streets, at this hour as empty as the streets of any village. The Bonn-Hangelar Airport is only a few minutes away; at each turn of the wheels, Hitler's choice becomes more and more ineluctably the fate of this town, and the country, so deeply asleep this short, last night of June.

On the shores of the Tegernsee, the air is sharper than in the valley of the Rhine. Some official cars have just driven away from the Pension Hanselbauer, where, as every night, there have been parties and singing. The SA leaders have drunk a great deal and have enjoyed themselves. The night is peaceful; its blackest hours seem to have already passed; the darkness is beginning to lighten. The last section of Roehm's personal guard, which stayed until all the guests had gone, has left in a closed truck. The Chief of Staff, Ernst Roehm, has nothing further to fear from this night, which has only a few more hours to run. Bad Wiessee is calm, with only the sound of the retreating truck to cover the rustle of the wind and the waves.

The Führer's cars have bypassed Bonn to the north, avoiding the center of town and leaving the banks of the Rhine. They pass the former castle of the Electors, whose heavy, massive shadow seems to absorb the darkness. Straight ahead the Poppelsdorfer Allee leads into the town; in the dim light, the double rows of Indian chestnut trees which line the streets are faintly visible. Now the drivers accelerate. The Führer wants to be done with this month and the hesitations which have haunted him since his return from Venice.

(Sunday, June 17)

Hitler's hesitations seem to have increased, despite Mussolini's advice. On Friday and Saturday, the fifteenth and sixteenth of June, the German papers are full of articles on the importance of the meeting between the Duce and the Führer. Nonetheless, Hitler is uneasy: his nervousness is noticed by everyone.

On his return to Germany on the sixteenth, Hitler goes to the Brown House in Munich, where he studies at length the trial of the murderers of Horst Wessel. This SA member has become a symbol of a new regime: Nazi Youth sing the "Horst Wessel Lied," while opponents abroad say that Horst Wessel was not killed, as his comrades claim, in a fight with the Communists, but after a quarrel between pimps. Whatever the facts, it is certain that during an evening in January, 1930, some men killed him at his home No. 62 Grosse Frankfurt Strasse. Two of them, Sally Epstein, twenty-seven, and Hans Ziegler, thirty-two, have been on trial. The murderer Höller has already been liquidated by the SA and the other accused have fled. Hitler is pleased with the results of the trial. Sentence is passed on June 15: Epstein and Ziegler are condemned to death. However, the Führer is not entirely satisfied. The papers have not sufficiently emphasized the international plot to portray Horst Wessel as a pimp. The honor of the regime and of the SA is at stake.

The trial brings Hitler back to his principal preoccupations. When he is told that on this same Friday, June 15, André François-Poncet left Berlin to spend two weeks in Paris, he is startled and disturbed: it is rather early to be leaving for summer vacation. Might not this departure confirm the rumors of a plot, allegedly instigated by François-Poncet, linking the SA leaders, Generals Schleicher and Bredow, and the French Embassy? François-Poncet, with his usual adroitness, would be likely to leave Berlin if his allies were about to strike.

Hitler gives the news of the Ambassador's departure even more attention as reports from the Gestapo and the SD multiply, bringing new intrigues to light. In Papen's entourage, too, action seems to be contemplated. Dr. Jung is increasing the moral pressure on the Vice Chancellor, hoping to push him into opposition to the regime. Tschirschky, also, is applying pressure. Himmler and Heydrich keep up a steady stream of warnings to Hitler. They alert him particularly to the visit Papen has planned for the next day, Sunday, June 17, to the University of Marburg. But how can Hitler act against Papen's plans, except by talking too? He will go to Gera and speak to the Party cadres and Nazi organizations of the industrial city—an old stronghold of socialism, now dedicated to Nazism.

This mid-June Sunday begins with another important moment in the drama which has been unfolding in Germany since the Nazi takeover.

In Berlin, however, it's a day of celebration. At the Tempelhof Airfield, thousands of people have assembled for a grand aerial meet. Hermann Goering had decided to give the capital of the Reich a huge, free-floating balloon, but, busy with his ministerial duties, or anxious to smooth over the mistrust and hostility of the SA, he has delegated his ceremonial functions to Obergruppen-führer SA Karl Ernst. Accompanied by cheering and a flourish of trumpets, Ernst christens the balloon the *Hermann Goering*. Then, climbing into the basket, he pilots it aloft. Hundreds of waving handkerchiefs and outstretched arms salute this flight symbolizing the unity of the Party leaders, the reconciliation between Goering and the SA. Nonetheless, Karl Ernst keeps his prominent position on Heydrich's list. Aerial celebrations change nothing.

THE MARBURG SPEECH

At the same moment that Karl Ernst delights in the physical proofs of his political importance, Franz von Papen, Vice Chancellor of the Reich, is entering the grand amphitheater of the University of Marburg. Marburg is one of the oldest universities in Germany: the pediment of the Gothic building is inscribed with the date 1527. The atmosphere is one of peace and calm. The university dominates the gentle river Lahn, the botanical gardens and the town, laid out like jewels in a jewel case. The history of Germany, mystic, dreamy, powerful and austere, is all there, recorded in the churches, the Town Hall, the low, heavy houses of the marketplace, and the castle, where the courageous reformers Luther, Zwingli and Melanchthon gathered in 1529 at the court of Philip the Magnanimous. It is against this ancient background that the Catholic Papen will speak.

"Knowing that the foremost personalities of the intellectual world would attend this meeting," Papen wrote later, "I prepared my talk, outlined by Ernst Jung, with particular care. I thought that this speech would give me my best opportunity to address the entire nation."

In fact, Papen was not as careful as he wished to believe years later.

He did not read the speech Jung had prepared for him with any care until he was on the train to Marburg. He turned then to his secretary, von Tschirschky, who understood from Papen's expression that he was afraid. Nonetheless it was necessary for Papen to speak out. During the preceding week, Jung and Tschirschky had met several times to make the wording of the speech as precise as possible. It was important to aim true, to hit the target squarely. Edgar Jung had reworked the beginning of the speech many times; the text was to be one of prime importance, a warning addressed to all Germany. "The speech took months of preparation," Tschirschky writes. "It was necessary to find the proper occasion for its delivery, and then everything had to be prepared with the greatest possible care." "If von Papen had come round to our point of view," his secretary adds with a note of contempt, "the speech would have been delivered much sooner."

But Franz von Papen was not a man of courage. His quick, piercing eyes betrayed a prudence which some did not hesitate to call cowardice. Extremely ambitious, he had preferred a government run by Hitler to one run by Schleicher; however, for several months now he has been feeling desperately anxious. Ernst Roehm's SA threatens a period of violent anarchy, of national Bolshevism, which would mean the end of the caste of aristocrats and Junkers to which Franz von Papen likes to think he belongs. Often, talking to Hitler after a cabinet meeting, he has warned him about the menace the SA poses to the regime and to Germany. But the warnings were always delivered in his allusive and indirect style, and the Führer invariably dismissed his Vice Chancellor's fears. On this point, Papen repeats what he said to the Ruhr industrialists: "Each time, Hitler ridiculed the demands of the leader of the Brown Shirts, and treated them as aberrations of no importance."

However, week by week, the situation has been growing worse. "During the month of June," Papen adds, "I came to the conclusion that the balance must be restored. My discussions of the subject at cabinet meetings, my arguments and direct insistence to Hitler had been absolutely in vain. I decided to make a public appeal to Hitler's conscience."

Franz von Papen could no longer evade the issue: his collaborators were there, pressing him to act. "We more or less forced him to make that speech," Tschirschky said later. They had wrung from Papen the promise to intervene at Marburg, at the ceremony to which the university had invited him. On the train en route, the Vice Chancellor looks anxiously at Tschirschky. Then he takes out a pencil and begins meticulously to "strike certain remarks which seem too pointed." Tschirschky immediately intervenes. "Herr von Papen, what are you doing?" The Vice Chancellor lifts his pencil from the page. The two men are alone in the compartment. Outside, a landscape of wooded hills moves past the window: they will soon arrive in Marburg. Papen looks at Tschirschky, silently interrogating him: can't Tschirschky see what he is doing? For a moment there is a sense of constraint between them. Then Tschirschky slowly tells Papen that the complete text of the speech has been transmitted to the foreign press, and that therefore the scandal would be even greater if there were noticeable differences between the two versions. Franz von Papen, among other things, is a realist. He puts away his pencil. The only choice open to him now is to press forward, to turn to his own advantage the courage imposed upon him.

In the large amphitheater of the University of Marburg, everyone is standing as Franz von Papen comes in. In the tiered rows of seats there are no empty places. Scattered and isolated, here and there, one can see a brown shirt, with a Nazi armband on the sleeve; there are not many, and they seem lost in this crowd of students and gowned professors. Papen coughs several times, and then begins to speak, into absolute silence:

"It appears that my part in the events which occurred in Prussia, and in the formation of the present government, has been extremely important—so important in its effects on the evolution of Germany that I am obliged to judge the present situation more severely, and with a sharper critical sense, than is required of most of my compatriots."

There is not a sound; the attention of the audience seems to grow. Papen continues more slowly, praising the new regime. Then: "Convinced of the necessity of a regeneration of public life, I would fail in my twofold duty as a citizen and a statesman if I suppressed things that should now be said." A series of criticisms of Nazi methods follows, all the more astonishing because for two years the country has been stupefied by propaganda, every pen and voice given public expression has been servile. Yet Franz von Papen is the Vice Chancellor of the government he is criticizing.

"The Minister of Propaganda [Goebbels] seems enchanted with the conformity and docility of the press. He forgets that a press worthy of the name must point out injustices, errors and abuse."

"From the first," Papen wrote later, "both professors and students seemed thunderstruck. They listened in silence as I enumerated my accusations, but I sensed that I held them by the freedom of my language."

Papen goes on to remark that the country has reached a crossroads. In the city to which Luther came, which still seems so close to the Reformation, he speaks of Christian principles, "for centuries the foundation of the nation." These phrases of Jung's sound like the free expression, at last, of what even the most conservative German intellectuals have been thinking since 1933, the year in which the country began to sink into a silence broken only by rhythmic acclamations which mark the rise of fanaticism.

"If we betray our traditions, if we ignore the lessons of our long history and forget the obligations flowing from our European position, we shall have lost the most beautiful and most magnificent opportunity offered to us in this century. . . . In a world in full evolution, let us accept the responsibilities imposed by our consciences."

The speech's conclusion is, naturally, vague, but it raises the room to its feet. "The thunder of applause greeting my peroration," Papen wrote, "completely drowning out the furious protests of the few Nazis, seemed to express the spirit of the German people." Tschirschky bows to him, and professors take his hand, formally but with warmth. Papen smiles. He has not yet had time to feel afraid. "I felt an enormous sense of relief," he writes. "At last, I had relieved my conscience."

While Papen is surrounded and beginning to judge how his speech will inevitably be taken, telephone communications between Marburg and official Berlin are rapidly multiplying. Goebbels is one of the first to be warned. He has been personally attacked by the Vice Chancellor. Is this the conservative offensive many Nazis fear? Goebbels takes immediate steps. Radio broadcast of Papen's speech, planned for the evening, is forbidden. Journalists at Marburg preparing to forward the text are asked to send nothing to their publications. On the following day copies of the daily papers will be seized. Only the *Frankfurter Zeitung* has time to publish a few extracts in its afternoon edition. Moreover, this censorship is being applied to the Vice Chancellor of the Reich, while around Jung, Papen's collaborators at the Vice Chancellory are trying to break the circle of silence in which Goebbels wishes to imprison Germany. Copies of the text have already been sent abroad. The presses of the paper *Germania* are printing complete versions, which are being distributed to diplomatic representatives and foreign press correspondents. "We also sent," Papen writes, "a great many copies by mail, to our friends in Germany itself." But the Vice Chancellory is under round-the-clock surveillance by the Gestapo. Heydrich, who suspected the intentions of Jung and Papen, was one of the first to be informed.

At No. 8 Prinz-Albrecht Strasse, the afternoon of Sunday, June 17, is one of concentrated work. There is a continuous series of meetings, and the switchboard is overloaded with calls to Marburg and Goering's presidential palace. Heydrich orders all suspect correspondence emanating from the Vice Chancellory seized: there might be an attempt to disseminate the Marburg speech. In the post offices, agents from the SD and the Gestapo give their orders, which are extremely effective. "I was to learn later," Papen wrote, "that the Gestapo succeeded in intercepting most of the letters" which enclosed a complete text of the speech.

Heydrich, whose informers at the Vice Chancellory have been well informed since the beginning of the week, has warned Hitler, still in Munich after his return from Italy. Perhaps it was then that the Führer made his decision to go to Gera to play tricks with Papen's speech and its possible consequences. At 8:15 Hitler arrives at the Munich Airport—to the same ceremonies, the same men, but with a different plane, the D 260, reserved for domestic travel. The weather report for June 17 between Munich and Leipzig is good, with a few low-altitude cloud banks above the Erzgebirge. At 8:25 the plane takes off, and at 10:15 lands at Leipzig. The plane is one of the Führer's new weapons. In this small country he can be anywhere within two hours: his enemies often forget this.

A car is waiting at the Leipzig Airport: it is early, barely 10:30, when Hitler crosses the great industrial and commercial city. The streets are nearly empty. On Sunday mornings the workers stay at home. The cars drive south through the valley of the Elster, toward Gera, with its textile and metalworking plants. Since the early hours of the morning big buses have been bringing SA and SS groups and youth organizations into the little town. Thousands of people have arrived, filling the streets with their songs and their high spirits, walking about while they wait for the time to assemble. On the gray walls of the houses typical of this industrial region hang the long swastika banners of the regime. They float upward, puffed and swollen by the spring wind. When the Führer's car appears and stops in front of the Hotel Victoria beside the station, there is a burst of cheering. Sauckel, the Gauleiter of Thuringia, receives the Führer, who salutes the crowd and goes into the hotel, where he will speak to the Party cadres. At 1 P.M. Hitler appears on the street again for the beginning of the parade, a large one for a small town like Gera. Goebbels and Ley are there, beside the Führer. Here, just a few years before, the "Reds" held the streets. Here and throughout the district, people voted Social-Democrat. Here the SA suffered serious losses in confrontations with organized and angry labor groups. But now, while at Marburg Franz von Papen is being congratulated by professors and applauded by students—here at Gera twenty thousand men are marching, nine abreast, behind Sauckel: SA, SS, Hitler Youth, RAD, Motorized SA—the Party paramilitary organizations.

They march to shouts of "Heil Hitler!" and the tramping of their boots seems an expression of the new regime's determination to yield neither to Papen nor to the return of any threat from the Left. It appears that the Nazi forces are once more united in response to the Marburg speech (almost not delivered) and that the compromise desired by Hitler has been realized. All the units converge toward the Schützenplatz, where more than seventy thousand people have gathered. The cannon is fired to announce the Führer's arrival, and the drum rolls of the "Badenweiler-marsch" resound through the cheers of the crowd.

No one in the crowd suspects that this scene is anything more than another of the meetings, perhaps somewhat unexpected in this industrial district, which are supposed to indoctrinate Germany; no one realizes that it is also a response to the Vice Chancellor, as well as a demonstration of force aimed at the conservatives, and at those who swarm about von Papen, hoping, perhaps, to overthrow the new regime.

Four hours of parades, hundreds of buses and the shouts of tens of thousands of men demonstrate the Führer's popularity and his Party's invincibility.

However, even to this ignorant and enthusiastic crowd, the Führer's hard, menacing voice is startling. It is a violent speech, emphasized by large gestures. Hitler is dripping with sweat, and seems to have rediscovered the vindictive, unbridled violence of his first verbal paroxysms in the smoke-filled bars of Munich.

"All these little dwarfs," Hitler shouts, "who think they have something to say against our idea will be swept away by its collective strength." Shouts ring out, and cries of "Heil! Sieg Heil!" "For all these dwarfs forget one thing: whatever criticisms they may think they can make, where is there anything better to replace what we have?"

Carried on a wave of emotion, Hitler multiplies his expressions of irony and scorn: "This ridiculous little worm . . . what would happen if these bellyachers had their way? Germany would disintegrate!" Thrusting his fist forward at the end of a taut, straight arm, Hitler rises to the tips of his toes and shouts: "This is the clenched fist of the nation, and it will crush whoever attempts any act of sabotage."

Shouts, trumpets: who will be struck by this fist which Hitler brandishes on Sunday, June 17, at the man who helped him to power, the gentleman-rider Franz von Papen, the enemy of Captain Ernst Roehm?

4

Saturday, June 30, 1934
Bonn-Hangelar Airport

1:45 A.M.

The approach to the airport at Hangelar is marked by huge signs warning motorists not to park along the embankments. For several minutes the cars have been moving at reduced speed along the road from Bonn, which skirts the airfield until it comes to the wide entrance framed by wooden buildings. Lit by yellow lights, the runways vanish into the darkness toward the north. When the cars pull up at the checkpoint, the Führer's trimotor Junker is immediately visible in the floodlights, the crew and the mechanics gathered in a group on the ground beneath the engines. Hitler salutes several officers in a distracted manner as he continues his conversation with Goebbels. Then he walks quickly toward the pilot who has come forward to meet his passenger and guide him to the plane. The pilot points out the scattering of light cloud in the sky; Hitler does not really listen, but strides toward the cockpit, his hands thrust deeply into the pockets of his leather coat, his shoulders slumped.

He knows that he has to hurry. Once a decision has been taken, a moment comes when further waiting is unbearable, especially if the decision has been in doubt for weeks. After this moment separating the decision to act from the act itself, hesitation becomes feverish, and turns into a rage for intervention. As Hitler climbs the metal ladder, he is undoubtedly aware of such feelings within himself; he is also afraid that it may already be too late, that he will be anticipated by one of the plots he has been warned about for months, in which statements from Roehm, François-Poncet's departure and Papen's talk at Marburg all seem to fit together.

(Monday, June 18, to Thursday, June 21)

In the Daluege report, submitted by Goering on Monday, June 18, the SS General has collected all the evidence of the SA leaders' guilt and their desire to seize power. Actually, the proof is somewhat tenuous, but the report includes copies of letters and recordings of telephone conversations which are revealing in tone; the SA leaders don't say anything precisely treasonable, but they mock the Führer and various cabinet ministers with heavy plebeian irony. For that Hitler cannot forgive them. Each day as he is surrounded by a more obvious show of humility and fawning, he feels more wounded by those gross, disrespectful words—and by the very fact that men like Ernst and Heines, who owe him everything, including their high positions, still dare to criticize him and want still more. Such men are certainly capable of plotting to further their ambitions and appetites. Hitler listens to Goering, Himmler and Heydrich with the Daluege report in his hand. But the report contains matter more serious than wounds to the Führer's pride: it reveals that on several occasions Obergruppenführer Ernst and Heines have alluded to their role in the Reichstag fire. They gossip between bouts of drinking, drop hints and behave like accomplices without talent, minor members of a gang who imagine they have some sort of hold over the chief because they have taken part in one of his dangerous enterprises. The rule by which gangs live allows no room for pity—a fact confirmed by a report Hitler receives at the end of that Monday from von Ribbentrop.

The Führer's personal representative for Foreign Affairs had met with the President of the French Council in Paris that afternoon. The information he has wired to Berlin relates to elements in the Daluege dossier, and to information supplied by Heydrich and Himmler. Ribbentrop points out that his conversation with the President of the French Council has confirmed his impression that French government circles are firmly convinced that Germany faces grave economic and other difficulties; for the moment, they prefer to await further developments. "Indeed, this rigid, negative attitude toward us on the part of the French government is based on the French view that serious internal difficulties are imminent in Germany."

Although hundreds of copies of Papen's Marburg speech attesting to the desire of the men close to the Vice Chancellor for an open campaign against the regime have been seized, and while the Gestapo and the SD continue to send out reports filled with negative information, both true and false, Ribbentrop's report is the next thing to positive proof.

However, the Führer has still not come to a final decision: he cannot seem to isolate the few hours necessary to make up his mind. Those who have already made their choice are equally jostled by events, dragged along by daily obligations, leaving to the men behind the scenes—Heydrich, Eicke, Sepp Dietrich—the organization of final details. However, Hermann Goering, who is one of the moving spirits behind the plot, seems to be concerned only with moving the body of his first wife, Karin, to the immense crypt he has built on his country estate.

The exhumation is scheduled for Tuesday, June 19, at the cemetery of Levöe. The weather is beautiful, the sky a pale blue, and it is unusually warm for Sweden, even for June. It seems also as if daylight has settled in so firmly it can never be driven out by night. Karin's coffin is a long box of gleaming zinc. At six o'clock in the morning, in the presence of a few close friends and relatives, there is a short religious ceremony. Also present are representatives from the three Swedish Nazi parties, their flags lowered. Slowly the mass of flowers grows larger: they come from all parts of Germany and every Party organization. The largest wreath is from Goering, and is inscribed "To my Karin." Slowly, the coffin is placed in a special car attached to the regular Berlin train, and the funeral procession sets out, bearing the mortal remains of this Swedish woman who pledged her life to Hermann Goering and Nazism. At Stockholm, a crowd throngs the platform, and bareheaded men give the Nazi salute. These maneuvers take place in complete silence. The special car is put on the ferry *Drottning Viktoria* with a special honor guard. The sea is calm, phosphorescent.

At 1:45 on Wednesday, June 20, Goering arrives at Sassnitz, where the ferry is already tied up in the harbor. The railway car is covered with wreaths, and after Goering has bowed to the coffin and left the boat, the heavy sound of muffled drums begins, like a long groan, announcing the grandiloquent ceremonies. Goering has neglected nothing. The transfer of Karin's body is to be an opportunity for him and the regime to organize a pagan rite celebrating the summer solstice that hearkens back to ancient Germanic traditions. Goering has invited all the Nazi leaders to Karinhall except one: Roehm. Thus what would seem to be simply the first ritual of the Karin cult has also become a political ploy: the meeting of the conspirators around a woman's coffin.

The special train, loaded with flowers, passes through the stations of Bergen, Stralsund, Greifswald, Ducherow, Pasewalk and Prenzlau, and on each station platform, frozen into postures of attention as rigid as marble, representatives of the various Nazi movements lower their flags and drums slowly roll. The countryside of North Germany, still and damp with spring, seems to be a reflection of these rites, alive with a certain savage grandeur but devoid of feeling. The sky is very high above the horizon, and the sandy heath stretches into infinity, cut here and there by a wave of hills, or a forest of pine or beech, black against the sand and the silvery sky.

At 8:30 the funeral car arrives at Eberswalde. There Goering, in full uniform, is joined by Countess Rosen Willamovitz Mollendorf, Karin's sister, officers, Prussian princes and Police General Wecke. In the square in front of the station, delegations from all the Nazi movements are drawn up, their flags draped in black. The band plays Beethoven's Funeral March, while Prince August Wilhelm Hohenzollern, the Gruppenführer SA and Gauleiter Wilhelm Kube salute Goering. A grand parade begins: the coffin is carried in turn by eight police officers, eight leaders of the national organization for aerial sport, eight forest guards—all men who belong to one or another of the groups directed by Hermann Goering. The population stands silent along the sides of the road; the women bow their heads, the men remove their hats. Dressed in peasant clothes, often in black, the people watch with respect as the "gentry" pass by. This procession represents one aspect of a regime which wishes to recall the hard, authoritarian times of the Teutonic epic.

At the Döllkranz forester's lodge the coffin is placed on a car drawn by six horses. Groups of riders from Goering's personal police head the procession, and also bring up the rear, as it winds its way through the thick, black woods. It is as if all of seigneurial Germany were trying to be reborn with Nazism. The descendant of the Hohenzollern marches beside Goering, as the crowd of peasants, silent and submissive, watch their masters pass by.

Gradually, high dignitaries and ministers have joined the procession. Hitler appears, followed by Brückner, Sepp Dietrich and Meissner, representing Hindenburg. The horns ring out; black uniforms, beeches and black pines, the death's-heads on the uniforms, the funeral march from *Die Götterdämmerung*, the solemn faces, the crypt surrounded by huge stones, German menhirs, the silver sand—elements composing a tableau in which

Nazism and the past are grafted together, united to honor a dead woman, announcing a time of violence. The choir stands up to sing Luther's *"Trutzlied,"* and the chorale "Take Me in Your Hands." Beyond the glade, one can see the glittering waters of the Wackersee. The woods ring with the sound of hunting horns which play the *hallali.* Around the crypt are large bowls of fire, their flames shuddering in the wind. The voice of the pastor, Dr. Fendt, speaks: "And now, Karin Goering, this German forest and German lake salute you; above you glitter the stars of our Fatherland, which has become your second Fatherland. You have sought with an ardent spirit, and you have suffered for your country at the side of your husband; you have struggled for it, and rejoiced in it even unto death."

The men standing around the crypt are motionless; the pastor's voice rings out clear and hard.

"The splendor of the German soil shall henceforth enclose you forever, and in the majestic solitude of its forests you shall hear the peace and well-being of Germany ring with gratitude toward you."

Suddenly, as the coffin is about to be lifted for its descent into the crypt, the crowd parts, and Himmler appears, his face working with anger and emotion. He walks over to Goering and Hitler, and speaks to them in a low voice. Brückner joins them, and then gives some orders. The ceremony resumes, and Goering, accompanied only by the Chancellor of the Reich, goes down into the crypt. Surrounded by a few high-ranking SS, Himmler speaks rapidly. On the road between Berlin and Karinhall, only a few miles from the house, someone fired on his car, piercing the windshield. A miracle he wasn't hurt or killed. Himmler demands reprisals: at least forty Communists should be executed, for it is Communists within the SA who have just tried to kill him. A group walks over to examine the car: the windshield is indeed broken. Karl Bodenschatz, one of Goering's ADCs, and like him a former pilot, examines the glass. A bullet could never have done so little damage; at most, the incident must have been caused by a stone on the road. But he says nothing. Himmler is still talking about the attempted assassination. By now, the word "Communist" has vanished: it is solely a question of an SA plot to kill the loyal Nazi leaders who follow Hitler.

Deep in the black forest, beside this massive crypt, Hitler, his face grave, walks beside Goering, joined with him in the pagan ceremony. Roehm's Sturmabteilung appears once again isolated and menacing, marked for punishment, a punishment that will be a violent reflection of this burial in the deep heart of the forest.

After the ceremony, Hitler returns to Berlin. Those who go with him, who see him when he arrives at the Chancellory at the end of the day, are struck by the somber, withdrawn expression of his face, more severe than usual. The Führer appears to have been deeply affected by the Teutonic setting and ceremony of burial, and by the position accorded him by Goering as Karin's coffin was taken down into the crypt. He undoubtedly feels the bonds of pagan mysticism which the ceremony has woven between Goering, himself and the dead woman. Goering has attained his goal: Roehm and the SA are excluded from that mysterious world of German mythology, and the Goering-Himmler clique has gained.

On Wednesday, June 20, at the Chancellory, Hitler reads the article which Alfred Rosenberg has published in the *Völkischer Beobachter*. It is one of the first replies to Papen's speech at Marburg. The Nazi theoretician affirms the Party's position in the Party's name: "We have not made the revolution of our time so that a superannuated epoch can proclaim a 'conservative revolution' under the guise of order, and the restoration of a state as it was conceived five hundred years ago. . . ." Hitler now orders Party leaders Goebbels and Hess to counterattack, to show that the regime will not be drained of its content by these gentlemanly conservatives.

As the Führer is getting ready to go to his rooms, Franz von Papen arrives and asks to see him immediately. In fact, the Vice

Chancellor has been waiting for several hours, and now Hitler is obliged to confront the man of Marburg against whom he is mounting a vigorous press campaign. The two men are afraid of each other. A few months ago, pointing out the Vice Chancellory building to Rosenberg, the Führer said: "All our troubles come from there; one day I'll have to clean it all up." But this evening the two men greet each other with formal politeness, aware of the tension of their differences behind the façade. The interview threatens to be stormy. Papen protests the censorship Goering has imposed: can a minister interdict the dissemination of a speech by the Vice Chancellor of the Reich? "I explained to Hitler," Papen recorded, "that I considered it my duty to take a firm position, for the situation had become critical. The moment had also come for him, I told him; he himself should make his position clear."

Hitler listens. He understands perfectly that he is being asked to uphold order, to restrain the extravagances of the SA and stop the Nazi violations of legality. Every organized force—the Reichswehr, the Gestapo, the conservatives—pushes him toward a breakup of the balance between the different currents that carried him to power. But each of the men wishing to destroy that balance turns to the Führer to do it. Franz von Papen is no exception. "Hitler should have understood," the Vice Chancellor continued, "that I still wished to maintain our association, and that that was why I was begging him to think about the problems I had just mentioned." All his supporters need him, including the SA: Hitler understands this very well.

Then Papen raises his voice, and his attitude becomes more arrogant. "In any event," he says, "the Vice Chancellor of the Reich cannot allow a new minister [Goebbels] to suppress the publication of an official speech."

Papen calculates the impression he is making, and then shouts: "I spoke at Marburg as an emissary of the President. Goebbels' intervention will force me to resign. I shall inform Hindenburg immediately."

That was the conservatives' trump card to force Hitler to yield—break with the SA and respect legality: Hindenburg, the commander who could crush Hitler by rallying around himself the Army, the conservatives and the mass of Germans. "I said I would do this," Papen continues, "unless the interdiction of my speech were rescinded, and Hitler himself agreed to adopt the line of conduct I recommended."

Hitler appears to hesitate. "He tried to calm me," Papen records. "He admitted that Goebbels had made a mistake in trying to avoid an aggravation of the tension that already existed." But Papen still threatens: he will resign, and von Neurath, the Minister for Foreign Affairs, and Schwerin von Krosigk, the Minister of Finance, will leave the government with him. "I am going to Neudeck," Papen added, "and I shall request that my speech be published." Hitler grabs at this opportunity: he will go to Neudeck with Papen. The Vice Chancellor's collaborators have warned him against this possibility. Papen must not accept a joint visit to Hindenburg; such a visit would rob the Marburg speech of all its significance. But Papen does not wish to break off his "association" with Hitler. The Führer insists. "The whole situation needs to be examined," he says. "The discussion can have no tangible results unless the Chancellor also takes part." Papen finally accepts the Führer's proposal, and Hitler promises to tell Goebbels to lift the ban on the Marburg speech. Then "he [Hitler] launched into a violent tirade against the general insubordination of the SA, who continued to complicate his work. Soon, he would be forced, by whatever means, to bring them to their senses."

Once again, the SA are caught in a backlash. To protect himself against Papen's attack and against Hindenburg, to avoid alienating the conservative wing of his government, Hitler blames the SA. Will he perhaps even sacrifice them?

Wednesday night, June 20, for Germany, a night without sleep. Bonfires have been lit in stadiums, squares and woodland glades, and members of Nazi organizations gather by the thousands. Young men carrying torches and singing hymns march in step. For the first time, on this the shortest night of the year, Germany is celebrating a new rite: the feast of the summer solstice. Karin's burial announced the opening and beginning of a new pagan cycle; now it approaches its zenith, to continue for the next several days.

At Verden, a small village in Westphalia on the Aller River, Alfred Rosenberg, the originator of this return to paganism, glorifies the memory of 4,500 Saxon rebels whom Charlemagne had executed in that place in 782. While the flames rise high into the freshness of the night, and the torches burn, Rosenberg delivers an inspired speech. "Hitler is our direct link with Hermann Chérusque and Duke Witikind. History has proved the Duke of the Saxons correct. Our Holy Land is not the Middle East, but all around us, here in Germany." Thus the summer festival becomes the exaltation of the Reich and its Führer.

On Thursday afternoon in Berlin, Goebbels takes up Rosenberg's theme. In the vast Neukölln stadium before tens of thousands of Brown Shirts, mythology is once again brought back to life for the solstice celebration. However, in this case, it is no longer a question of the past, but of the present: "A small circle of critics has decided to sabotage our efforts, from the mysterious shadows of the Café de Commerce. They are ridiculous. . . ." To wild applause, Goebbels adds: "These men conducting serious discussions of politics from the depths of their comfortable armchairs have no monopoly on intelligence. . . . They represent reaction. History will remember our names, not theirs."

Papen, a member of the Herrenklub, is clearly one of Goebbels' targets. The Minister of Propaganda cannot speak without Hitler's approval. Papen rereads Goebbels' final phrases: "No crown prince, no councilor, no big banker and no parliamentary chieftains!"

Does this mean that Hitler has once again turned his hat, and chosen the route of the second Revolution? That he wishes to break with those traditional and reasonable elements within his coalition? Has Hitler decided to rejoin Roehm's camp? Or does it indicate simply that the Führer is hesitating? There is anxiety everywhere: around Papen, in the circle close to Himmler, around Goering and in the Bendlerstrasse. Therefore, it is necessary, once again, to "sound out" Hitler—and the occasion presents itself almost immediately. On Thursday, June 21, Hitler sees the Reich President at Neudeck.

Hitler goes to see Hindenburg alone. Papen learns of the trip later. Officially, Hitler's visit to the President has a precise goal: to inform the highest authority in Germany of the substance of his talks with Mussolini. At Neudeck, at the end of a long avenue of trees stands the massive, austere house of the Field Marshal. Meissner, the President's secretary, Count Fritz von der Schulenburg and Colonel Oskar von Hindenburg receive the Führer ceremoniously on the steps. The vast, cold rooms already seem heavy with the silence of a mausoleum. Hitler is told that his visit with the President must be brief. Moreover, for the moment, Hindenburg is resting: he cannot receive the Chancellor until evening, after the doctors have examined him. The Führer thinks once again how close they are to the end of Hindenburg's life; he must be ready to seize supreme power the moment Hindenburg is dead, and for that move the Army must be firmly behind him.

The Führer wanders into the garden. The air is fresh, and the colors of this first day of summer are sharp and clean, the dry soil crunches underfoot; the countryside looks sharp and clear, almost gay. Hitler meets General von Blomberg in the garden. The Minister of War has just been on an inspection tour of East Prussia, and hearing that Hitler is at Neudeck, he has come here on the pretext of paying his respects to Field Marshal Hindenburg. At the home of Hindenburg, symbol of an older Germany almost buried by time, the Führer of the New Reich and the representative of the Army can only speak of the future, recalling the "*Deutschland* Pact." The elegant General would like to know if Hitler's position has changed since April, if he is still ready to sacrifice the SA. The two men walk side by side through a seemingly endless day: the old-line officer and the former corporal who has risen from the lower ranks of society to the summit of power, but who is still vulnerable. Blomberg has to speak to the point because Hindenburg's strength is declining rapidly; tension is rising in Germany; Papen, Bose, Jung, Klausener and Schleicher are putting pressure on certain elements in the Army; and the Bendlerstrasse is afraid that this tension may provoke an invasion from either Poland in the East or France in the West. It is essential to put an end to the disorder stirred up by the SA, and to assure the Army a stable reserve of recruits, over which it will have full control. The two men walk down the path side by side. Naturally, if Hitler renews their compact, the Reichswehr will swear fidelity to the new Head of State.

Secretary Meissner is waiting for Hitler on the front steps: Hindenburg is awake now, and can receive Hitler for a few minutes.

The old Marshal is sitting in a large straight-backed armchair, wearing a long black frock coat. A white collar, held in place with a black tie, lies loosely around a neck deeply furrowed with age. When Hitler appears, Hindenburg rises, his left fist clenched, his right hand resting on the head of his cane. He nods to his visitor, his heavy square face, crowned by short white hair, as expressionless as marble. Hindenburg sits down again, and a uniformed chamberlain pulls out a chair for the Chancellor. Hitler begins to speak of Venice, of the Duce, of the friendliness of Italy, but Hindenburg interrupts with a few words and questions which are, in fact, orders: Roehm? The second Revolution? The tranquillity of Germany is essential; its re-establishment and maintenance must be the first business of the Chancellor, the mission of the President. The country must have order, and the Army must have calm to prepare properly the defense of the Reich. Then with the help of the chamberlain, Hindenburg rises again, to walk slowly, heavily through the house. By his side, Hitler looks frail and insignificant, with no ties to German history, which Hindenburg radiates by the very way he stands, by his face. He accompanies

Hitler to the front steps, surrounded by his entourage of officers and chamberlains, leaning on his cane. He watches the Führer leave with the stern indifference and empty eyes of powerful old men, which always alarms those dependent upon them.

As he travels through the flat countryside of East Prussia, a sheep-flecked sea of heath and sand which fringes the Baltic, Hitler realizes that for a few weeks longer his fate will continue to depend on Hindenburg, on the old man's entourage and, above all, on the Army. Since April, since the cruise of the *Deutschland*, nothing fundamental has changed; everything has simply accelerated. Choices are now imminent; gears are shifting; he will have to act or the Army may. Hindenburg could declare martial law, giving the real power to the generals, sweeping out the SA. What would happen to Hitler's power then?

While Hitler is boarding his plane for his return flight, in Berlin Goebbels is giving a "political" tea. His social gatherings are a convenient meeting ground for men from different segments of society, where ideas can be exchanged, contacts renewed and influences brought to bear. Goering and Goebbels, as well as Hitler, favor this kind of occasion. On June 21 Goebbels has collected a group of businessmen and politicians: the industrialist Dr. Dorpmüller, the financial wizard Dr. Hjalmar Schacht and, somewhat apart, Vice Chancellor Franz von Papen. His acceptance of an invitation from the Minister of Propaganda, who censored his speech, is a measure of his "political flexibility." Also present is Councilor of State Görlitzer, Ambassador von Bülow, Field Marshal Guenther Hans von Kluge, and Fritz Gördeler. It is a carefully chosen group, combining, in the image of the Third Reich, traditional, Prussian Germany, Army representatives, business magnates, conservative politicians and Nazis. Goebbels asks for a few moments of silence: Schacht wishes to speak about the reparations question. The president of the Reichsbank has an ambitious program: a moratorium to enable the transfer of shares belonging to foreign creditors of the Reich, thereby encouraging them to buy German products. The resultant accumulated exports would facilitate German purchase of new materials, which would in turn facilitate rearmament. Papen and Kluge listen with passionate interest: one is linked to the heavy industry of the Ruhr, the other to the Army. Schacht enjoys the total support of the General Staff, and the organized metallurgy industry. However, Schacht has an adversary in the person of Schmitt, the Minister of Economics, who favors the development of a domestic consumers' market—and Schmitt is supported by Roehm. Goebbels' "political tea"—a device for presenting Schacht's ideas and the aide-mémoire he is preparing for the Führer with the support of the Reichswehr—is far from an idle occasion. Schacht's economic options also make it necessary to get rid of Roehm, in order to proceed unimpeded along the road to rearmament.

When his last guests have gone, Goebbels is driven to Tempelhof. Rudolf Hess has already arrived, and the two men walk up and down the cement runway beneath the crimson sky. Goebbels is smiling and chattering nervously, trying to hold himself as tall as Hess, who listens with an anxious look, his head tilted to one side, his hands behind his back. Hess' face is set in its usual expression of haggard obstinacy. In the vast sky of North Germany, Hitler's plane finally appears, a black speck in the dusk. Soon the two men can hear the throbbing of the plane's engines; after a preliminary pass over the field, the gray, three-engined Junker touches down and rolls slowly toward the group of officials. The plane comes to a stop; Hitler is the first one out. He salutes Goebbels and Hess, thanks the pilot and then begins to talk to his ministers. He tells them about the interview at Neudeck, evoking the massive, authoritarian silhouette of Hindenburg, and the ironic smile of Blomberg, the Gummilöwe. Even if he doesn't stress the choice that has been imposed on him, those who listen to him and see his tense, anxious face understand the moment for decision has come.

On this field of Tempelhof, Hitler, with his uneven gait, resembles an artillery commander walking up and down behind his gunners, listening to intelligence reports, taking in all the details yet deciding to withhold fire a little longer because experience has taught him that once the shells are fired, they cannot be recalled.

5

Saturday, June 30, 1934
Bonn-Hangelar Airport

1:50 A.M.

A gentle breeze comes up from the Rhine, pushing the wet fog toward the mountains. Various Nazi Party officials are gathered around the plane. Goebbels clenches his fists. Anxiously and mechanically Hitler salutes them, and then climbs the narrow metal ladder. In the plane, the pilot stretches out his hand to him. Goebbels, having trouble with his stiff leg, climbs in next. Brückner bends nearly double to get through the plane door. 1:50 A.M. From the control tower, a luminous signal confirms the radio instructions. The pilot turns on his engines, one by one, and their harsh throbbing settles into a regular hum, which echoes back from the distant hills beyond the river. Jolting a little, the plane slowly begins to roll along the runway toward the Rhine, into the wind, accelerating, lifting its tail from the ground, then increasing its speed still more to take off, passing over the barriers, making the long grasses bend double. From the control tower, it is soon impossible to see anything but its red and green navigation lights, glowing in the gray night. While the Nazi leaders return to their cars, the plane flies down the valley of the Rhine, and then curves to the ᶜoutheast toward Munich.

(Friday, June 22, to Monday, June 25)

Bonn: Barely a week before, the city university was the scene of an incident greatly disturbing to the Nazis. On this Friday morning, June 22, the Nazi Gauleiter Grohé is received at the university. Around the ancient castle of the Archbishop Electors of Cologne, housing the university, police of each Nazi group are stationed: boys from the Hitler Youth, the SS and the SA stand near the main entrance and through the gardens behind the castle, while regular policemen patrol the walks. Grohé is to speak in the ceremonial hall, the monumental Aula. Professors and Nazi dignitaries sit in the first tier of seats. As the Gauleiter comes in, the students rise. Representatives of each faculty are seated along one side of the amphitheater. The Gauleiter begins his speech in absolute silence: he speaks of the conflict between the Hitler Youth and the student organizations and touches on certain incidents, excusing the violence of the Hitler Youth. "If the Hitler Youth has sometimes been clumsy in its methods, it is a fault of youth. Those responsible for the Hitler Youth must guide this youthful, revolutionary spirit back within the necessary limits." He absolves the Hitler Youth of the excessive vindictiveness of which they have often been guilty. Suddenly, while Gauleiter Grohé is still talking, the faculty representatives get up without a word and in a body leave the hall. Grohé stops as a murmur runs through the audience. Finally he begins again, but there is a perceptible feeling of uneasiness, and he cuts his speech short. He makes a rapid departure from the castle in his heavy black car, saluted by the university authorities.

The snub he has just received is important: there will be no mention of it in the press, but the Nazis feel uneasy. After the triumphant reception of the Papen speech at Marburg by both students and professors, the Bonn incident indicates that the Nazis will not be able to stop the growth of opposition in intellectual circles: it indicates that the moderate, conservative, intellectual and religious groups are drawing away from the regime.

It seems to indicate that swift action will be necessary to show the opposition that Nazism will neither dissolve nor be swept away—that it controls Germany, and will assure order, no matter what the price.

Berlin is informed of the incident in Bonn. Himmler and Heydrich immediately call a meeting of their General Staff. General Reichenau is also present at the meeting at Gestapo headquarters. The first decisions concerning implementation of the plan for the liquidation of opponents—beginning with the SA— are made and passed on. On Friday, June 22, the SS Military District Commander, Freiherr von Eberstein, receives the order to place his troops in a state of alert. Reichenau warns the higher officers of the Reichswehr that action is imminent. Efforts are made to inform the Chancellory, but the Führer has just left Berlin. Almost immediately following his return from Neudeck early Friday morning, after one night in the austere and massive official residence, Hitler flew to Bavaria and the soothing mountains of Obersalzberg and Berchtesgaden. Is the flight a refusal to choose or a desire to let time and others make the decisions? Hitler seems like one of the hesitant kings of history, taking refuge far from the center of power, from the plots and conspiracies they wished to ignore—or, perhaps, like one of those birds of prey circling high in the sky before plummeting like a stone onto its victims.

He has just left Berlin, and the heads of the SS, Gestapo and Army again remain dangling in uncertainty. But in the SS barracks Freiherr von Eberstein's men check their weapons, the guard is reinforced, and leave canceled, even though Hitler seems to want to ignore all these preparations for assault.

Every event and circumstance is used to increase the general anxiety. An atrociously mutilated corpse is found at Gollmütz, near Schwerin, in that region of wooded hills and lakes which give Mecklenburg the look of a gentle, smiling countryside. The body is lying in the grass: the arms have been almost severed from the trunk, and the neck is cut half through, as if the murderer had been trying to chop the corpse into pieces. Police, a medical expert and judicial officials observe the body. The victim is finally identified as one Elsholtz, the administrator of an estate run on the old principles of exploitation, rough on the soil, animals and men. But he was more than that, he was also treasurer of the local Nazi Party. The murder is therefore a political crime. A man called Meissner is arrested, probably the murderer, motivated by the desire for vengeance, ulcerated by one of those peasant rivalries which gnaw at men attached to the soil. However, this explanation is not considered satisfactory by the Nazis. Meissner must also be close to Catholic circles. This is denied, but the rumor is spread in Berlin by agents of Heydrich and Himmler. The inquiry is therefore slanted toward a theory of political murder: eleven people are arrested, nine of them members of the Deutsche Jugendkraft, a Catholic youth organization. On Saturday, June 23, the *Westdeutscher Beobachter* publishes an inflammatory article: the Catholic party Zentrum, and Zentrum's paper, *Germania,* are declared responsible for the assassination of Elsholtz. If it were not for their continual attacks on the Nazis, the Nazi journal states, such acts would not happen. The Catholic conservatives are forcing good Germans to their deaths. The accusation is explicit, and contains a serious menace. The members of Zentrum protest, but their denials are lost in a flood of biased news. Tension rises, and the Nazis use it to influence public opinion.

On Saturday in Potsdam, Frederick the Great's city, Elsholtz's burial takes place. The ceremony is impressive: drums resound lugubriously through the wide avenue leading to the Nikolaikirche, the large, domed church in the Altmarkt Square. The funeral cortege moves at a slow, ceremonial pace; groups divide, passing on either side of the obelisk in the middle of the square.

The obelisk is decorated with medallions of the Great Elector and the first three kings of Prussia. The cortege is led by Minister Ley, and the Gauleiter of Berlin, Kube. After the ceremony at the church, the procession moves off again to the Potsdam cemetery. There, as the burial takes place, Nazi flags are lowered.

After the ceremony at Potsdam, the dignitaries return immediately to Berlin: most of them are expected to speak at one or another of the grand displays the Nazis are organizing to celebrate the summer solstice.

Everything seems to be preparing for the summer festival. The sky over Germany on Saturday, June 23, is filled with light; the colors of the lakes and fields are gentle, more like the colors of spring than of high summer. Ley's journey doesn't end at Berlin. He proceeds immediately to Tempelhof, where a Junker is waiting for him. In the plane he reads through his speech: he is to speak in the early afternoon at Oberhausen, in the Ruhr. From the narrow cabin of the plane, one can see the mountain peaks to the south marking the beginning of the Hercynian heart of Germany, with its somber masses of forest and billowing white clouds rising over the snowy mountaintops. Ahead in the distance, a gray cloud cover pierced by columns of black smoke announces the Ruhr with its steel works, the domain of the Krupps, the pounding heart of German power.

This same June 23, General Blomberg sends to the Chancellory a memorandum for the Führer prepared by General Thomas, a Reichswehr specialist in economics, who proposes an economic dictatorship to organize the rearmament of Germany. The director of this effort should be Schacht. Schmitt, the present Economics Minister, who wants to raise the standard of living, should be liquidated. With Schacht, production would count for more than consumption, and industry would be oriented toward the manufacture of steel bars which could be turned into gun barrels, or gun mounts, made for more than a century in the Ruhr.

Ley's flight is another example of the use made of planes by

Hitler and the Nazis in order to visit several German cities in one day: bury Elsholtz in Potsdam in the morning, speak to the workers of Oberhausen in the afternoon.

"National Socialism," Ley shouts, "will watch to see that everyone takes part in the necessary sacrifices; it will not allow a few hyenas on the battlefield to profit from these sacrifices."

The Nazi groups applaud, the workers are more reserved. "Let no one imagine that he will be able to live as before. . . . He who hopes to take refuge on an Isle of the Blest is greatly mistaken."

The build-up continues: no pity for the world of the past; the survival of former attitudes is impossible.

At Duisburg, the great, smoky port of the Ruhr, only a few miles from Oberhausen, where Minister Ley is speaking, Joseph Goebbels has been given the job of injecting life into the Gauparteitag (the Party Day of the district of Essen). He arrives at the flag-decked airport at two o'clock in the afternoon. There is a series of receptions and a visit to the exposition hall of the Essen Fair, where members of the female Party organizations have gathered. The president, Frau Scholz-Klink, is presented to the puny Goebbels; bands play, and young girls wave Nazi banners. Goebbels is delighted; his smiling face is even more set in a grimace than usual. Between four and five o'clock, through a din of sirens, Goebbels takes a boat across the dark waters of Duisburg Harbor, where heavy barges loaded with coal and minerals pass close to him. Finally, in the large Duisburg stadium there is the expected parade, with 150 fanfares by the Hitler Youth brass bands playing in turn. It is cool: the flames of the torches lengthen in the wind. At 8:57 P.M. one thousand members of Nazi youth groups intone the old military hymn, "Song of the Reiters." The bitter, stinging vigor of ancient Germany seems to rise beneath the gray smoggy sky. The song soars above this setting of chimneys, girders, cranes and mine shafts.

At nine o'clock, Terboven, Nazi leader of Essen, begins to speak, a few words drowned in cheers, announcing Joseph Goebbels, small, pale and nervous. In the glare of the lights, Goebbels walks up to the speakers' platform. He does not mince words. "It will be necessary to maintain low wages, because we have had to find work for four million unemployed." Loudspeakers carry his voice out into the night. He outlines the Party's program: "to build a future of happiness . . . the realization of this future will be the mission of our youth." Cries of enthusiasm rise from thousands of youthful listeners: the night seems to burst with their fervor. "Our movement has become our second fatherland; we have fought and struggled to ensure its greatness. The desire of each of us is to watch over our movement, cherishing it as we cherish our loved ones." Goebbels concludes his speech, hammering out his words. For some twenty minutes he has spoken of fidelity, constancy and a simple style of life. At 9:30 the parade begins with the singing of the "Horst Wessel Lied." The 150 brass bands accompany the march, and at 10:05 the feast of the solstice begins. Nazism has German youth firmly in its grasp, and youth rejoices, believing with all its ardor that it has rediscovered a profound and natural force. At 10:30 Goebbels leaves the stadium and its atmosphere of excitement and sets out for Osnabrück, where he is to speak the next day.

When he arrives at Osnabrück late at night, Goebbels finds the local Nazis preoccupied and worried. Word has arrived from Quentzin, a small, gray town near Greifenhagen, of an incident between the SA and the National Socialist veterans' organization. Sturmführer Moltzahn, one of the SA leaders of longest standing in Pomerania, was being honored on Saturday, June 23, at the same time the feast of the summer solstice was being celebrated. Members of the SA and various youth organizations were listening to the Sturmführer's speech, accompanying it with rhythmic shouts of "Heil!" When the SA leader tried to give an order to Kummerow, the leader of the veterans' group, Kummerow refused to obey, grabbing an oak stick and threatening the SA officer. A fist fight began between the two men, which was ended by Kummerow, who seized Sturmführer Moltzahn's sword and stabbed him in the stomach. The SA threw themselves into the fray; Moltzahn, his tunic red with blood, collapsed; Kummerow was arrested.

At Osnabrück Goebbels reads the first reports. The SA demand dissolution of the veterans' association: "The sword thrust at Quentzin has struck every German." Other SA bulletins condemn in advance all those who may view the incident as an isolated occurrence. To the SA, it is a political matter. "I don't know anything worse than you and your SA," Kummerow is alleged to have repeated several times. After stabbing Moltzahn, he is said to have shouted: "If only I'd just been able to get him in the guts!" "A leader of the SA, which has fought for Germany, has been killed," say the SA. Clearly, they want to present themselves as victims: they are not responsible for the disorder; when National Socialism is attacked, they are attacked. This is the result of the politics of moderation of the men advising the Führer. A strong reaction to the Quentzin incident is essential as a warning to everyone. The heroes of National Socialism, the brave leaders of the SA, cannot be allowed to be massacred.

What will the SA do? In the tense atmosphere of the final days of June, the question is repeated at the Bendlerstrasse and at No. 8 Prinz-Albrecht Strasse, Gestapo headquarters. At the Gestapo itself, the originators of the rumors of an SA plot have begun to worry: what if Roehm's men take their enemies by surprise and strike, using the Quentzin incident as a pretext? On June 23 efforts are made to reach Hitler, but he is on the way to his chalet at Berchtesgaden, and is not available. Goebbels confers at length with Heydrich, and then Himmler.

On this same Saturday, toward the end of the day, General Friedrich Fromm, Chief of General Services of the Army, has called together the officers under his command for a confidential conference at the Bendlerstrasse; no one is present in the large marble-floored room except ranking officers, stiffly seated on their high-backed chairs, symmetrically arranged around the long, black table. After a brief word of greeting, the General solemnly announces that he has learned from reliable sources that a plot for an imminent coup d'état has been organized by Captain Roehm and his SA. The Army must be ready to intervene to assure the maintenance of law and order. The officers sit motionless, silent: it is no time for comment.

The following day, General Fromm's information is confirmed: General von Fritsch calls together the higher officers in Berlin, and orders them to prepare to resist a putsch by the SA. There is every indication, Fritsch declares, that the SA plan to act very quickly—perhaps in a few hours, at most in a few days, and certainly before the general leave of the Sturmabteilung, which is supposed to begin on July 1. The officers will be expected to assemble their troops with maximum discretion, keeping them in a state of combat readiness. Thus, following the example of the SS, the Reichswehr assumes a wartime posture. In Berlin, on Sunday, June 24, strollers along Unter den Linden see many police cars on the street. Since early morning the police, too, have been ready to fight. The trap is closing around the Sturmabteilung.

The earliest fighters for Nazism, however, men who took part in assassinations, some even who were involved in the Reichstag fire—these "old fighters" do not seem in the least suspicious.

In front of the Pension Hanselbauer, facing the lake, cars are parked; there is a succession of visitors. The local SA, and the officers who arrive from all parts of Germany, are relaxed and in good humor. Some leap into the water of the Tegernsee; others nap or drink. Roehm swaggers about, posturing, surrounded by his young aides-de-camp. Several times, each time to a new audience, he declares that he has confidence in the judgment of the Führer, his old comrade Adolf Hitler, who will eventually move in favor of the Sturmabteilung. Some of the SA leaders express their doubts and anxieties: Roehm laughs and sweeps their objections away with a large gesture. When the Führer has heard their grievances here in the drawing room of the Pension Hanselbauer, he will see things their way and agree with them. And then if . . . But Captain Roehm does not complete these half-formulated threats, which only exist in the realm of the impossible. This last Sunday in June is a day of celebration, spent drinking the light beer of Munich and singing the "Horst Wessel Lied." One by one, the SA leaders raise their beer steins and make speeches to the glory of the Sturmabteilung, damning the veterans' associations responsible for the death at Quentzin. Roehm says a few words, and then in chorus the group begins to sing war songs. In the small spa, patients taking the cure walk peacefully beside the lake. People have driven out from Munich to spend Sunday in the mountains: some applaud or salute when they pass the SA cars. The weather is beautiful, the air is tonic.

While the SA are splashing naked in the blue waters of the Tegernsee, Himmler and Heydrich receive the superior officers of the National SS at Gestapo headquarters in Berlin. Most of them arrived in Berlin the day before and spent the night in SS barracks, or at 8 Prinz-Albrecht Strasse. Now while ordinary Berliners prepare to spend a relaxed summer Sunday, the officers of the Black Guard have gathered around their leaders. Heydrich is speaking: as aways icily efficient, he goes straight to the point. The General Staff of the Sturmabteilung is preparing a revolt which will break out very shortly—perhaps within a few days. His words fall like hammer blows. This SA revolt must be foiled —Heydrich insists upon the term—and put down with extreme harshness. Sealed lists of the SA conspirators have already been given to various SS units. When the moment comes, orders will be executed without the slightest hesitation, with full National Socialist severity. Accomplices in the plot who do not belong to the SA will also be tracked down. Orders are to be followed without considering the past record of anyone, including his rank in the SA or the Reichswehr.

The SS leaders listen and take in the determination of Heydrich and Himmler. There are some in the audience who, for various reasons, have suffered at the hands of the SA, or been damaged by the success of one of their former comrades. Their feeling of release mounts: the day is drawing near when their accumulated anger can be expressed in political action for the good of Germany. They will also liquidate those pretentious figures—the Reichswehr generals or advisers of Franz von Papen.

It is also on this tranquil June Sunday that General von Schleicher returns to Berlin. Friends, probably working at the Bendlerstrasse, had warned him in the spring that he might be in danger. He had taken a long automobile trip following his stay on the peaceful shores of Lake Starnberg.

Now, with his wife, he returns to his comfortable suburban villa in the capital. Once again it seems to him that his political instinct has served him well: everything is calm. His friends' anxiety had been mistaken. Life will resume its normal course. Schleicher has no idea that on that very day Heydrich, Himmler and the leaders of the SS are completing their final preparations. He does not know that his name is on their list, or that this Sunday, colored by his pleasure in returning to Berlin, will be the last Sunday of his life.

He, who imagines himself the most "political" and able general in the Reichswehr, does not notice the accumulating signs: not only the police cars prowling slowly through the tranquil city, but also the interview with Hitler published in the *News Chronicle,* in which the Führer speaks of the "sacrifice of friends from the early days" which may be necessary. Undoubtedly General Schleicher, like so many other Germans, including the leaders of the SA, is reassured by Hitler's absence from the capital, announced on the radio and in the press, which state that he has gone to rest in his chalet at Berchtesgaden. How can preparations for brutal action be under way when the Führer is not in Berlin, when he is posing for photographers in Tyrolean costume and receiving friends in his drawing room with its impressive view of the Alps?

The fifty thousand people who have collected in the park on the southern outskirts of Berlin to attend Sunday Mass celebrated by Monsignor Barres are also calm. They kneel in long lines on the short, thick grass, then move to the altar to take Communion. Dr. Klausener, the Reich's Director of Public Works, speaks. His talk is moderate in tone: he makes a few remarks complimentary to the government, and contents himself with claiming the right of Catholics to celebrate their religion in dignity and respect, precisely as they are doing now. This surely must be proof that all is calm in the Third Reich. Dr. Klausener is applauded vigorously by the peaceful audience.

At the same time, a large audience in the Berlin stadium is gripped with enthusiasm. Tens of thousands of spectators shout with joy, waving Bavarian flags and Nazi swastikas. During the last minutes of the soccer game, the Oberhausen team, the celebrated Schalke 04, breaks a tie and scores a goal against the Nuremberg team, winning the German championship. The crowd starts for home in a joyous mood, children perched on their fathers' shoulders, while laborers out for a day of Sunday enjoyment continue their discussions of the game before retiring to one of the local beer halls. Everything seems to be normal, even joyous, in the capital this long summer day. At the edge of town, the black cars of the SS leaders returning to their districts pass groups going home from the Catholic rally and from the stadium.

What do the Brown Shirts have to fear? Nothing has changed: they are still the powerful "old fighters" to whom even ministers defer. The SA of the Ruhr, mixed in with a crowd of strong-faced workers, skins toughened and darkened by long hours beside furnaces and forges, have been gathered since 8:45 A.M. in hall No. 5 of the Essen-Mülheim Fair. The large vaulted building of reinforced concrete, disproportionately long, gray and dreary, looks like a stern temple of industry, powerful and sinister. A wide passageway has been arranged down the middle of the hall with seats on each side. Flags and enormous banners stamped with swastikas hang from the balcony and the speakers' stand which has been placed in the middle of the hall. The SA, workmen and

Nazi Youth groups have been waiting since morning. The hall echoes with thousands of voices and is filled with the breath from thousands of lungs: it is not yet really warm. At 8:40 the regional leader of the Hitler Youth appears on the speakers' platform and the grand demonstration begins. It is necessary, he shouts, that the struggle against social prejudice and class spirit begin in earnest. The caps of university and high school students, for instance, representing a dated hierarchy, must be burned. Some of the audience begins to respond with enthusiastic approval; the shouts grow louder at the announcement that Rudolf Hess has arrived. "Youth needs discipline," he declares, to a storm of vociferous approval and applause. When Hess finishes his talk, the audience bursts into song, the SA joining the students. At ten o'clock an open car brings Ley and Goebbels to the hall. They enter to more applause.

The two ministers are wearing caps. Goebbels also wears an armband stamped with a swastika. He sits next to Ley, stunted, grimacing, somehow incomplete beside Ley's massive corpulence. "Power reaches its peak when violence is no longer necessary," Ley declares. After opening with much the same idea, Goebbels launches into an attack against the enemies of the regime, waving his clenched fist as he talks. "They appear in many guises, sometimes as reserve officers or intellectuals, sometimes as journalists, sometimes as priests." The SA roar their approval. Karl Kuhder, who was at the back of the hall, remembers that when Goebbels added: "It is always the same clique . . . they have learned nothing . . . they will act tomorrow just as they did yesterday," he and his comrades "recognized *our* Goebbels and *our* Reich." After Goebbels' attack on the Junkers, officers and intellectuals, Kuhder and his SA comrades cheered. "We shouted so hard that we lost our voices." They hadn't listened when Goebbels talked about revolutionary discipline and loyalty, but they shouted with joy when he cried: "I am convinced that we have the power to do anything we consider useful. Our power has no limits."

"Our power has no limits." The SA and the Hitler Youth take

up the refrain. They run down the wide central aisle to see Goebbels to his car. "We thought that at last they were telling us we were right; we were sure of it," Karl Kuhder remembers. Hadn't Goebbels just condemned all the Papens in Germany, all the people Roehm and his followers had been denouncing for months? Kuhder adds: "Goebbels left the hall at Essen around twelve o'clock. It was said that he was flying to Hamburg, on his way to the German Derby."

The sky over Hamburg is gray, with light clouds broken into parallel bands. A fine rain is falling, but the crowd is considerable. Begun in 1869, the Derby attracts all social classes. Workers crowd the lawn despite the rain. A special train has brought members of the diplomatic corps from Berlin; they will also be attending the Kiel Regatta. There are numerous public figures in the grandstand, in uniform, saluting each other. There are members of the Reich government and of the government of Prussia, including National Sports Director Tschammer von Osten. On the road to Hamburg there is a line of cars almost a mile long. Suddenly an official car flanked by two motorcycles passes the other cars. It is Franz von Papen on his way to the Derby. He reaches the central stand. People come up to him from all parts of the stand, and there is a burst of applause. The Vice Chancellor gives this account: "I went to Hamburg to watch the German Derby. As soon as I reached the stands, thousands of people came running toward me shouting 'Heil Marburg, Heil Marburg!'—a completely unexpected demonstration because Hamburgers are generally phlegmatic, and because the occasion was purely a sporting event." As the significance of the demonstration dawns on the crowd, their applause grows louder. They keep pressing toward the stand. "I could scarcely take a step without finding my way blocked by hundreds of enthusiastic people, until finally I began to feel hemmed in."

The SS officers make no secret of their displeasure, and bemedaled SA leave their seats. The spontaneous demonstration is clearly political. Papen is being applauded because he has dared speak certain truths about the functioning of the Third Reich. Then the horses appear, and Papen is no longer the center of attention. It is the first race: Orchauf on the outside, a magnificent, high-strung creature, nervously pawing the ground, Agalire on the inside, skillfully held in by his jockey; and Palander in the second row. Count Almaviva quickly takes the lead, running under the low sky, in a silence broken from time to time by distant cheering, which breaks out suddenly when Athanasius, one of the favorites, spurts ahead, spurred on by Blintzen. It is a magnificent race, no longer disturbed even by the weather, because the rain has stopped—just wet mud splattered in all directions by the horses' flying hooves. At the end of the first race there are cheers at the track entrance: Joseph Goebbels has just arrived from Essen, where he has been making a speech. He is gesticulating grandly, and appears to be indignant. Associates have just told him about the demonstration for von Papen. He refuses to sit in the box beside the man he has just been attacking, who symbolizes the "clique which has learned nothing." He goes down onto the grass, joining the crowd of laborers. He is recognized and applauded. Papen notes simply: "There were a few isolated outbursts of applause—Hamburgers are polite people—but that was all."

Papen hesitates a moment, and then, sensing that the crowd is with him, decides to confront Goebbels. "I decided to reap the maximum benefit from the friendly attitude of the crowd. This was an excellent opportunity for me to find out whether my Marburg speech had pleased only the upper classes, or whether it had also pleased the masses. Therefore I followed Goebbels to the cheaper seats, where my reception was even warmer. Stevedores, students and workers gave me an overwhelming ovation. This time, it was too much for Goebbels. Green with rage, he decided not to attend the official banquet."

The Minister of Propaganda leaves the racetrack and returns to the capital. He instructs Görlitzer, the assistant Gauleiter of

Berlin, to make Papen look ridiculous in his newspaper. Heydrich and Himmler are immediately told about the demonstrations at the Derby, while Hitler, in his chalet at Berchtesgaden, receives a detailed report. In spite of the enthusiasm of Essen, the joyful Hitler Youth and the pagan festival of the solstice, the von Papens and Klauseners still exist, an uncertain grouping of more or less determined opposition. As do the SA who wait with Roehm at Bad Wiessee, hoping to profit from the agitation of the reactionary "clique" denounced by Goebbels.

The Führer listens, thinks and rests, gazing out at the icy peaks. He must choose: he senses the growing impatience of both sides. Papen pushes his advantage, Roehm gathers his forces, Himmler and Heydrich are already sending their killers out all over the Reich, while the soldiers of the Black Guard make ready to track their victims whenever the order is given. While the attention of the country is fixed on ordinary summer pleasures, while Germany lives through this last Sunday in June in ignorance and tranquillity, the Führer's moment of choice and action has drawn very close.

Franz von Papen returns to Berlin a few hours after Goebbels. The banquet given by the town of Hamburg for the various public figures attending the Derby had been a lively occasion. A few officers of the Sturmabteilung, aggressive and drinking heavily, conspicuously avoided the Vice Chancellor. After a short night's sleep, Papen leaves the capital again, on Monday morning, June 25. He has to go to Westphalia, for his niece's marriage.

During the ceremony, which is attended by several Reichswehr officers, von Papen seems distracted and anxious. Several times his private secretary brings him messages and dispatches. The Vice Chancellor's face is tense: he smiles at the young couple and their parents, but his thoughts seem to be elsewhere. From Nuremberg to Cologne, the attacks against him are multiplying. Papen is too practiced in the ways of governments and politics not to understand that the atmosphere in Germany is growing tenser, that the Nazis, who have the power, are preparing to act.

Goering speaks in Nuremberg, hammering out the message: "We need ardor, not the chill of reason." The flesh of his pale, heavy face trembles with his effort. He threatens large events. "We shall soon see that Germany, so often betrayed and defamed, is the greatest of the civilized nations." Papen wonders about these forthcoming events. He receives the text of another speech. At that very moment, Hess is speaking on the Cologne radio, and his talk is being broadcast throughout Germany. A Monday speech by the second man in the Party is extremely unusual. Why has Hess made this unexpected visit to Cologne? Why were all those officials assembled so hastily at the Butzweilerhof Airfield? Why was the SA honor guard called out at the last minute with Gauleiter Grohé and Brigadeführer Hovel, and driven out to the airfield to welcome the Minister of the Reich? He was there for one reason: to go to the radio station, make his speech and then return to Berlin. It is a curious proceeding, indicating improvisation and determination, as if a long-deferred decision had finally been made and now called for immediate execution. Hess' speech is violent, highly excited, but also vague, threatening to everyone, Papen as well as Roehm, repeating and emphasizing a single idea: "There is only one man above all criticism—the Führer. Everyone knows that he has always been right and that he always will be right. In unquestioning fidelity and obedience to the Führer, in complete execution of his orders, lies the strength of our National Socialism. The Führer follows his calling; the call of a higher vocation. His task is to shape the destiny of Germany." Hess attacks the critics, and then, carefully emphasizing his words, he utters a series of phrases, each of which contains a dark warning. "Woe unto those who, with heavy boots, crash clumsily through the fragile web of the Führer's strategic plans, thinking that they can reach our goal more quickly. These people are enemies of the Revolution." Whom does Hess mean, if not Roehm and his impatient SA? The warning rings out again: "Only the orders of the Führer, to whom we have sworn fidelity, are valid. Woe to him who loses faith, woe to him who thinks he can serve the Revolution by rebellion."

Who else but Roehm is this threat aimed at? Franz von Papen is anxious: he knows that in practice revolutions often force strange alliances, that in the carts which clattered down the streets of Paris in 1794 heading for the same guillotine, side by side sat former noblemen, Royal Army officers, Girondists and rejected revolutionaries. Hitler might just as easily toss into the same basket the heads of the brigand Roehm and the country gentleman Papen.

At Oberhausen few people are thinking about Hess' speech. Everyone is in the streets to welcome the soccer team returning from Berlin after its victorious match. The station is besieged; the SS, SA and the railway police are overwhelmed by the human tide welcoming the players, above all the forward, Kuzonna, who made the winning goal. An enormous wreath is draped over his shoulders. The parade proceeds through the town. The team is piled into two open cars, and the populace greets them with enthusiasm. Who thinks of Hess, the SA or the Gestapo? The crowd is caught up in a festival of rejoicing, the whole town, relaxed and joyous, waving its banners and applauding the winners of a sports event as in any democratic country where there is no fear of the brutal intervention of armed men or the persecutions of the SS and the SA, who salute with stiff arms, but whom the crowd ignores. One might have been in one of the steel towns of England, or in Sweden. Oberhausen might be any city of a calm and orderly country passionate about sports, and which for centuries has not thought of such things as putsches, plots or secret police and their hired killers.

While the crowd shouts in the streets of Oberhausen, the Reichswehr is in a state of watchfulness. It expects an SA putsch. The officers are under orders to keep a weapon within arm's reach. A few object; they do not believe in the threat, and refuse to be dupes in what they sense is merely a maneuver. When a Lieutenant under orders arrives to leave a gun in the office of Colonel Gotthard Heinrici of the Army's General Services, Henrici loses his temper. There are similar reactions in many barracks and staff offices.

In Silesia, General Ewald von Kleist commands the troops of the military district. He is a remarkable officer, a soldier with a high sense of honor and principle. For several days he has been receiving warnings from the Bendlerstrasse and the Gestapo that the Sturmabteilung is about to act. Finally the General gets in touch with Heines, commander of the SA in Silesia. Heines denies all the rumors, and swears ignorance of any plot. Kleist, who was skeptical, is convinced by Heines: could all these false alarms and rumors not be part of a scheme organized by the SS, perhaps, to set the Army against the SA, in order to profit from the confrontation? Kleist goes immediately to Berlin. At the Bendlerstrasse it is impossible for him to wait patiently: he paces up and down the antechamber to General von Fritsch's office. Von Fritsch, on the basis of his reports, has sent out orders for a general alert to the various units. At last he receives Kleist. After a few opening remarks, Kleist plunges in without hesitation. He tells Fritsch of his uncertainties, and analyzes the situation in Silesia, where the SA is entirely calm. He presses his argument. Gradually Fritsch is shaken: could the Reichswehr be deceived?

Reichenau is called in. He arrives, stiffly belted into his uniform, and listens, absolutely motionless, without showing the slightest surprise. Reichenau is at the heart of the plot. He knows everything, but beneath his impassive façade he is disturbed: the scruples of men like Kleist could very well put a brake on the action, if not thoroughly compromise it. The more time passes, the more the doubts and hesitations of such officers will grow. It is necessary to head them off, catch the hesitant by surprise, and move into action to create an irreversible situation. In General Fritsch's office Reichenau looks at Kleist, then at Fritsch, and doesn't bother to discuss their argument. "In any case," Reichenau says dryly, "it's too late now."

6

Saturday, June 30, 1934
In Flight Over Taunus

2:30 A.M.

In the plane the noise of the engines makes conversation difficult. Joseph Goebbels is shouting, trying to talk to Lutze. Since leaving Bonn-Hangelar, the plane has been in the air for about half an hour. The sky is clear. Hitler sits in the cabin beside the pilot, the collar of his leather coat turned up. He is leaning forward, and, as Goebbels remembers later, "stares fixedly ahead into the infinite darkness." The Führer says nothing. From time to time the pilot calls out the name of a town, pointing to an irregular checkerboard of winking lights. They have flown over Ems and Nassau, which appeared briefly on the plane's right. The plane has been gradually climbing; now it is flying over the Feldberg Mountain. Slightly to the right the faint gleam of the converging Rhine and Main is visible, and seemingly side by side, Wiesbaden and Mainz are surrounded by a luminous halo. At regular intervals, a voice from flight control resounds through the cabin with information about the weather over the Steigerwald or Frankenhöhe, mountains of moderate height like all those running like veins across Germany. Throughout the region as far as Munich, the air is clear: the pilot tells the Führer he is turning more sharply southeast, for a direct approach to Munich.

It is 2:30 A.M. In the Pension Hanselbauer everyone is asleep. In one of the little rooms, Edmund Heines has slipped his arm around the shoulders of a young SA, pulling the boy against him, asking him not to leave but to stay and sleep with him, prolonging their amorous encounter. There will be plenty of time to leave the room discreetly in the morning. The young SA is exhausted and falls asleep.

At Kaufering, orders are barked out. The SS of the Leibstandarte, their boots hammering the floor, mechanically fall in, merging into a single unit, each carefully selected and trained man linked to the next. Gruppenführer SS Sepp Dietrich has arrived. He speaks in a low voice: obedience is vital; traitors must be eliminated no matter what their present position or what their past record. The staff of the SA is a nest of treachery and debauch; the Leibstandarte must clean it out, defend the honor of Germany, protect the Führer. "Heil Hitler!" Their cries weld the men together. The trucks arrive, and the two SS companies board them in silence. Surrounded by officers, his hands behind his back, his legs apart, Gruppenführer Sepp Dietrich surveys the scene with a smile of satisfaction. He knows where the trucks are headed: Pension Hanselbauer, Bad Wiessee, by the Tegernsee.

(Tuesday, June 26, to Thursday, June 28)

Sepp Dietrich does not simply obey orders: he is one of the SS leaders on whom Heydrich and Himmler particularly depend as they construct their trap—a trap which must be adjusted daily to the continual threats posed by the imponderables which can undo a political alliance made up of so many different interests, causing its collapse: an imprudent confidence or the unexpected action of a man suddenly seized by scruple. Heydrich understands this: he is a man of method. When Reichenau warns him that Generals von Kleist and von Fritsch are beginning to doubt the actuality of the SA plot, he acts. They must play on the officers' anxieties, show them that the SA really does threaten them. The Gestapo is already expert in the fabrication of documents.

On Tuesday, June 26, Sepp Dietrich goes to the Bendler-strasse and asks to see an officer in General Blomberg's office, giving him a confidential document which, he says, he obtained from an SA Führer who was outraged by its contents. When Blomberg reads the document, he is frightened and angry: during the putsch, the General Staff of the Sturmabteilung intends to liquidate all ranking Reichswehr officers. The Army must be purged of these rigid conservatives, the text states; they must be replaced by revolutionaries. Generals Beck and Fritsch are specifically mentioned among the first victims.

The same day Captain Patzig walks into his office. He has served in the Navy for many years, but for the last few months he has been directing the Abwehr, the Army's Intelligence Service, which even the defeat of 1918 failed to dismantle, and which, during the black years that followed, constituted a secret core of the Reichswehr, itself the heart of the defeated nation. On his work table, in plain sight, Captain Patzig sees a document. The sentries and other officers all say they know nothing about it. This mysterious and explosive paper is a copy of an order given by Roehm to the SA—a secret order decreeing the immediate re-armament of the SA. Is this not decisive proof of the preparation of an SA putsch? Patzig warns his superiors. A short time later, General von Reichenau arrives at Patzig's office. Reichenau, his monocle fixed over his right eye, reads the document, and then says, casting a glance at Patzig: "This is the last straw. I'm going to the Führer."

But Hitler has not yet returned to Berlin. He lingers at Berchtesgaden, letting the others show their hands; surely there is only one rule for winning, and the Führer does not forget it:

you must know your adversary's game. So Hitler stays in his chalet, and receives delegations from neighboring villages, patting the cheeks of the children. At the secretariat of the Chancellory General von Reichenau insists, and is told that Hitler will undoubtedly return the next day, Wednesday, June 27, but that he will not be staying in the capital.

Reichenau returns to the Bendlerstrasse. Hitler's absence aggravates the general unease, the feeling that anything is possible. The Abwehr has further information for Reichenau. In one of the buildings assigned to the SA (the headquarters of Reiterstandarte 28), located opposite the home of a French diplomat, members of the Sturmabteilung practice regularly, firing their heavy machine guns. The French diplomat has surely sent a report to Paris, for the firing can be heard in the streets. It began less than a week ago, and is a sign of something serious—more serious than anything in the documents delivered by Sepp Dietrich, or accidentally left on the desk of Captain Patzig.

The firing of the SA machine guns resounds through the heads of all the men preparing the action against Roehm. Himmler, Heydrich, Reichenau—all those who fabricated or used documents compromising the Sturmabteilung now face facts seeming to prove the reality of their accusations. Training with heavy machine guns, the SA may indeed initiate action, may actually *be* planning a putsch. As always, those who operate in a world of shadows imagine there are others in the shadows, also conspiring. For Himmler and Heydrich fear is now added to determination.

Goering himself seems to be anxious. On Tuesday, June 26, he speaks at Hamburg. It is a mixed audience, combining members of wealthy shipping families and local Nazis, some of whom were formerly employees of these wealthy families. Goering is all affability. He is no longer the thundering demagogue of Nuremberg. He no longer threatens or insults the conservatives, but preaches unity behind Hitler, suggesting that he, too, has been touched by fear. "To those who long for order in the country, to those who remember the grandeur and discipline of the Imperial epoch," Goering says, "I affirm that Adolf Hitler is the only man capable of returning Germany to its strength, of making the former soldiers of the Hohenzollerns once again objects of respect. . . . We who are alive today should rejoice that we have Adolf Hitler with us." The sound of the Sturmabteilung's machine guns may, for Goering, counter the words of Franz von Papen at Marburg. Hermann Goering, hero of 1914–1918, raised to the rank of general by Hindenburg, widower of Karin, the Swedish aristocrat, is the most conservative Nazi of all, the closest in spirit to the Junkers, the Officers' Corp and the Reichswehr. It is not surprising that he should try to maintain his links with the conservatives.

Sometimes he is suspected of being too interested in his own future, of caring less about the Nazi regime than about his own career. He is closely watched; General von Reichenau, icily ambitious, is afraid that one day Goering may be Chief Minister of the Reichswehr—perhaps in a new Reich. Reichenau's hatred for the SA, the ties he has formed with the Gestapo, Himmler and Heydrich's Black Guard, may be simply a means of defending himself against General Goering.

In the seething brew of ambition, intrigue and rivalry which constitutes the Third Reich of the Nazis, each man must defend himself against everyone else. Whoever one can hold is an ally. Hermann Goering, because he needs the conservatives, can forgive the Marburg speech; others remember it, however, and do not forgive.

Vice Chancellor Franz von Papen has decided to spend Tuesday, June 26, in Westphalia with his relatives. The banquet which followed the wedding lasted late into the night, and Papen, tired after several taxing and active days, is counting on Tuesday as a day of rest. In the morning he took a long walk with his secretary, but early in the afternoon a communiqué from Berlin puts an end to this brief calm. "On June 26 Tschirschky called me to the telephone to tell me that Edgar Jung had just been arrested by the Gestapo." Jung is a journalist, a brilliant stylist with real political courage. On Papen's behalf, he had maintained liaison with Marshal Hindenburg at Neudeck. He had also written the Marburg speech, which Papen and his collaborators modified only slightly. The Gestapo knows all this. It would like to know more; it never forgives.

Jung's friends reconstruct the movements of Himmler's and Heydrich's men. Jung's housekeeper gave the alarm. She arrived on Tuesday morning around nine o'clock. As soon as she opened the door, she was terrified. Clothes were strewn over the floor of the entrance hall; in the study, drawers were open, and the disorderly scatter of papers suggested a hasty search. In the bedroom, furniture was overturned and the bed was unmade. Undoubtedly, Jung had been surprised in his sleep, and had tried to resist. In horror, the housekeeper telephoned everyone she knew to be a friend of Jung's. She did not telephone the police; on a wall, she had recognized Jung's handwriting. He must have been allowed to go into the bathroom for a moment, and had been able to write in pencil one word: "GESTAPO." In the ransacked apartment the Vice Chancellor's collaborators and Jung's close friends are appalled. The chaos of the crumpled clothes and scattered papers with its implied violence seems like a sinister warning of the misery to come. What can be done? First, locate Papen. Tschirschky is finally able to reach him in Westphalia. Papen makes him repeat the details of their discovery to give himself time to think. But in fact, as soon as he hears the word "Gestapo" he understands what has happened. Heydrich and Himmler have begun their offensive; they are beginning to set their snares, to seize their victims. But how far will they go? Papen decides to return to Berlin immediately. He must try to rescue Jung from his torturers; he must find out who else they want and why. Papen thinks, too, of his own safety. In the official world of Berlin, the Vice Chancellor will be somewhat protected from clandestine arrest and anonymous killers. Tuesday, June 26: with Jung's arrest, the struggle is joined.

Papen arrives in Berlin on Wednesday, June 27. Black storm clouds bear down on the capital from the southwest. As the plane lands, it is buffeted by wind. The Vice Chancellor, in the grip of an anxiety increased by exhaustion, meets Tschirschky, waiting on the runway. The two men have to hold onto their hats, as the damp wind billows up under their raincoats, stirring up eddies of dust. After a quick consultation, Papen decides on a series of maneuvers designed to help his collaborator: to save Jung is also to protect himself. But Franz von Papen is unable to meet with Hitler; at the Chancellory he is told that the Führer has just returned from Munich and is resting. Goering is away, making a speech in Cologne. Papen is driven to 8 Prinz-Albrecht Strasse, and finally manages to see Reichsführer SS Himmler. The head of the Black Guard is coldly correct, reassuring: it's a question of a simple inquiry, about which he can say nothing for the moment. Later, Papen writes an account of this day, in which tragedy is very close: "When I returned to Berlin, I tried in vain to see Hitler or Goering. In despair, I protested vehemently to Himmler, who replied that Jung had been arrested on a charge of illegal contacts with foreign powers. An inquiry was in process. Himmler said he could give no further details for the moment, but promised the rapid release of my colleague."

Papen is a prudent man. He knows one must often wait, accept the impossibility of insistence, maintain appearances, accept official declarations. He is an experienced man. Himmler's attitude and the evasions of Hitler and Goering convince him the climate is no longer one of conciliation. He returns to his Berlin home while Jung remains in the hands of the Gestapo. No one will ever know what Jung suffered in the cellars of the big building at No. 8 Prinz-Albrecht Strasse; no one knew then that he was the first victim of the Night of Long Knives.

Only an insider could sense the rising desire for vengeance. For most Germans, everything is calm. Readers of the *National Zeitung* are reassured: on the first page, under the title, "The German Situation," a radiant future is promised. The Germany of the Third Reich is triumphing over poverty and unemployment—a triumph once thought unobtainable. "Let us give thanks to our Führer, Adolf Hitler, who has found work for everyone."

Over Radio Berlin, Rosenberg speaks to schoolchildren and high school students. Pupils are assembled in classrooms everywhere to hear the Party ideologist, who affirms that "Germany finds herself involved in a political struggle which is also a spiritual struggle without historical precedent. . . . It is necessary that all our fellow countrymen appreciate German unity. You must serve this unity by maintaining amongst yourselves true camaraderie." In class, teachers discuss the talk with their pupils: what is true camaraderie in the New Reich? The Hitler Youth are the first to answer: the camaraderie of soldiers at the front, the indestructible camaraderie of the "old fighters." The audience of youthful blonds, in white shirts and black shorts, let their imaginations wander while Rosenberg speaks; they live in the virile fellowship of wartime, fostered by the Nazi Party.

A few hundred yards from one of the Berlin schools Himmler presides at a conference in his office at Gestapo headquarters. He is meeting with the military district leaders of the Sicherheitsdienst (the Security Service of the SS), who watch over the Sturmabteilung. The action, Himmler says, will occur very soon now. Each of the regional leaders of the SD describes his particular part of the action, whose details are then completed by Himmler with a final set of orders. On the same day, Sepp Dietrich is received at the Bendlerstrasse, where he asks for arms for his units of the Leibstandarte Adolf Hitler, so that he can carry out a very important mission entrusted to him by the Führer.

Meanwhile, at the Chancellory in Berlin, Adolf Hitler is giving a tea to honor government dignitaries and foreign diplomats. He appears relaxed—still tanned by the mountain sunshine of Berchtesgaden—but is nervous. One of the guests at the tea hears him speaking to a Nazi leader in a furious voice: "Each group considers itself capable of striking first." Who does he mean if not Roehm's SA and their adversaries? This remark, widely repeated throughout Berlin, makes Himmler and Heydrich uneasy. It suggests that the Führer has not yet made his choice. Everything may still be settled by compromise, and the SA themselves seem convinced of Hitler's good will and neutrality.

On Wednesday evening, June 27, there is a party at Roehm's Berlin residence. Shouts of laughter and bursts of song mix with the clink of glasses and the fizz of champagne. Passers-by slow down as they approach the house, looking up at the open windows at the sound of music and singing, Roehm's men are celebrating their approaching leave, Ernst's marriage and the engagement of another of his companions, Lieutenant Scholz. The police who stand guard in front of the house go about their work with an air of casual indifference. They walk along the pavement in groups of two, asking pedestrians to move on, directing cars, without lifting their heads. They are Hermann Goering's men. Their leader, at the moment Ernst and Scholz toast the future of the Sturmabteilung, is speaking at Cologne.

Thousands of men and women are in the convention hall there, pressed tightly against each other in the crushing heat. Since morning, the town has been paralyzed by parades and receptions in honor of the Minister of the Reich. At 1:20 his red Junker landed, circling the airfield three times at a low altitude before touching down and taxiing up to those who have come to meet him: Gauleiter Grohé, Rudolf Diels, Hake and Major Generals Weizel and Knickmann. The first minutes of Goering's visit to Cologne are marked by Goering's evident cordiality toward his former collaborator, Diels. The SS form a double line before the meeting room in the Town Hall. The Lord Mayor, Dr. Reisen, presents Goering with a Celtic sword which is at least three thousand years old. There is a dinner before the grand parade which begins in front of the Opera: police, SS, SA and the Labor Corps of the Hitler Youth, all march by with mechanical precision, carrying hundreds of banners stamped with the swastika. The pounding of their boots against the gray asphalt sometimes drowns out the music of the bands. On the speakers' platform, Goering swivels his heavy body to the left and to the right, smiling expansively, his huge vanity revealed in his whole bearing.

In the evening, the main hall of the fair is crowded with people who have come to applaud Goering, to feel reassured: "No one, abroad or here in Germany, has the right to argue that results can be produced by a rule of bloody terror." Nothing seems to reflect "bloody terror," and nothing seems to suggest its imminence.

A few miles from Cologne, in Essen, it is also a gala holiday. Never before, from Berlin to Cologne, from Hamburg to Nuremberg and Essen, has Germany heard so many speeches, watched so many parades.

In Essen, the Huyssenallee has been closed to traffic since 9 P.M., in homage to Gauleiter Terboven, who will be married the next day. The new lords allow their people to participate in their intimate joys. In front of the Park Hotel, a triumphal arch has been erected, and a torchlight parade moves toward it in a writhing of flames stirred up by the wind. The parade follows the Holzstrasse and Adolf-Hitler Strasse before passing the reviewing stand: thousands of young men and brass bands, miners, Hitler Youth, the SA and the police corps, which goose-steps by, and then an elite unit which all eyes follow: the Sturmbann SS No. 1, who, with their black uniforms and white gloves, appear to have sprung from some evil mythological creation.

Gauleiter Terboven stands beside his fiancée, his back straight, his bearing youthful. The girl is pretty in her long, flowered dress. She smiles. This pair perfectly symbolizes the elite of the new regime. A crowd of uniformed officers has gathered around them. From 6:10 to 7:15 the units march by, while the population of Essen applauds such a demonstration of order and strength. The regime of the Third Reich appears to these thousands of spectators like a monolith: the precision of the marching, the immobility of the faces and the shoulders make it impossible to separate an individual from the whole. One can see only a black mass, bristling with guns, covered with steel, relentlessly advancing: the Sturmbann SS No. 1 is an image of the new regime, it is power on the march, power which gradually must swallow and control everything. In Cologne Goering insisted that the Third Reich was not a regime of "bloody terror," but he had also added: "Everyone here may sleep peacefully in his bed." And the others? Those who act, or wish to? What will their fate be? Goering speaks in Cologne at the end of the day, Wednesday, June 27. Since dawn this same day, Dr. Edgar Jung has known the price of taking action.

A NAZI WEDDING

Dawn, Thursday, June 28, 1934. The sky east of Berlin whitens like an immense beach covered by an ebb tide, as the darkness slowly withdraws. In the streets the footsteps of the first people going to work echo in the silence. In front of the Chancellory, the guard is changing. A noncom and three helmeted men, goose-stepping like little wooden figures on German clocks, execute the first orders of the day. In these moments of dawn, as motionless as a calm sea, the two groups salute, and the soldiers take up their positions on either side of the wide entrance.

In the courtyard of the Bendlerstrasse building another platoon of soldiers responds to the first orders of the day. The men line up around the flagpole on which every morning the German flag is raised. In every barracks the same gestures are repeated, heels click, metaled boots clatter on the paving of courtyards in which, a century earlier, the soldiers of Prussia lined up with similar discipline under the eyes of implacable young officers.

At 7:30 A.M. the streets are full of life. Long lines of cyclists move through the suburbs: in the courtyard companies present arms as their commanders arrive. They salute while the flag is slowly raised, stopping halfway up the mast, dangling its full length, only faintly stirred by the fresh wind. Throughout Germany, from Cologne to Dresden, on the flagpoles of public buildings, the flag is at half-mast. It is exactly fifteen years since June 28, 1919, when Germany was forced to sign the Treaty of Versailles, accepting the dictated terms of the victors. Since then, Erzberger, who signed the Treaty, has been assassinated by officers on half-pay who bitterly felt the country's humiliation and dreamed of revenge. Since then, the Reichswehr has been reconstituted, a vital force which can be reduced but not destroyed; since then, Hitler has come to power and Versailles has become a national shame, a symbol of treachery. This official mourning of flags at half-mast proclaims against the pale sky that the Third Reich has not forgotten, and does not intend to forget, the shame of defeat. "Fifteen years ago," states the order of the day read in every barracks, "the glorious German Army was betrayed, stabbed in the back. It must never happen again."

At the airport at Tempelhof the flags are at half-mast. The SS in parade dress, their white cross-belts and gloves standing out against their black uniforms, line both sides of the path to the plane. The sky has clouded over, and the first drops of rain have begun to fall when Goering and Hitler arrive, shortly before nine o'clock. A short metal ladder is drawn up beside the plane, marked in black letters with Field Marshal von Hindenburg's name. Hitler and Goering are in high spirits. Goering is wearing the uniform of full general, with a cape thrown over his shoulders, and is speaking with evident animation. Hitler wears his leather coat; his white shirt accentuates his pallor. He is holding his hat. The Führer salutes the crew, and Goering jokes with the pilot. Then the two men disappear into the plane. It is nine o'clock. The vast, heavy red flag with the black swastika beats in the wind. The rain falls steadily.

It is pouring when the plane lands at Essen-Mülheim. The Führer's arrival was kept secret until the last moment. Nonetheless, the SA have been there since morning, standing at intervals of thirty feet along the road to Essen, down which the official cars proceed. In the city, garlands, flags and thickly crowded streets proclaim a public holiday. Yesterday there was a torchlight parade, and today is the wedding day of Gauleiter Terboven. The crowd, standing in the street despite the rain, is especially heavy in front of the Hotel Kaiserhof, cheering Goering and Hitler, and then waiting for more than an hour to catch another glimpse of them as they leave for the office of the Mayor. They are followed by ADC Brückner, Dr. Dietrich and Oberführer Schaub.

In front of the Town Hall, the crowd is enormous, shouting its loyalty to the Führer. Ilse Stahl, the bride, has arrived, wearing a long dress of white silk, with a diadem in her hair. Her eyes are glazed, as in a state of ecstasy; she holds a bouquet of roses. Gauleiter Terboven walks beside her, a swastika armband around his sleeve, the Iron Cross on his breast. With his glossy hair parted on the side, and his resolute clean-shaven face, he looks like a very young man. A boy and a girl—both Hitler Youth—hold the bride's train, and behind them, solemn-faced, walk Hitler and Goering. Everything is slow, heavy and emphatic, in this large chamber in the Essen Town Hall. At the back of the room, the women all wear long dresses, the men are in uniform. There are several SA officers among the guests, including Karl Ernst, the SA Obergruppenführer from Berlin, who was still celebrating in the capital yesterday evening, and who wanted to attend this wedding before leaving on his own honeymoon. The SA and SS are there, side by side, undoubtedly wondering why the Führer and Goering honor this marriage by their presence. Ernst leans to speak to his neighbor, an officer in the Black Guard: political and human accord are the note here. A woman in a long dress salutes with outstretched arm, staring at the Führer while Ilse Stahl and Gauleiter Terboven stand motionless before Dr. Reismann-Grone, the Mayor of Essen. Side by side, the SS and SA listen to the speech celebrating this new-style wedding, solemn and symbolic, and which, in a few hours, will be known as "the bloody nuptials" of Essen.

"A curious happiness fills Essen today," Reismann-Grone begins. "Since 1550 the ancient trunk of the oak, the genealogic tree of the Dar-Boven, has thrust its roots down into our hard soil, the soil of our monastery. Today, Joseph Terboven, one of the scions of this tree, has been married."

Everyone is now seated. Hitler, his hands folded, seems to be listening attentively. Goering sits beside him, his face set in a frozen smile. The Mayor of Essen continues: "The political leader of the Northwest Rhine Province is, for us veteran politicians, a promise of the future." Ernst and SA Prince August Wilhelm sit calmly side by side; next to them, impassive, sit several SS officers. Who, in this room in the Essen Town Hall, knows that a secret mobilization order has already been sent out to all SS units? Who knows that Captain Ernst Roehm, right now taking his usual morning walk beside the lake at Tegernsee, has just been excluded from the veterans' associations as well as the Officers' Corps? "Gauleiter Joseph Terboven," the Mayor continues, "is marrying a young girl who has come from the farthest eastern provinces, whose forebears were fighters as hard as steel [her name is Stahl—steel]. It is a propitious symbol, and this tender flower of a distant province is no foreigner here. She, too, is a member of our Party, and we feel such love and respect for her that she shall feel she has found a new Fatherland."

The dull howl of distant sirens marks the changing shift in the soot-blackened factories around Essen. There, in noisy sheds echoing with the deafening blows of power-hammers, amid dazzling showers of sparks as molten steel flows onto the rolling mill, the power of Nazi Germany, of the Third Reich, is being forged. "This ceremony constitutes an event of historical and political importance," Dr. Reismann-Grone continues. "Our city of Essen, of Assindi, is a solid fortress. It has already witnessed a thousand years of history, has seen Charlemagne, Otto the Great and the last of the Hohenzollern. It is also a place of peaceable welcome. Mein Führer, and you, Herr Prime Minister, are welcome guests of this great metallurgical center."

Outside, there are shouts of "Sieg Heil!" for the Führer and the bridal couple. Hitler and Goering rise, and sign the city's new golden book. Then the official procession moves across town to the cathedral, for the religious ceremony. In front of the church, on the Adolf-Hitler Platz, the young members of the Hitler Youth maintain an incessant, cadenced cry of enthusiasm, waiting for the Führer to come out. They disperse only when the last cars have left the square.

The wedding dinner is a solemn occasion. Goering speaks first, there are cheers and cries of "Sieg Heil!" and then SS Gruppenführer Zech, in a short speech, turns to the SA and declares: "I celebrate here our long friendship, the long-standing friendship of the battlefield, which binds the SS and the SA to the workers and intellectuals alike."

It is about 4:30 in the afternoon, Thursday, June 28, exactly the moment when General Beck, Army Chief of Staff, reminds his officers that they must keep a weapon within reach. The courtyard at the Bendlerstrasse resounds with the sudden blast of a whistle. Soldiers run to line up rapidly before the captain on duty. In the courtyard guns are stacked, and barbed-wire barriers have been set up. Officers returning from leave are meticulously checked at the entrance and look with astonishment into the courtyard, which seems to be preparing for a long siege. They are told that they are being confined to barracks because of the serious threat of a putsch by the SA, or by the Communist elements which have infiltrated the SA. Final instructions are telephoned from the Bendlerstrasse to the General Staffs of all the military districts. They are very precise:

1. In each barracks warn a reliable officer of the threat of an SA putsch.
2. Check instructions for an alert.
3. Check the guard at all barracks.
4. Check the guard at all arms and munitions depots.
5. The above is to be done without arousing attention.

The last order seems astonishing to some officers, but perhaps the idea is to catch the SA red-handed.

At five o'clock that afternoon, Hitler, accompanied by Brückner and Oberführers Dietrich and Schaub, arrives at the Krupp works. The tall chimney, which rises some 225 feet, is decorated with a Nazi flag. In the reception hall of the principal administrative building of the Krupp von Bohlen und Halbach Industries, Fräulein Irmgard von Bohlen receives the Führer as other Krupps have received German Emperors and Kings. An eminent technician shows the Führer through the works: the forges, the workshops, the rolling mills, the truck factory. In the cool or burning shadows, in air heavy with the strong, acid smell of molten steel, Hitler is fascinated, and scarcely listens to the technician's explanations. He looks at the fountains of red and gold spurting from the crucibles, the incandescent ingots which roll out and are flattened beneath the deafening pressure of the power-hammers, two stories tall. He breathes in the sense of power, the power of the Krupp empire, which his empire, and therefore the Reich, must be able to rely on, must have. Krupp shows the Führer a commemorative plaque which reads: "To the memory of our comrades who, on March 31, 1923, fell before French bullets on this site."

It was Good Friday, 1923. French troops occupied the Ruhr. A detachment entered the strike-bound factory at about nine in the morning, marching into the shop where Krupp trucks were assembled. The workers protested, gathering in menacing groups. At eleven, the French opened fire. Eleven died, and thirty were seriously injured. The workers, said Krupp, had been expressing their solidarity with the company and with Germany.

Hitler listens: 1923, the occupation of the Ruhr—a time of beginnings, when, inflamed by the French, German nationalism experienced a strong recovery; from that nationalism Nazism drew its first strength. Today, fifteen years after Versailles, the Reich is on its feet once again, and the Krupp factories once more are powerful. The workers gather around the Führer, to applaud him. Then Hitler has a long talk with Krupp; perhaps, as is alleged, the head of German metallurgy has complained about the activities of the SA, their statements, the disorder they create, and their incessant calls for a second Revolution.

Hitler seems preoccupied as he leaves the Krupp complex. The official cars drive quickly to the center of Essen, to the Hotel Kaiserhof. There, in the hotel's large drawing room, transformed into an office, the Führer reads his messages. Himmler is responsible for a great many of these, all attesting to an SA putsch in preparation. The messages contain precise information about the arming of particular units, and thoughts expressed by particular members of the Sturmabteilung. Hitler calls his collaborators together. Goering is present, and Lutze, the SA leader who is worthy of confidence. Himmler calls on the telephone. He says that the SA will attack the Reichswehr. At the same moment, the SD service for the Rhine sends in information that the SA have molested a foreign diplomat in the Rhine district. Everything about the story is vague, and suggests provocation or falsehood. But Hitler explodes: the SA is a danger to the security of Germany. If it is true that Krupp warned him against the SA, the Führer's anger is understandable. The three essential elements of his political calculations—economic power, military power and foreign relations—have been disturbed by the SA.

At the Hotel Kaiserhof he asks to be put through immediately to the Pension Hanselbauer at Bad Wiessee. He demands an immediate explanation from Roehm. He will be at Bad Wiessee as planned on June 30 at eleven o'clock. All the SA Obergruppenführers and Gruppenführers and the SA inspectors should be called together to attend the meeting. Roehm is not surprised. He has ordered a large banquet at the Hotel Vierjahreszeiten. For Hitler there will be a vegetarian menu.

After this telephone call, Hitler seems to relax. He speaks for a few moments with the hotel staff, and accompanies Goering to the building's front steps as the Prime Minister of Prussia leaves for Berlin. Goering's car drives off, and Hitler salutes the cheering crowd. However, back in the hotel, Lutze has the impression that the Führer becomes anxious again, and hesitant, as if, now that Goering has gone, he finds himself once more grappling with a decision engaging all his energy, weighted by the past, affecting his long-time comrade, Roehm.

But if Hitler is still irresolute and hesitating as June 28 draws to a close, others know exactly what they want, why they want it, and how to get it. "It was my impression," Lutze was to say later, "that certain people wished to profit by Hitler's absence, to accelerate the train of events and reach a rapid conclusion."

For these people, every hour counts. They create and magnify the most alarming rumors they can imagine, putting pressure on sympathetic officers at the General Staff of the Reichswehr so that signals for the alert are strengthened, made more specific. They must create a state of crisis.

During the night of June 28–29, at Munich, Reichswehr Officer Stapf, who commands No. 7, the new motorized reconnaissance section, receives instructions from the General Staff—officers may not leave their barracks—the order is imperative. The text adds that officers are directly threatened, that the SA has drawn up lists of officers to be killed. Live ammunition is issued to men on guard duty. In the courtyards of the Munich barracks, men in guard companies collect their cartridges. Officers watch the distribution. The older among them summon up memories of '23, the year of the putsch.

While ammunition is being distributed in the Munich barracks, Roehm, now abandoned by the Officers' Corp, sends out the first telegrams addressed to SA Obergruppenführers, and the principal leaders and inspectors of the Assault Sections, calling them to the meeting with the Führer set for Saturday, June 30, 1934, at eleven o'clock. In the Pension Hanselbauer, the atmosphere is still one of confidence and calm. Roehm has gone in person to the Hotel Vierjahreszeiten to inform the director that the Führer's arrival has been confirmed, and that it is important to take particular pains with the banquet. Roehm's personal guard will assure the Führer's protection, and from Friday, June 29, will also protect the hotel.

In Berlin, the first proofs of a text on whose pages the ink has not yet dried have just been placed on the large tables at the printing house. Two officers of the Bendlerstrasse staff read the pages carefully with the head printer, while the presses turn:

> The Reichswehr considers itself in close harmony with the Reich of Adolf Hitler. The time has passed when people from various camps could pose as spokesmen of the Reichswehr. The role of the Army is clearly determined: it must serve the National Socialist State, which it recognizes. The hearts of the Reich and the Army beat in unison. . . . The Reichswehr wears with pride the symbols of Germany. It stands, disciplined and faithful, behind the leaders of the State, behind the Marshal of the Great War, President von Hindenburg, its supreme leader, and behind the Führer of the Reich, Adolf Hitler, who, coming from the ranks of the Army, is and always will be one of us.

At the bottom of the page, the article is signed by a name in large letters: "General von Blomberg, Minister of Defense"—the Gummilöwe.

The officers OK the proof. This article by the man who is the Army incarnate will be printed on the first page of the *Völkischer Beobachter* on Friday, June 29. By the pen of its highest authority, the Reichswehr approves the Führer's actions in advance. That morning the Reichswehr had already ejected Roehm from its ranks, and now it proclaims itself ready to follow Hitler, accepting all his decisions even before the first bullets are fired. While the first copies of the paper pile up at the printer's, the moment of decision and action remains the Führer's.

7

Saturday, June 30, 1934
In Flight Over Augsburg

3:30 A.M.

The pilot leans toward the Führer and points out, to the left of the plane, the town of Augsburg, whose lighted streets are clearly visible until they recede into darkness. But already the dawn of Saturday, June 30, 1934, is beginning to break. In the Chancellor's Junker, interrupted conversations resume. The radio has just announced that the plane is now within range of the control tower at Munich; everything is ready for its landing at the Munich-Oberwiesenfeld field. The Führer asks the pilot how soon the plane will be landing; he is told in about twenty-five minutes.

Twenty-five minutes: a minuscule fragment of time, the last, brief respite before the plunge into action, before seeing the men at the airfield who wait for his orders. Hitler has sunk back into his seat beside the pilot. With each moment daylight grows, as if, symbolically, the long hesitation of weeks and months ends and is dissipated with the darkness. In a few minutes the plane will be landing at Munich, where the violent men of both the SA and SS are waiting for him.

(Friday, June 29, to Saturday, June 30)

Scarcely twenty-four hours ago, on Friday, June 29, before his inspection tour of Westphalian work camps, everything could still have been stopped. At the Hotel Kaiserhof in Essen, however, Hitler learned that on his return to Berlin Hermann Goering had strengthened the battle-readiness of his police: Goering had multiplied his patrols, doubling the guards. The Führer, therefore, knew that in the capital on this last Friday in June Heydrich, Himmler and Goering were pushing through their final preparations. He is also aware of the fear which has swept over some: Franz von Papen, who accepts a speaking engagement at the Kroll Opera before representatives of German and foreign Chambers of Commerce, and proclaims that "No one in Germany doubts that the Chancellor and Führer Adolf Hitler will lead the work of the nation's material and moral revival to a victorious conclusion." Papen is making amends for his Marburg speech, forgetting Jung, who wrote it, in the cellars of No. 8 Prinz-Albrecht Strasse. Early on the morning of the twenty-ninth, a copy of the *Völkischer Beobachter* with General Blomberg's article is on the large table of the drawing room of the Kaiserhof in Essen. Hitler reads it slowly; he was aware of the general drift of the piece, but the printed text takes on a fresh aspect. Blomberg has given him a free hand. There is also the news from Breslau. Goering has ordered the SS Oberabschnittsführer Udo von Woyrsch, who commands the southeast sector, to place all the SA leaders in his district under arrest, to occupy the prefecture at Breslau, and to place himself and his men at the disposition of the Commandant of Police.

Friday morning, June 29, the sky over Essen is gray; the humidity of the warm summer air holds down the heavy smoke and haze, keeping it from rising. In the drawing room of the Kaiserhof, Hitler has ordered a light breakfast with tea. At ten, he is expected at the work camp of Schloss Buddenberg: the young men must already have gathered in the fine rain to wait for their Führer.

Roehm walks beside the lake with his orderly, pleased that he will be able to explain his feelings to the Führer. The first SA leaders are about to arrive; he will have to speak with them before meeting with Hitler.

Friday, June 29, 1934, between nine and ten in the morning, nothing had been settled. Hitler's day moved through the "Sieg Heils" of youthful enthusiasts, along the road to Bad Godesberg, to the Rhine with its ruined castles beneath the terrace of the Hotel Dreesen. It continued with the arrival of Goebbels, and Viktor Lutze, the telephone calls from Himmler and Wagner, a decision made, and the road taken toward Bonn-Hangelar, the plane and flight through the night to Munich. Now tomorrow has become today, Saturday, June 30, 1934. It is 3:55 A.M.

Day has almost broken. The sky is a pale gray, joyless, the color of cement. The plane begins its descent. One can see the blue and red lights along the runway, forming a continuous twinkling trail; in front of the control tower, three black trucks and a group of people. The Junker makes a preliminary pass, and then approaches the runway from the north, touching down at its extreme end, taxiing slowly to the arrival area, a few yards from the trucks. The propellers of the three engines continue to turn slowly in the silence. Through the plane's windows one can see the uniformed SS walking toward the plane. A mechanic opens the door from the inside, onto the hesitant dawn of this last day in June.

PART THREE

Until the Living Flesh
Was Burned

Saturday, June 30, to Monday, July 2, 1934

1

First to appear at the door of the Junker, Hitler quickly steps down the metal ladder and walks toward the cars; the Nazis and SS who have been waiting hurry to keep up with him. He takes long, nervous strides, holding his hat in his hand, arms swinging rapidly. He has saluted no one. Goebbels, far behind, tries to catch up, with his awkward, limping gait.

A short way off, their gray masses almost invisible in the early dawn, are two armored cars which the commanding general of the Wehrkreis VII, the Munich military district, has parked on the field to protect the Führer. A military truck is parked beside the cars. Helmeted soldiers, their guns between their knees, have been waiting for more than an hour. The truck and the armored cars will follow the Führer's official party as a military escort. The commanding officer of the detachment walks toward Hitler. Beside him is an Abwehr officer. Hitler salutes them rapidly. His brusque manner suggests an edgy determination. He listens to the report of the two officers, and then an SS officer on the situation in Munich. The SA who had demonstrated in the streets have all gone home and are waiting for orders. Hitler barely seems to listen. He begins to talk: his voice is breathy, and his words tumble out. No military cover: the Reichswehr must remain uninvolved. He repeats the words, insisting, emphasizing his meaning with a gesture. Turning to the Abwehr officer Hitler adds, "This is the hardest, the worst day of my life. But believe me, I know how to do justice. I am going to Bad Wiessee." He brandishes his left fist, takes a few steps and finishes: "Inform General Adam of our plans immediately."

Adam commands the Wehrkreis VII. Messages have been coming into his staff headquarters in quick succession because the Munich district plays a principal role in the development of the action. Lieutenant Colonel Kübler, Adam's chief of staff, has stayed in his office all night, waiting for orders. Shortly after 4 A.M. he received from the Bendlerstrasse confirmation of the orders placing several units—artillery, engineers, communications, supply—in a state of alert. The 19th Infantry Regiment must be kept under arms, ready to move out to re-establish order along the route connecting Bad Tölz to the two lakes of Schliersee and Tegernsee. At 4:15 the Munich central barracks echo to the blasts of a whistle. The men race through the corridors, helmets in their hands. Lieutenant Colonel Kübler is in the courtyard, listening to the familiar sound of hundreds of heavy boots pounding down the stairs, of voices shouting orders. Soon the companies are drawn up, and once again there is silence, while Lieutenant Colonel Kübler reviews his men.

Dawn has spread quickly across the sky, but on the ground, solid objects, silhouettes, trees, remain enveloped in darkness. The cold light gives an impression of uncertainty. The Führer has with him Wagner, Minister of the Interior and Gauleiter of Bavaria. His pale, heavy face is marked with tension, anxiety and fatigue. Since yesterday evening every hour has brought a new development: the telephone from Berlin and Godesberg, with instructions from Himmler, has been ringing continuously. Wagner stands beside a car, explaining the situation in Munich. All is calm. Obergruppenführer SA Schneidhuber must still be confined at the Ministry of the Interior. Hitler listens, and then gives a few brief orders: the famous Bay Po Po (Bavarian Political Police), organized by Heydrich and Himmler, will move into action, arrest the SA leaders and, with the SS, watch the Munich station to stop the men invited by Roehm from going to Bad Wiessee.

Finally the doors slam, and the cars start off. The two Reichswehr officers salute. After a few minutes on the road the cars pass the first buildings on the outskirts of Munich, the birthplace of Nazism. Hitler had his start here in 1923 with the first attempted putsch. Roehm was in the thick of the action, having occupied the War Ministry. Hitler had walked through the streets of Munich, his revolver in his hand, into the narrow Residenzstrasse toward the Odeonplatz and the War Ministry, where Roehm was waiting. The police refused to open the barriers; Hitler shouted "Surrender!" Firing broke out. Hitler fled toward the rear of the column, diving into a yellow car parked on the Max-Josef Platz. Now he can't help but think of that eighth and ninth of November, his failed Brumaire coup. Now he moves again through the same gray, empty treeless streets. At a crossroad a few small groups of SA are talking, some men sitting on the curb, others standing on the pavement. "We saw only the last remnants of the SA formations, who, dispirited and uncertain, appeared to need nothing more to make them disperse than a reassuring word from the Führer," Goebbels was to report.

The cars drive by. The men in the brown shirts do not see Hitler and Goebbels, Germany's destiny and their own. Many have been drinking since last evening; some are talking loudly in the quiet streets, others are singing. No one interferes: for a long time now, the police have been cautious, and the citizens of Munich know that one does not argue with the SA.

Some of the SA have gone to Party headquarters, the Brown House, where Hitler has so often celebrated the events of 1923, or the founding of the Party. It is the general headquarters of the Sturmabteilung, and since yesterday evening it has been full of men, drinking and singing. Tomorrow the Führer is to meet Roehm, and everything will be clarified between the Sturmabteilung and the Party. Some of the SA have taken off their boots and cross-belts and unbuttoned their shirts, and are sleeping on the benches. These corpulent men who seek fraternity and the illusion of solidarity bestowed by belonging to a group and wearing a uniform, who forgot themselves in ritual, drinking and song, are free of anxiety this morning. The last ones to enter the Brown House after carousing through the night in Munich beer gardens don't notice the SS and police quietly taking up positions in front of the building, harmless-looking sentries. They don't know that the Minister of the Interior has been ordered to allow anyone into the Brown House who wants to enter, but to prevent everyone from leaving after five o'clock in the morning.

It is not yet 5 A.M. The cars carrying Hitler, Goebbels, Lutze, Otto Dietrich, Schaub and Wagner stop in front of the Ministry. Again, Hitler is the first to get out, with a step down which is almost a leap. Now that the battle is joined, he knows he must move fast, play his hand without giving the enemy any respite, destroy them. The SS are there in front of the Ministry: Emil Maurice, with his battered boxer's face, and Buch and Esser— loyal men who have been warned of Hitler's arrival, who have been waiting, in some cases for years, to settle accounts with their former comrades. Other SS arrive in small groups: men attached to Himmler and Heydrich, whom Wagner called before leaving for the airport. Most of them understand that the hour for action has come, and know that they are behind Hitler.

The Führer walks into the Ministry. Brückner is behind him, his expression veiled, his eyes suspicious. The corridors are badly lit, so that it is almost like night again. Orders are shouted out, and men start to run as the building comes to life.

On the third floor, Obergruppenführer SA Schneidhuber is waiting, half-asleep, in the outer room of Wagner's office. When he sees the Führer, he begins a salute, but Hitler rushes at him, his hands open, as if to seize him. Schneidhuber draws back, and Hitler shouts: "Lock him up!" The Führer's strained features are agitated by a tic, and he continues to shout as the Obergruppenführer is dragged to Munich's Stadelheim prison.

"They are traitors!" Everyone is silent. In a corner of the office, Goebbels and Wagner are drawing up lists of men to be arrested. Wagner himself telephones Gruppenführer SA Schmidt. The order is precise: he must come immediately to the Ministry of the Interior, where the Führer is waiting for him. Hitler silently paces up and down. Groups separate to let him through. There are now nearly thirty men in the room; their nervous yet resolute faces lend the atmosphere an unbearable intensity. Outside, the city is calm and empty. The Ministry of the Interior is a small island of activity. Several cars are parked in front of the entry.

A few moments later, Schmidt comes into the office. Hitler goes up to him, and before the Gruppenführer has a chance to speak rips off his gold braid. "You are under arrest. Traitor! You will be shot." Schmidt's expression is one of stunned surprise. The witnesses' faces are fixed in frozen smiles combining fear and joy at being on the right side, the side which will survive. "You will be shot." The sentence rings in the air while Schmidt is on his way to Stadelheim Prison.

It is no longer possible to leave the Brown House. A few of the SA who had wanted to go home were firmly pushed back—with no violence, the sentries' only explanation: "The Führer's orders." In the huge, low-ceilinged rooms, stale with smoke, the men still sleeping are wakened. There is a buzz of talk, and windows are thrown open. The sky over Munich has turned blue. It is now almost six o'clock. Shop boys are lifting the iron grilles. The SA, leaning over the window ledges, now see the truckloads of police and SS: the Brown House is surrounded.

At about the same time, the Reichswehr trucks are parking in the interior courtyards of the Munich railway station. Only

NCOs are authorized to leave the vehicles. The soldiers have been brought as reinforcements and are to intervene only if the SS is unable to manage the job. The SS have taken up their positions along the station platforms, to the surprise of the first travelers of the day on their way to work, carrying the traditional black leather briefcases. The SS must intercept the SA leaders as they arrive.

Other SS have gathered in front of the Ministry of the Interior. From time to time a single man, or a group of two or three accompanied by men from the Bay Po Po, get into their cars, which rapidly drive off: the teams of killers are beginning to hunt their prey.

Shortly before six o'clock the early morning light turns into the broad light of full day, striking the upper stories of the buildings without banishing the gray shadows which cling to the depths of the streets. Adolf Hitler leaves the Ministry of the Interior. His leather coat belted at the waist is creased, and he still carries his hat. His movements are sudden and somewhat jerky; he looks up and down the street, to the left and to the right, seemingly nervous and uneasy. Goebbels is behind him, pale-faced and smiling. The SS salute. The Führer hesitates for a few moments. Some of the SS requisition taxis; others take the last of the official cars. Hitler has not yet given the signal to depart. Wagner stands, with his arms crossed, on the top step of the Ministry. He is to stay in Munich to control the situation, and prevent any action by the SA. One of his particular duties is to imprison the men who are still in the Brown House. A few moments later, the convoy starts off, with the Führer's car in the lead.

In the center of town the city is beginning to stir. The cars move rapidly along the wide Avenue Thal, approaching the curve which, after the Isar-Thor Platz, leads to the Isar bridges. The river waters are high at this time of year, pulled along by a strong current which breaks into little white waves against the piles of the Ludwigs-Brücke. Once the bridges have been crossed there is the long, straight line of the Rosenheimerstrasse and, some thirty-five miles to the south, beside the Tegernsee, the Pension Hanselbauer, where Roehm and his comrades are sleeping. The cars reach the outskirts of Munich, and the road opens suddenly into the country. In the distance, one can see the somber mass of the forest, wrapped in gray fog.

In Berlin, in von Tschirschky's apartment, the telephone rings. Vice Chancellor Papen's secretary picks up the receiver, and after a few moments asks who is on the line. The caller at the other end hangs up without answering, as if he had only been checking to make sure that Tschirschky is at home.

At No. 8 Prinz-Albrecht Strasse, messages are coming in. Despite the early hour, Heydrich and Himmler have already been there for a long time—since shortly after the Führer took off from Bonn-Hangelar. Only a few moments ago, a telephone call from Wagner warned them that Hitler has left for Bad Wiessee, and that he requires the presence of Rudolf Hess in Munich.

2

Saturday, June 30, 1934
Bad Wiessee: Pension Hanselbauer

6:30 A.M.

The road climbs quickly through farmland; the level golden light glances off the polished automobiles. Behind to the north, Munich has become a collection of gray cubes rising from the plain, with an occasional building distinctly piercing the zone of mist stagnating over the town. Soon the road enters the darkness of the forest, with its closely grown trees and intermingled branches, its black beeches spreading to meet the trees on the other side of the road. The cool, damp air of the shadowy underbrush envelops the cars, whose engines lose their strident sound. The Führer sits in silence beside the driver of the first car. Behind him, Joseph Goebbels talks tirelessly, reconstructing the story of the Sturmabteilung plot. Hitler says nothing. It is now more than twenty-four hours since he has had any sleep: his wakeful night at Bad Godesberg weighs on him now—that night of hesitation, choice and waiting. Then the long trip on land and in the air. The fatigue and irritation of long sleeplessness are visible in Hitler's swollen face, and in his eyes and puffy lids. He has left the window beside him open, and the cool damp wind smelling of the forest whips his face and hair. His coat collar turned up, his arms crossed, he slumps down into his seat, staring straight ahead at the road which will take him to his old comrade, Ernst Roehm.

After about eighteen miles, the driver turns right onto another road, which seems to cut deeper into the forest. The road is narrow, and the trees beside it meet overhead in a low, uneven vault. Sometimes the branches scrape against the cars. Lake Tegernsee is at the end of this road, still in shadow, with night clinging to its shores. The reflections of the forested slopes begin very close to the banks of the water. The higher slopes, near the peaks, are already bathed in early morning light.

The driver has slowed down; the road follows the western shore of the lake. The sound of the engines in the open air is suddenly enormous after the silence of the forest, like a warning broadcast to the whole district. The Führer leans slightly out of the window as they pass through the first village, Gmund, a group of wooden houses clustered around a church—a fanciful construction from the seventeenth century. A few peasants are busy in front of the village barns, and an old woman is driving a herd of cows. Beyond the village they pass a sign indicating another three miles to Bad Wiessee.

In the back seat of the Führer's car, sitting beside Goebbels, a Reichswehr officer, sent to represent General Adam and the Abwehr, has been listening silently to the impassioned perorations of the Propaganda Minister. Suddenly Hitler turns to him: "I know that for a long time you were a colleague of General von Schleicher." The officer has no time to reply to this, as the Führer talks fast. "I am sorry to tell you," he continues, "that the government is obliged to open a preliminary inquiry against him. He is suspected of contact with Roehm and with a foreign power." The Führer falls silent, withdrawing to his own seat.

At this hour, the Griebnitzseestrasse in Potsdam, where Schleicher's comfortable villa stands, is quiet and empty. General von

Schleicher is preparing for his usual early morning workout of gymnastic exercises; he feels no anxiety. The wooded hill of Babelsberg which he can see from his window is wrapped in a light fog under the blue sky of June.

The blue sky is also reflected in the dark waters of the Tegernsee. The cars have slowed down, but the noise of their engines still fills the air, echoing from the slopes surrounding the lake. The cars pass the first houses of Bad Wiessee. A truckload of SS of the Leibstandarte Adolf Hitler, and their leader, Sepp Dietrich, are waiting at the last bend in the road. The column of cars does not stop: now each second counts. In front of the Pension Hanselbauer, even before the trucks have stopped, the men jump out and run toward the building, carrying their revolvers. The shutters are closed. The mossy grass muffles their footsteps; they encircle the large, white building, the SS officers guiding the maneuver with gestures. The silence is made even more noticeable by the cheerful twittering of the birds.

Hitler stands in front of the main door, surrounded by SS Brückner and Emil Maurice; both are armed. Suddenly it begins. The door is kicked open; there are guttural cries, slamming doors, maids roughly shoved aside. Later, Goebbels remembers: "Meeting no resistance, we were able to penetrate the house and surprise the gang of plotters while they slept, arresting them immediately. The Führer himself began the arrests."

In the Pension Hanselbauer, everyone is sleeping. Brutally, doors are knocked open, some smashed in, and the SS, their revolvers drawn, shout as they rush through the Pension. In the semidarkness, the SA, dazed and half-asleep, are driven through the corridor with blows and shouts. Count Spreti, Standartenführer of Munich, doesn't have time to get up. He is hauled, half-naked, from his bed and pushed into the corridor, with a stream of insults. Further on, Edmund Heines is surprised in bed with the young SA he has kept with him all night. Goebbels commented later: "A disgusting scene, which made me feel like vomiting." Heines, insulted, arrested and threatened with immediate death, tries to resist. Brückner smashes him with his fists and knocks him down. Stunned, Heines doesn't understand what is happening. "I haven't done anything," he shouts to Lutze. "You know that. Help me. I haven't done anything." Lutze simply replies, "I can do nothing."

Outside in the corridor, there is a sudden silence; Hitler and several SS stand at the door to Roehm's room. Hitler is holding a revolver. Behind the thin wooden barrier lies a comrade, his past, a part of his life about to be destroyed. A policeman knocks at the door, and then the Führer himself begins to pound on it, answering when Roehm asks who is there, giving his name. The SA Chief of Staff opens his door, and Hitler rushes into the room, screaming insults, accusing Roehm of treason, threatening him, and shouting again of treason. Roehm is naked to the waist. His red face is swollen by too little sleep; faint traces of his scars show in his flabby flesh. At first he is silent; then, slowly waking, slowly grasping the situation, he begins to protest. Hitler shouts, accusing Roehm of arrogance, and announces that he is under arrest. Then he rushes off to other rooms, other victims, leaving the SS to guard Ernst Roehm, whose power has just collapsed, who is now merely a corpulent man dressing with difficulty beneath the ironic eyes of the SS. In another room, Standartenführer Julius Uhl is arrested. Later, commenting on the liquidation of the SA, Hitler will declare: "One of them had been picked to kill me: Standartenführer Uhl admitted, several hours before his death, that he was ready to carry out such an order against me."

The prisoners are pushed one by one into the cellar, where they are kept under strong guard by the SS and agents of the Bay Po Po. Hitler, Goebbels, Lutze, Brückner, Maurice and Dietrich go out into the garden. Facing them is the lake, now cut by a pale band of light, and faintly stirred by a gentle breeze. There is the quiet, the big trees, the moss and the dewy grass. Goebbels laughs, and the SS begin to talk loudly, with the joy of those who have won more easily than they had hoped. Hitler is surrounded, but doesn't talk. He seems to be listening to these men as they discuss the moments they have just lived through. He keeps his peace. He has played his cards and won. Around him there is a general atmosphere of relaxing tension. But Hitler knows that a game is never won until it is finished, until all adversaries are dead.

Suddenly, there is the sound of an engine. Goebbels gives an account: "At that moment the Stabswache, Roehm's personal guard, arrived from Munich. Hitler ordered them to about-face." These two short sentences indicate that destiny hesitated that morning, beside the Tegernsee. The SA of the Stabswache are faithful to Roehm and will stand by him in any circumstance. They jump down from the truck, heavily armed. Their officers stare with surprise at the SS and the Pension Hanselbauer. They do not know that their leader, Julius Uhl, is a prisoner like Roehm. They hesitate uncertainly. The SS, facing them, stare back, suddenly silent. Everything could be upset. Hitler takes a few steps toward them. Among all these armed men he is the sole will and power. The SA officers salute him. He begins to talk, and as he talks his voice grows firmer. "I am your Führer. You are responsible to me. Go back to Munich and wait for my orders." The SA officers glance at each other and then climb back into the truck, which slowly drives away, past the gate of the Pension Hanselbauer. For a few minutes the noise of the engine can be heard, and then once again there is silence and peace.

No one speaks of the incident, but there is no more laughter. Everyone is silent. There are a few more orders, and then the prisoners—Uhl, Spreti, Roehm and their comrades—are pushed toward the cars, the doors slam shut, and the truck loaded with the SS of the Leibstandarte pulls in at the end of the procession. The Führer is in the first car, resuming his place beside the chauffeur. He gives the signal to start.

It is broad daylight. The lake is almost entirely in sunshine. The light wind has died away, and the water is smooth, not a ripple. The air itself seems motionless, as often during summer in the mountains just after sunrise, before the heat has stirred nature into motion. The cars once again follow the lake shore, but by a gesture the Führer changes the route. They will return to Munich by the south, making a complete tour of the Tegernsee. Hitler is prudent, and the departure of Roehm's personal guard has not entirely reassured him. The SA might turn back to the Pension Hanselbauer and cross the route of the prisoner convoy. By turning south, the chances of running into Roehm's guard are diminished. The SA officers must be anxious and uncertain. Everything must strike them as unusual, strange: the early morning presence of Hitler, the armed SS and the seemingly empty Pension Hanselbauer. In fact, they do decide to stop the truck between Wiessee and Gmund, but Hitler's column passes on the other bank.

Wiessee, Rottach-Egern, Tegernsee: the little towns gradually waken. It is shortly after seven, and as they pass through these towns the procession is forced to slow down: the narrow streets are partly blocked by delivery vans making their morning rounds. The contrast is great between this black column, personally directed by the Chancellor of the Reich, of armed men driving others to their deaths, this column which is history itself, and the ordinary citizens standing in the doorways of their shops, unloading cases, tying up parcels, eating breakfast under the trees, unaware that the Führer and their destiny have just passed by. They don't see Hitler, nor could they imagine his appearance here, enclosed as they are in their ignorance, their illusions, the routine of their daily lives. Hitler does not see them either, the isolated, anonymous, unknown particles which make up the German people. He is entirely caught up in an action which gathers together many elements of his life, on which his fate depends. He is personally involved, just as on the evening of November 8, 1923, when with his gun in hand, he interrupted the speech by the President of the Bavarian Council, leaping onto a chair, firing into the air and shouting: "The national revolution has begun." That time, however, he had lost.

They reach the village of Gmund again, at the end of the lake, and the road through the forest leading to the junction with the main road into Munich. Hitler slows down the convoy. It is likely that they will cross the route of the leaders of the Sturmabteilung on their way to join Roehm at Bad Weissee for the meeting with the Führer. They must be intercepted on the road. Some vehicles in the column turn to the left, so that traffic headed for Wiessee will be forced to stop. As Goebbels later told it, "As they passed the checkpoint the cars were asked to stop, and their occupants questioned. If they were obviously guilty, they were taken prisoner immediately and sent to the SS in the convoy. Otherwise, they were ordered to join the column and return with it to Munich."

These peremptory interrogations in the fresh forest air, with the SS stopping cars with guns at the ready, seem less like a police action in a great modern state than like a raid by mercenary soldiers of a legendary Germany, behaving with the brutality of the brigands who ravaged the country during the Thirty Years' War. One of the first cars to be stopped is Peter Heydebreck's. Brückner and Hitler himself, and then some SS, run toward Heydebreck. The SA Obergruppenführer is a thin, bony man. He lost an arm during the war and was one of the moving spirits in the Freikorps. He fought in Silesia and has been a Party member since 1922. A soldier-adventurer, he is a man of war. In June of this year, 1934, Hitler honored him by naming a village on the Polish frontier after him. In 1919 in the surrounding forest, Heydebreck and his troops had fought ferociously against the Poles in defiance of the dictated terms of Versailles. Heydebreck stares at the SS, their guns pointed toward him. The Chancellor questions him: are you with Roehm? Heydebreck replies affirmatively. Immediately he is disarmed, cursed and shoved toward one of the cars where Uhl and Spreti are already under guard. Spreti looks haggard and defeated, and Uhl's face is set in a grimace of bitterness and desperation; both have understood that they will be killed. Suddenly Peter Heydebreck understands, too, and lets himself be pushed into the car without a word.

On the road near Munich, the convoy crosses the path of the Reichswehr trucks. The soldiers belong to the 19th Infantry Regiments, which is moving toward Tegernsee and Bad Tölz. The trucks proceed slowly; they are on patrol—but everything is calm.

Entering Munich, the traffic is heavy. It is a little after eight o'clock. Streetcars filled with workers on their way to work move toward the center of town in the bright sunshine which glitters on the waters of the Isar. Despite the early hour, the city is already covered by a warm smog. At each stop, long files of pedestrians wait patiently. There are also cyclists, impatient, waiting for a signal from the traffic police to turn into a crossroad. The convoy slows down and then stops. An SS officer runs toward the Führer's car. No one seems to notice Adolf Hitler. The citizens of Munich do not even turn their heads. They already know it is often better not to see.

The stop lasts for a few seconds at most. The SS set off again for the Stadelheim Prison with the arrested SA leaders. The Führer and the other Nazi leaders proceed to the Hauptbahnhof, the main Munich railway station. The train from Berlin, filled with Sturmabteilung officers, must have come in. The Führer wishes to be there. Like the leader of a brigand band, an adventurer or a Chief of State, he knows that there are some actions one must control oneself.

The Hauptbahnhof is an immense grayish building near the court house in the heart of Munich, in one of the old quarters of town gutted by the railways at the end of the nineteenth century. The cars of the convoy park in one of the interior courtyards at the north end of the station. The Reichswehr trucks are still there; some of the soldiers have pushed their helmets to the backs of their heads, others are dozing. The SS run toward the cars as Hitler climbs out, his face still tense and drawn. He is told that Hess has arrived from Berlin, that he is waiting for Hitler in the station-master's office. Hitler's group, dominated by the tall figure of Brückner, moves toward the interior of the station, escorted by armed SS. Goebbels follows behind as quickly as he can. Above the hum and noise of the station, the loudspeaker invites arriving SA leaders to present themselves at the verification desk located in office No. 1 for further instructions. On every platform, SS scrutinize incoming passengers. When the Berlin train enters the station,

SS officers jump onto the steps of each car, checking the passengers one by one, and visiting every compartment. Any SA asked to follow the SS Standartenführers and Oberführers complies without hesitation. They are entirely unaware of what awaits them, and imagine that the SS will take them to Bad Wiessee, where Roehm and Hitler are waiting. They are not in the least anxious, thinking instead of the month's holiday beginning tomorrow. Most of them are still half-asleep after a night on the train and walk heavily beside the SS, surrounded by travelers used to the mix of black and brown uniforms. In this way Obergruppenführers von Krausser and Hayn are taken, as well as Gruppenführer Georg von Detten and Hans Joachim von Falkenhausen and many others. By the time they begin to question the proceedings or to protest, it is already too late: they are disarmed and led to the black cars waiting for them. Hemmed in by the SS or the Bay Po Po, they are asked to get into the SS cars. Anyone who resists is roughly shoved in anyway. Then the cars set out through the indifference of the busy city, to the Stadelheim Prison.

Dr. Robert Koch, the director of the prison, is a model civil servant: he is a Nazi, but like many Germans, a Nazi without exaggeration or excess. He is very respectful of laws and regulations, and this day, Saturday, June 30, 1934, will be one of the most difficult of his career. Toward six in the morning, he receives a telephone message from the Ministry of the Interior. Minister Wagner himself tells him that during the day he will receive many SA officers accused of conspiracy; he must keep them under strong guard. Koch immediately apprises himself of the number of empty cells available and settles down to await developments. During the morning his astonishment grows: a few hours after Schneidhuber and Schmidt arrive, Roehm himself is brought in, with Heines, Spreti and Heydebreck: the entire elite of the Sturmabteilung, escorted by the SS. Standartenführer Uhl is the most bitter, voicing his regret in front of Dr. Koch that he did not kill Hitler during the night, while he still had his revolver. Then the lesser SA, picked up at the railroad station, are brought in. By nine all the cells are full, and after consulting his officers, Koch puts the prisoners in the prison courtyard. The SS mount a heavy guard; their attitude clearly indicates that the men in brown shirts, these SA officers with Nazi armbands and numerous decorations, these glorious "old fighters," only yesterday respected comrades, are now nothing more than beaten men, abandoned and imprisoned. When a group of SA leaders, exhausted by the long wait in the sun, ask for something to drink, the SS, without a word, with their guns in their hands, drive them back to the center of the courtyard.

Some of the SA sit on the ground, sheltering in the shadow of the high prison walls. Exhausted by the journey and the shock of their arrest, they sink into the fatalism so common among professional soldiers, who know there are moments when one can only wait passively, without trying to think or anticipate events. Some protest, ask questions. A few wonder about an Army putsch supported by the conservatives. Others still count on Hitler, who they think must have acted on false information but who will quickly recognize the truth. Those who have seen Hitler at the Pension Hanselbauer are silent: they know Hitler has abandoned them, and they no longer understand what is happening. The man whose political fortunes they made, who is personally acquainted with them, who has paid them so many informal and fraternal visits at the Brown House, who wrote Roehm a letter of congratulations—this man, Hitler, came with his revolver to arrest them.

While fear and futile anger begin to grow among the imprisoned SA, Hitler is at the station listening to reports from the SS and Minister Wagner. Hess, Goebbels and Lutze are with him. Everything is proceeding normally, without the least difficulty. The SA accused of preparing a putsch are unsuspecting: they allow themselves to be arrested without reacting. From time to time, as if to convince those present, Goebbels repeats that the SA putsch has been nipped in the bud, but in fact it is clear that the pretext no longer has any importance. The action is its own justification, since it has been begun and seems to be succeeding. General von Epp, Statthalter of Bavaria, an old, hawk-faced Reichswehr officer, who, from the beginning has supported the Nazi Party, confirms by telephone to the Führer that everything is calm. The troops remain in a state of alert, but it is clear that they will not have to intervene. They remain at the disposition of the Chancellor of the Reich.

The Führer decides to return to the Brown House, only a few hundred yards from the station in the Briennerstrasse. The procession of cars sets off again, leaving the Hauptbahnhof shortly before ten o'clock. Everything is calm in the streets. The crowds are thick, dressed in light summer colors, the men often in white shirts, carrying their jackets. The center of Munich, with its parks and luxury stores, restaurants and monuments, has an atmosphere of festival, of summer gaiety. The cars pass the statue of the Elector Maximilian I, the leader of the Catholic League during the torment of the Thirty Years' War, when war plagued Germany like a bloody epidemic. Now another leader of another league, Chancellor Hitler, arrives at the Brown House, in the Briennerstrasse. The building is guarded by the SS, while Reichswehr troops have taken up positions in the neighboring streets. The pavements in front of the Brown House have been cleared by police and pedestrians are sent to the other side of the street.

At exactly ten o'clock, Saturday, June 30, Hitler enters the Party headquarters. After a brief conversation with the Führer, whom he has been following like a shadow, Goebbels asks to be put through to Goering's headquarters in Berlin. On the telephone, the Minister of Propaganda pronounces only one word: "Colibrì."

Colibrì: three syllables to notify Berlin that there, too, the killers may go into action.

3

Saturday, June 30, 1934
Berlin

About seven in the morning, Tschirschky goes to the Vice Chancellory, anxious about a telephone call he received during the night from a mysterious caller who immediately hung up. Berlin, for the most part, is still asleep, and the summer day just beginning is bright and hot. The municipal water trucks sprinkle the streets; the water glitters in the sunlight. Everything seems peaceful. Tschirschky notices, however, that police cars are stationed around official buildings; in fact, those interested have been aware of these reinforced security measures for several days now. The Berlin police are in a state of alert, ready for action, although twice, at the end of the day, they have been released. Yesterday evening, however, the state of alert was continued; today the police cars are still in position; the patrols go on. Two or three black cars and a few Army vehicles transporting impassive SS move slowly down the nearly empty streets.

Tschirschky tries to find out what is happening, but the Ministry of the Interior knows nothing of the various police alerts.

Daluege, the director of the Ministry's police services, has not even been consulted by Goering, who has made all the decisions himself. All these facts interest Tschirschky, who knows that in informed circles major events are anticipated. There have been plenty of signs: even the night's mysterious phone call hadn't really surprised him, but had simply confirmed his feeling that whatever was to happen was nearly upon them.

That is why he has come to the Vice Chancellory so early and is striding down the empty corridor to his office. He has been there only a few minutes when the telephone rings. It is Goering, asking to see the Vice Chancellor on a matter of extreme urgency. For Tschirschky there are no more doubts: something serious has already happened, or is just about to.

Each day, Franz von Papen comes to his office at nine o'clock, with the methodical regularity of a Prussian officer trained at the Lichterfelde Cadet School. Tschirschky, however, does not hesitate to call him earlier. As Papen remembered it later: ". . . he called me from the Vice Chancellory to ask me to come as quickly as possible. . . . When I arrived at my office, I learned that Goering wanted to see me urgently."

It is barely 8:30 in the morning, but Berlin is coming to life. In the section of town where the ministries are located, the employees are beginning to emerge in waves from the subway.

On the Wilhelmplatz, a cigar-seller casually pulls his cart into a corner of the square. He settles there every day, in front of Prince Leopold's palace, waiting for the flood of ministerial employees to pour down the Wilhelmstrasse at lunchtime, to stroll about the Wilhelmplatz before the columns of the Kaiserhof and the statues of the heroes of the Seven Years' War.

It is already hot when Papen and Tschirschky cross the square on the way from the Vice Chancellory to the building generally referred to as "Goering's Palace," on the Leipzigerplatz. The building sits back from the street, in a garden separated from the pavement by a high, gilded iron fence. Up to within thirty yards of the palace, everything looks perfectly normal; then suddenly, the groups of police and SS become visible. "Still without the least idea of what was happening," Papen writes, "I went to Goering's apartment in the gardens of the Air Ministry. It was only then that I was struck by the fact that the grounds around the building swarmed with SS carrying machine guns." In the courtyard, police and SS are heavily armed. Men are on the balconies and lying on the roof, with machine guns trained at the entrance, ready to fire. It is necessary to pass several barriers to get into the big reception hall. Arrogant SS sentries watch everyone who comes and goes. Vice Chancellor Papen and Tschirschky are peremptorily questioned several times. Finally, they are admitted into Hermann Goering's study, cluttered with bibelots. A feverish atmosphere reigns. Messages pour in, in quick succession; ADCs, SS and Gestapo agents run in and out. Goering is there with Himmler. Gisevius remembers Goering delivering a continuous stream of speeches, his hair in disorder: "With his white blouse, his gray-blue military trousers, and jackboots reaching high up his bloated legs . . . he made one think of Puss-in-Boots, or some character in a fairy tale." Himmler, on the other hand, is discreet and reserved as usual, but his eyes, behind thin glasses, speak of determination and crafty patience. Goering receives Papen with ironic condescension: the Minister-President of Prussia, former pilot and drug addict, is finally playing a part commensurate with his capacity for passion and violence. He speaks with the assurance of someone at the heart of the action, who knows what is happening. "He told me," Papen writes, "that Hitler had been obliged to fly to Munich to stop a revolt fomented by Roehm, and that he himself had been given full powers to put down the insurrection in the capital."

Goering is often interrupted by messages brought from the Ministry's telephone exchange. Pili Körner, Goering's secretary of state, has just arrived with a large dossier. Goering begins to leaf through it as Papen walks over to him. "I protested at once that Hitler could delegate his powers only to me, the Vice Chancellor," Papen writes.

That is the law, but Goering barely listens. The Vice Chancellor must understand that for months now in Germany, since the Nazis have been making the laws, the articles of the Constitution are no longer what count, but the force of arms. All Papen and Tschirschky need do is look around the room at the innumerable sentries, SS and police—or through the window at the cars leaving Goering's residence to bring gangs of armed men into the capital. Naturally, Goering refuses to yield his place to Papen, just as he refuses the Vice Chancellor's suggestion that he inform Hindenburg and proclaim a state of emergency, returning the duty of restoring order to the Reichswehr. The Reichswehr itself, however, under Generals Blomberg and Reichenau, is not an impartial force. Papen is either extremely innocent or badly informed. Goering dismisses the Vice Chancellor's arguments with a large gesture, and busies himself with the latest messages, paying no further attention to his illustrious visitor. "I had to give way," Papen records. "With the police and the Air Force behind him, Goering enjoyed a position far more solid than mine." When Papen insists again that Hindenburg be informed, Goering, irritated and condescending, ends the interview. There is no point in disturbing Hindenburg, he says. Thanks to the SS, he, Goering, is in perfect command of the situation.

Outside, in the hall, the commotion is as great as ever. The bells at the telephone exchange desk ring continually. Himmler had left Goering's office while Papen was protesting the violations of law. In the waiting room, Tschirschky observes the Reichsführer talking on the telephone, engaged in a conversation of evident substance. He looks absorbed and determined. Although Himmler is talking softly, Papen's secretary overhears one remark: "Now we've got to get down to it; you can clean up all that." Is he talking about the Vice Chancellory, which the Gestapo looks on as a nest of opposition? Tschirschky tries to warn Papen, returning to Goering's study right behind Himmler, but Goering is now almost shouting at the Vice Chancellor: "You would do better to think of your personal security. Go home immediately, and stay there. Don't go out without telling me."

Himmler passes Goering a message, as Papen once again tries

to argue: "I shall look after my own security. I have no intention of accepting a barely disguised arrest." This time Goering doesn't even answer; he ignores Papen, as if the message from Himmler had further weighted his already scornful attitude. Tschirschky tells Papen of his anxieties, and the two men leave the room. In the waiting room, an SA officer is sitting collapsed in a chair, with his face in his hands, guarded by an SS. It is Gruppenführer Kasche, who was picked up in the street as he left his home and brought here. He doesn't understand why, but he is definitely afraid. Outside in the courtyard, the sunlight of a magnificent summer day is dazzling after the semidarkness of Goering's office. Papen and Tschirschky cross the noisy court. The guard seems to have been strengthened.

When the two men present themselves at the gate to leave the Ministry, an SS officer and two sentries bar their way. They have the hard, closed faces of those with orders they will not discuss.

"No one may leave," the officer declares curtly.

He looks straight at Tschirschky. With his hands behind his back and a man on either side, he is a perfect representative of brute force. Tschirschky is not in the habit of being intimidated.

"What's going on here? Herr von Papen surely has the right to leave?"

His tone is peremptory, contemptuous. The officer, evidently unaffected, doesn't move.

"No one is allowed to leave."

The lips of the young officer barely move. His eyes are motionless, and his face, cut by the edge of his helmet, is anonymous, an unreal face emptied of all personality and individuality, as if it no longer expresses a man but a disembodied force temporarily incarnated in a living form.

"Are you afraid we'll be killed?" Tschirschky shouts.

The question receives no reply. Papen's secretary hurries back into the building. As he crosses the hall, he runs into Goering's ADC, Karl Bodenschatz, who is astonished to see him.

"You back already?"

Around them, the atmosphere of urgency and violence persists. Orders, clicking heels, the ringing of telephones—tension which is almost unbearable.

"They won't let us leave," Tschirschky says simply.

Papen is waiting in the sunny courtyard, smiling a bitter, scornful smile. Bodenschatz shouts, ordering the gate opened: "We shall see who gives orders here, the Prime Minister or the SS."

Finally, after an SS has gone to check orders, the heavy gate is pushed open, and Papen and Tschirschky find themselves on the street.

Except for the presence of a few groups of policemen, the day seems to be proceeding peacefully. In the Wilhelmplatz, the cigarseller is sitting in the shade of his cart, his open boxes neatly arranged under the hood. As yet he has had no clients; he is reading the newspaper, which gives a long description of Hitler's visit to the work camps in Westphalia.

It is just after nine o'clock. From the windows of the Ministry of the Interior one can see the leaves of the lime and chestnut trees of Unter den Linden gently stirring in the breeze moving down the length of the avenue from the Brandenburg Gate. Gisevius stands looking out at the magnificent boulevard.

He arrived at the Ministry very early this morning. He, too, knows that the police were kept on alert last night, and his friend Nebe has told him of the mission of surveillance and security Goering has given him. Nebe was supposed to telephone him during the evening, but did not. Something unusual must be happening. Now, staring at the limes and chestnuts, he is listening to his boss, Karl Daluege, express his indignation. Goering has alerted the Prussian police three times without informing him, which is a grave breach of customary procedure. He has decided to complain directly to Goering and, as an "old fighter," tell him, for once, exactly what he thinks. As Gisevius approves what his boss says, the telephone rings. It is Goering, asking Daluege to come to his office.

Gisevius is left alone with his questions and doubts. By now the Ministry has assumed its normal workday pace. The sentries are at their posts, and one can hear the ceaseless clatter of typewriters: the central mechanism of the police of the Reich seems to be functioning perfectly and efficiently. The momentous events which are taking place are beyond its jurisdiction. Goebbels, Goering, Himmler, Heydrich, the Gestapo, the SS and the SD have together set a trap beyond the control of traditional authority, and now that Hitler has given the signal for action, the trap has begun to crush its victims. The Ministry is functioning normally but in a void.

When Karl Daluege returns to the Ministry, Gisevius notes that his face is as "white as a sheet." It is not yet ten o'clock. At this moment Hitler is leaving the Munich Hauptbahnhof to go to the Brown House. Daluege talks rapidly: an SA putsch was expected during the coming night. "In any case," he concludes, "there is going to be a bloody purge of the SA." Daluege's voice and face indicate that he, too, is afraid. When he informs Secretary of State Grauert of the facts, he realizes Grauert is also afraid: machinery has been set in motion which could crush anyone. It respects no law. Daluege and Grauert decide to warn Minister Frick; Gisevius joins in their decision.

They must go out, walk back along Unter den Linden, through the still gentle heat of the radiant summer morning. The three men walk rapidly, in silence. The black cars of the Gestapo are parked on the Pariser Platz, from which they can observe Unter den Linden and the Wilhelmstrasse, which cuts obliquely through this central quarter of Berlin where the ministries and government buildings are concentrated. Beyond the Brandenburg Gate lies the Tiergarten, with its shrubberies, tranquil tree-lined walks, and innocent strollers, some of whom might notice these three solemn-faced gentlemen walking down the Friedensallee to the Königsplatz.

A great many visitors are standing around the Siegessäule, the immense victory column. A line has already formed to visit the top, to see the panoramic view of the city. The column, of sandstone, bronze and gold, celebrates the victory of Prussia, and the birth of the Prussian empire. Now another empire is being born in blood and violence, expected to endure for a millennium—the Third Reich, today systematically destroying its creators, the SA.

Frick's office is near the Königsplatz. The Minister, too, has been left in ignorance. Gisevius is not admitted to Frick's office, but Grauert and Frick quickly come out, on their way to see Goering. Daluege rejoins Gisevius, and the two men walk back to Unter den Linden. By now it is a little after ten o'clock.

Only a few moments before, Goebbels has telephoned Goering from Munich, pronouncing the three syllables: "Colibrì."

THE TIME OF ASSASSINS

At 8 Prinz-Albrecht Strasse, Heydrich receives the same signal, and immediately sends it out to the various towns and districts of the Reich, where his men are eager to go into action, like impatient dogs pulling at their leashes. For several days they have had their sealed envelopes; this morning they break the seals, stamped with the eagle and the swastika, and read the lists of names, former comrades with whom they have fought side by side, whom they now must arrest or liquidate. They find names of respected persons, covered with honors, whom they must take to concentration camps or cause to "disappear" in woods or marshes. They pursue their prey, sending teams of killers working in twos or threes, implacable, anonymous, knocking at doors like salesmen, then firing—no explanation, no remorse. They are indeed salesmen, these efficient, remorseless SS and SD—commercial travelers of the New Reich, dealing in death, one of its most common commodities.

In Berlin, Gestapo agents receive lists of numbers, each referring to the name of a particular public figure. Eighteen SS, commanded by Hauptsturmführer Gildisch, a former police officer, are charged with the immediate murder of specific persons who are to be given no form of trial. Himmler, Heydrich and Goering have made their orders precise. From his office on the Leipziger Strasse, Goering freely condemns opponents of the regime to summary execution. To Gildisch he said simply: "Find Klausener and kill him." The Hauptsturmführer SS clicked his heels and went to the Ministry of Communications to find the Director of Catholic Action. While liveried agents bring Goering and Himmler sandwiches and drinks, Gestapo agents place on the table beside the bottles of beer little white slips of paper marked with the names of men who have been arrested and taken to the Cadet School at Lichterfelde. Goering shouts with violent delight: "Shoot them! Shoot them!"

At this moment, Gisevius, arriving at Goering's palace in the Leipzigerplatz, is struck by the atmosphere there. "A sudden sense of pain grabbed me by the throat," he remembers. "I breathed in an air of hate and tension, of civil war and, above all, of blood—lots of blood. On every face, from the sentries' to the humblest orderlies', one perceived the knowledge of terrible things."

In Goering's waiting room, another bunch of arrested men have joined Kasche, still there, trembling with apprehension. An SA officer sits with his teeth chattering beneath the cold gaze of an SS. Summoned by phone, the SA had arrived calmly to be met with a flood of abuse from Goering, who called him a "homosexual pig," and told him he would be shot. Anxiously, Nebe and Gisevius meet near Goering's office. "We greeted each other," Gisevius remembers, "with our agreed signal: a tight hand squeeze, and a blink." Nebe tells Gisevius what he knows, in a few apparently colorless phrases: the first men to be killed were those already in the camps or in the cellars of the Gestapo. While still at the Ministry, Gisevius learned that most of the SA leaders had been arrested—or would be: "Fräulein" Schmidt, Heines' ADC, Gehrt, Sander and Voss. Karl Ernst's men were the first to be taken. Now they are at Lichterfelde, perhaps dead already, their bodies lying on the paving stones worn smooth by generations of young cadets drilling to the shouts of Prussian noncoms.

Gisevius watches and listens. Anyone not directly involved in the action at the killers' sides cannot help but be anxious. It is clear that a grand settling of accounts has begun, and Gisevius has already had a few run-ins with Heydrich and the Gestapo. "I could smell danger," he says, "and considered it wise, during those hot June days, to avoid solitary interrogations, to stay in the company of people who could save me, should that necessity arise. I preferred, therefore, to stick close to Daluege." But Daluege is afraid, and Nebe, too, "believing it was not impossible that before the day was over he might be killed as an accomplice."

Papen is afraid, too, and Tschirschky, for the assassins have begun to strike. When they arrive at the Vice Chancellory to find it occupied by SS and Gestapo agents, they understand they were called to Goering's to make it easier for his men to occupy the Vice Chancellory. To reach Papen's office, they walk through Tschirschky's office, which has been searched and left in a state of total disorder, with drawers pulled open and papers scattered over the floor. The search was brutal, and Himmler's men, arrogantly triumphant, are still there. They have even set up a machine gun. One of the office personnel manages to inform Papen that Herbert Bose, one of the Vice Chancellor's closest collaborators, who worked on the Marburg speech with Jung, has been killed only a few moments before. Two men dressed in black had asked to see him; when he came to the door, they shot him wordlessly, leaving the body in his office. An SS is now stationed at the door, forbidding all entry. When Papen asks what happened, he is told that Bose resisted the police.

Suddenly they hear the rumble of an explosion: it is the Gestapo agents blowing the locks off the strong boxes in the cellar of the building—at one time a bank—hoping to find compromising documents. A short time later, SD agents place Tschirschky under arrest. He and the Vice Chancellor exchange a long handshake; then Tschirschky and the two SS walk away. He is the third of Papen's colleagues to be arrested. As Tschirschky is walking down the staircase of the Vice Chancellory, followed by the two SS, two new policemen appear and ask for him: they are Goering's men.

"It's already been done," Tschirschky says, pointing to the SS. "Gentlemen, you will have to settle this matter between yourselves." He waits for their decision, his face lit by a scornful smile. Finally, the SS take him to the Gestapo headquarters in their car, with Goering's men following immediately behind. This repression, plotted and calculated for so long, nevertheless includes improvisation, uncertainty, last-minute rescue and chance executions, because each of the leaders of the plot has his own interests, his chosen victims, as well as protégés, kept alive because they may be useful in the future.

Goering protects Papen in this way. The Vice Chancellor is escorted to his house, guarded by a detachment of SS. "The telephone was cut," Papen remembers, "and in my drawing room I found a police captain whose responsibility it was to ensure my complete isolation. He told me that I was forbidden all contact with the outside world, that I could receive no visitors." In fact, the officer is there to prevent Himmler's men from liquidating Papen. He is forbidden to release the Vice Chancellor to anyone without a personal and formal order from Goering. Papen is kept a prisoner with his son in his own home for three days, guarded by the SS, who keep everyone away from the house. But Papen remains alive. Goering shelters the Vice Chancellor in exchange for services rendered, and because Papen has Hindenburg's private ear. Papen knows this. "One man interposed himself between me and the executioner: Goering."

There are very few who can thank Goering. On the contrary, his attention that morning means death for a score or more, death falling on them like destiny in antiquity—blind and ineluctable. Goering liquidates anyone who has annoyed him, or whose life in some way represents a threat. Himmler and Heydrich do the same, and the list of bullet-ridden victims grows rapidly. The fact that a man may have abandoned political life and renounced all ambition does him no good. Nazi revenge does not forgive. The leaders of the Reich do not take chances. They know that, contrary to the pious fables of idealists, a dead adversary is easier to handle than a living one.

Gregor Strasser, formerly an intimate companion of Hitler's and creator of the Nazi Party, was that Saturday lunching at home with his family. For months he has only been on the edge of any real activity, even if his name has been repeated frequently during the last few weeks, and even if, as is rumored, he met with Hitler sometime toward the middle of June. All this only condemns him. His doorbell rings. He answers it. Eight men are there with revolvers. One word is pronounced: "Gestapo." Strasser is dragged off without a chance to say good-bye to his family. Tschirschky, surrounded by the SS taking him to be interrogated before leaving for Dachau, passes him inside the Gestapo building, on Prinz-Albrecht Strasse, at the end of the morning.

It is nearly one o'clock. On the Wilhelmplatz, the cigar seller is standing beside his wares: this is the best time for his trade. The employees of the ministries have come out for their lunch break and are strolling through the square. It will soon be the moment for a cigar, a moment of relaxation, the euphoria of tobacco on a fine summer day. People are chatting about their lives, about what they will do tomorrow. Many have the afternoon off, but they linger for a few moments before going home.

A few hundred yards from the square, at the Ministry of Communications, Hauptsturmführer SS Gildisch is asking for the office of Director Klausener. The sentries hesitate, then give the SS directions. Slowly, he climbs the stairs and in the corridor passes Klausener, who has just come from washing his hands. Klausener looks at Gildisch, and perhaps grasps the threat. In his office higher up, a telephone call, very unusual at this hour, startles Dr. Othmar Fessler. It is Klausener, and his voice sounds anxious. "Will you please come see me right away." Then he hangs up. Fessler, quite surprised, gets ready to go downstairs, but it is already too late. Gildisch has entered Klausener's office. The Director of Catholic Action is startled when the SS informs him he is under arrest. As he turns toward the closet to get his hat and follow the SS officer, Gildisch fires a single bullet into Klausener's head. While the blood spreads slowly across the floor, Gildisch telephones Heydrich, giving a plain police-style report, and asks for further orders. They are simple: simulate a suicide. The Hauptsturmführer puts his revolver in Klausener's right hand, and then telephones the SS who accompanied him to the building and are waiting downstairs. A few minutes later, two young militiamen dressed in black stand guard in front of Klausener's office, blocking the door. Gildisch leaves calmly without looking back, undoubtedly hearing the clerk speaking in a terrified voice to Herr Fessler, who is questioning him: "The Herr Director killed himself; he has just shot himself with a revolver!" Impassive and immobile, the two SS stand in front of the office door, hearing and seeing nothing.

It is barely 1:15. Hauptsturmführer SS Gildisch is a quick and efficient man. He is back at Goering's residence almost as soon as his mission is completed, ready for a new assignment. The atmosphere is still heavy and tense. Goering shouts, "Shoot him!" and Police Major Jakobi runs across the room shouting orders to arrest Paul Schulz, a friend of Strasser, and one of the Party members of longest standing, who has not been found, although his name is on a list of men to be killed. In the waiting room, ADCs keep coming and going between the central switchboard and Goering's office.

At about this time, throughout the city the sense that something unusual is happening begins to grow; ministries, embassies and foreign journalists ask for information.

Since eleven o'clock the inhabitants of the affluent section of Berlin, between Tiergartenstrasse and Königin-Augusta Strasse, the avenue bordering the quiet, picturesque canal, have been uneasy. The district is, in fact, under siege. Goering's police have set up machine guns at the corner of Tiergartenstrasse and Standartenstrasse, and the street is closed to traffic. It is a quiet street, opening into a quiet square halfway down its length, in the center of which stands the pretty Matthaïkirche. At its northern end near the Tiergarten stands the General Staff headquarters of the

Sturmabteilung. The building is besieged, occupied and ransacked by the Gestapo, the SS and Goering's men.

In the same street, behind small gardens, stand Roehm's house, the headquarters of the Stahlhelm, the French Consulate and the Italian Embassy. The French Consul is trying to evaluate the actions he has observed, trying to obtain information to telephone the embassy. But André François-Poncet has been on holiday in Paris since the fifteenth of June; the Consul can only send out urgent telegrams. People in the neighboring building are similarly preoccupied; from the windows of the Italian Embassy the Fascist diplomats can see the machine guns which have been set up on the sidewalk in front of Roehm's house. Signora Cerutti, the Ambassador's wife, asks a stream of questions: she is giving a reception in the early afternoon. Will her guests be able to get past the roadblocks? She consults the Ministry of Foreign Affairs, but neither the Secretary of State for Foreign Affairs, Herr von Bülow, nor the Chief of Protocol, Herr von Bassewitz, can give her any information. They know nothing. The foreign journalists ask questions too. Some say they saw the police ransacking Roehm's house, that Papen himself will be arrested, that high officials have been killed in their offices. The journalists turn to Aschmann, the head of the Ministerial Press Service, but he also knows nothing. In the face of this flood of events and questions, the diplomats of the Wilhelmstrasse are forced to recognize that something serious is going on, that a time of bloodletting has begun whose limits and objectives are yet unknown but which is clearly brutal, pitiless, unchecked by any law; that it may fall on anyone, striking down the opposition without distinction; that it has already swept through the ranks of the SA and the conservatives.

Almost 11:30. General Kurt von Schleicher is in his study on the ground floor. From his desk he can see not only down Griebnitzseestrasse, but also the vast expanse of the Griebnitzsee itself, which is one of the principal charms of the Neubabelsberg district. There are many boats on the lake this Saturday morning;

white and orange sails make vivid splashes of color against the water and against the green of the fields and gardens. Here at Neubabelsberg there are still green spaces in front of the luxurious villas belonging to company directors and high government officials, men who have attained wealth and power. Kurt von Schleicher is certainly one of these—former Chancellor of the Reich, "éminence grise" of the Reichswehr and the intimate of President Hindenburg, with whom he had served in the same regiment. On the sidelines since Hitler's rise to power, he returned a few days ago from a holiday trip with his young wife and is already giving evening parties, which, he assures well-wishers who question him uneasily, are "purely social." His friends do not like to see him openly mixing in the world of politics. But Kurt von Schleicher is a gambler, and finds it impossible to forget the taste of power, the exhilaration of deference and intrigue. Schleicher is flattered when he is told in discreetly lowered tones that he is being "held in reserve, for the nation." However, warnings and recommendations of caution have not been lacking. Yesterday evening, June 29, a friend from his cadet days telephoned. At the Bendlerstrasse, his friend said, there was talk of intrigue between Schleicher and Roehm. The officer went on to specify: the next few days would be very dangerous for Schleicher.

To his worried wife Schleicher remarked that he hadn't seen Roehm for months, and that such gossip was without importance.

Maria Güntel, the governess, remembered the General's casual manner perfectly. She had opened the big sliding door connecting the dining room and the General's study. Schleicher and his wife were sitting on a leather sofa, and as Maria served them after-dinner liqueurs, she had listened to Kurt von Schleicher, joking about the gossip and fears of the Bendlerstrasse officers, as cautious and timid as young girls.

That was yesterday evening.

This morning, Schleicher is sitting in his study looking out at Griebnitzseestrasse, flooded with hot summer sunlight. The last radio announcement predicted 86 degrees for Berlin; there was also a lengthy reading of extracts from General Blomberg's article affirming the loyalty of the Reichswehr to the Führer. The extracts irritate Schleicher. He has never liked the Gummilöwe, his ingratiating courtier's manners toward Hitler, and the way in which he drove Schleicher's men from the Bendlerstrasse.

At that moment, the telephone rings. It is an old military friend of Schleicher calling to welcome him back from his trip. They talk for several minutes. Schleicher tells his caller of the accident from which he escaped unhurt, as if by a miracle. Then he excuses himself for a moment, explaining that someone is ringing the doorbell. In a front room, Maria Güntel opens a little window beside the front door, and sees five men in long raincoats. A black car is drawn up before the door.

"We would like to speak to General Schleicher."

The voice is authoritarian, and expresses, like the silhouetted figures, official power, with which there is no arguing. Hesitantly, the governess half-opens the door. Then, before Maria Güntel quite realizes what is happening, the door is pushed wide, and she herself backed against the wall by one of the men. The others go straight to Schleicher's study.

At the other end of the telephone wire, Schleicher's caller hears a click, which is undoubtedly the receiver touching the table. Distantly but distinctly, he hears the General's voice: "Yes, I am General von Schleicher." Then, immediately, a burst of gunfire before someone replaces the receiver.

Fascinated and terrified, Maria Güntel walks into the room. Schleicher is lying on the rug, his legs slightly bent. A wound on the right side of his neck is clearly visible, and others on the left side of his back. He is lying on his stomach, as if having suddenly recognized his visitors he had also understood why they had come and had tried to escape. Suddenly there is a scream; Frau von Schleicher, coming from the adjoining dining room, screams again. The killers are still holding their revolvers. The young woman walks toward them, her arms raised, staring at her husband's body. She screams once more, but her voice breaks in a dry burst of fire.

She, too, falls dead. Maria Güntel stands petrified in the doorway. One of the killers walks over to her. "Don't be afraid, Fräulein. We won't kill you."

The others make a rapid search of the General's study and then, without a word, leave the house, not even shutting the door to the study, leaving Maria Güntel in the doorway, her huge eyes staring at Frau Schleicher and Kurt von Schleicher lying on the blood-soaked carpet.

A chambermaid, hiding on the second floor, comes downstairs to find the governess sitting motionless, holding her face in her hands. The maid telephones the police.

The prefect himself comes to Schleicher's house, and investigators collect evidence. At the Ministry of the Interior, Gisevius is informed by the prefect. Daluege questions Goering and Himmler, but as he is turning back to Gisevius, a new phone call from Potsdam informs him that the prefect has received instructions which enable him to write his report: General Schleicher, compromised in Roehm's treason, had resisted the Gestapo agents who came to arrest him. There was a struggle during which the General and his wife were killed. The inquiry is closed. The investigators are already sealing the study door of the former Chancellor of the Reich. The villa is quiet. A policeman remains on duty at the front door, observing the governess still sitting where she was. She is the only witness.

A few months later her lifeless body is found, death allegedly self-inflicted out of despair and fear. Whatever the truth, it is a suicide which the press does not discuss. In the Third Reich no one really wants to know about such things, or to remember the violent death of General Kurt von Schleicher and his wife on Saturday morning, June 30, 1934, in their comfortable and quiet villa at Neubabelsberg.

4

Saturday, June 30, 1934
Munich

In Munich, as in Berlin, it is hot; in Munich, as in Berlin, the killers are at work. Black cars drive rapidly through the streets in the center of town, ignoring traffic lights at crossroads. Suddenly a car door flings open and SS jump out, opening fire. SA officers fall dead—or conservatives or old enemies.

Two cars stop in front of Ritter von Kahr's villa. He had not been involved in politics for years, and is now only a shadow of the man who in November, 1923, managed to fool Hitler and still escape. Because of Ritter von Kahr, nearly eleven years ago the Munich putsch failed.

Von Kahr's doorbell rings. It is not quite ten o'clock. Von Kahr is still in his dressing gown. Three men stand in his doorway, looking at him. Without a word, they seize him and drag him to one of the cars; their movements are so decisive that von Kahr scarcely protests. He has not been seized by human hands, but by the violent vindictiveness of triumphant Nazism. On the street passers-by look away, trying not to see the men pulling him into a car. It is a beautiful day and the sun is hot. This afternoon crowded trains will carry contented families to weekend outings at the Bavarian lakes. Why bother about Ritter von Kahr, an old man of seventy-three, whose body will be found in a few days' time, savagely mutilated by an ax and thrust into the mud at Dachau?

In the same mud, a few hundred yards away, another body is discovered, with three bullets near the heart—7.65 millimeter, the SS caliber—and a broken spine. The police are able to identify the body without difficulty: it is the corpse of Bernhard Stempfle, who had the misfortune of being close to Hitler. In 1924–1925, Stempfle, who had a facile pen and vigorous anti-Semitic opinions, edited a little weekly in Miesbach which specialized in attacking Jews. Nazism had attracted him. He had corrected the proofs of *Mein Kampf*, rewritten certain passages, improved the style, refined the thought. When the book became the Bible of the regime, the Führer found this interference hard to forgive. Stempfle had also known about some of the Führer's amorous passions. He knew Hitler had idolized Geli Raubal, one of his own half-sister's daughters, that he had terrified her with his obsessive jealousy, and that on the morning of September 17, 1931, Geli had killed herself. Her death had plunged Hitler into a long crisis of depression from which he only gradually recovered. The circumstances of Geli's death were kept from the public. But Stempfle knew about it. He knew too many secrets. Former member of the Order of Hieronymites, Stempfle understood his danger and tried to disappear. But his efforts were in vain. This Saturday morning the killers find him and drag him to Dachau. Hitler and the other Nazi leaders have long memories. They need to blot out their troubled pasts, to see that any witness who has lost his sense of complicity disappears. A dead man is worth more than a living one, an error better than an oversight, a useless death preferred to an enemy who goes free.

Frau Schmidt learns this lesson. It is she who opens the door that Saturday morning when the bell rings. Four gentlemen ask to see her husband. She is surprised; she doesn't recognize them, for they don't look like their usual visitors—musicians, journalists, professors. Wilhelm Eduard Schmidt is, in fact, a well-known music critic, respected even in Berlin. Goering, for instance, is said to admire his articles in the *Münchener Neuste Nachrichten*.

The three Schmidt children cluster around their mother. From the drawing room, they can all hear the sound of Schmidt's cello. One of the gentlemen insists, and Frau Schmidt goes to get her husband. He appears smiling, prepared to inquire what the visitors want. He is immediately seized and dragged away. His wife looks on, stupefied by this eruption of history into their tranquil life of art and culture. Wilhelm Eduard Schmidt has never thought about politics, but politics have destroyed him. The SS and the Gestapo are looking for a Munich doctor, a friend of Otto Strasser, Dr. Ludwig Schmitt. Since they cannot find him, they arrest Wilhelm Schmidt hoping that he will do instead, sending Frau Schmidt his coffin a few days later from Dachau. The SS eventually proposes a pension for Frau Schmidt to redress the error, and finds her refusal difficult to understand. What does one life more or less mean to the Black Guard? So the last morning of June, 1934, passes in Munich.

While the SS are tracking down their victims in Munich, Hitler is still at the Brown House, Briennerstrasse. He hears of Schleicher's death, starting nervously at the news. One of the SS in his escort remembers this reaction, which shows on his face. Then Hitler begins to talk again.

He has been talking for a long time to the SA gathered around him, listening with the look of helpless animals. Roehm, Heydebreck, Heines, Spreti—the leaders to whom they had shouted their faith and sworn their loyalty are now struck down, imprisoned, insulted, addressed as homosexual pigs. And they—the SA—must submit like cowards. For all their virile posturing, their swollen pride, brown shirts, armbands, decorations and weapons, they are afraid. They have been fighting for too long against defenseless adversaries, terrorizing peaceable Germans who could not fight back, and they have lost their taste for genuine combat. They are afraid, and hang their heads. And then this man talking to them, shivering in his raincoat, is their Führer.

So they approve what he says, and the Brown House rings with their enthusiastic shouts: "Sieg Heil! Sieg Heil! Heil Hitler!" Rudolf Hess approaches them with the brusque gestures and stern face of one who represents justice. "You are all suspect," he tells them. "Those who are innocent must suffer for a few days for the faults of the guilty. Until the inquiry has established the roles played by each of you, you are all under arrest."

An SS officer who has been standing behind Hess speaks next. Each SA must be searched, he says; then, if the Führer decides, they will be allowed to return home. One by one, without protest, the SA present themselves to the SS, who search them thoroughly. The defeat and humiliation of the Sturmabteilung are complete. The SS are meticulous, and the silence in the long line of SA is total. It is no longer the time, nor yet the time, for songs of triumph: for each man now, the question is simply survival.

The Führer has withdrawn into another room. The windows are open wide, but today Briennerstrasse is quiet. The Reichswehr is still responsible for keeping order on the street, and isolating the Brown House. Hitler walks up and down the room: his fatigue has grown, exhaustion brought on by prolonged nervous tension and sleeplessness. Lutze, Goebbels, Party Judge Buch, Martin Bormann, Sepp Dietrich, Rudolf Hess, Wagner, Max Amann (the editor of *Mein Kampf* and director of Party publications)—all are in the room, watching and listening to Hitler, forcing him by their very presence into a position of intransigence. All these men are long-term adversaries of the SA and of Roehm. Now that the Führer has decided to take severe measures, they are determined to guarantee their future security and power.

Hitler continues to pace the room, heaping insults on Roehm and the SA leaders, declaring that there will be no clemency. Viktor Lutze, who has played the smallest part in the plot, holds himself somewhat aloof, surprised by the violence of the scenes he is witnessing. He had never thought the day would end with the deaths of Roehm and his men. Yet that is what is under consideration. Rudolf Hess and Max Amann each request the honor of killing Roehm with their own hands. The Führer motions them to be quiet. Then, in a halting voice he dictates to Lutze the new course of the Sturmabteilung.

"I want the officers of the SA to conduct themselves henceforth like men, not like repulsive, grotesque monkeys. I want blind obedience from the SA, from its leaders down to its most humble ranks. I can no longer permit leaders of the SA to organize costly dinners or accept invitations to them."

The Führer's voice rises, the insults multiply. "Champagne has been flung from windows during these orgies," he shouts. All the gossip collected by Heydrich's agents suddenly surges into his memory. "They have been wasting Party funds!

"Henceforth, I forbid SA leaders to drive about in expensive cars. No more diplomatic dinners." Without comment, Lutze appends this to the dictation, and reads the whole back to the Führer, who initials it.

There is a moment of silence. Then Buch, the great judge from whom Roehm escaped in 1932, asks once again what the fate of the SA leaders imprisoned in Stadelheim will be. "The dogs should be shot!" Hitler shouts. He takes a list handed to him by Wagner, the Minister of the Interior, and in a gesture of fury, makes an "X" before several names. Sometimes he hesitates before making the mark of death. Everyone is quiet; everyone can hear the Führer's pen scratching the paper. When he has finished, Hitler gives the list to Sepp Dietrich.

"Go to Stadelheim at once," he says. "Take six men and an SS officer with you, and have the SA leaders executed for high treason."

The list of prisoners is the one drawn up by the director of the prison, Dr. Koch. The names of five high-ranking officers of the SA have been marked with an "X." Sepp Dietrich reads them out slowly:

Edmund Schmidt, Gruppenführer SA, Cell 497

Hans Joachim von Spreti-Weilbach, Standartenführer SA, Cell 501

Hans Peter von Heydebreck, Gruppenführer SA, Cell 502

Hans Hayn, Gruppenführer SA, Cell 503

August Schneidhuber, Obergruppenführer SA, Munich police prefect, Cell 504

The Führer adds dryly: "I have spared Roehm for past services rendered."

At the last moment, then, Hitler has hesitated again. Is it political acumen, scruple, a Machiavellian sense of balance keeping a card to play against the other power groups, or is it the memory of Captain Roehm, who helped him take his first steps as a politician in Munich? Whatever the reason for his clemency, consternation is visible on the faces of Buch, Goebbels and Bormann: Roehm escapes them once more, and as long as he is alive, it is always possible that the Führer may change course. Only Roehm's death can assure their safety. They must obtain that death, whatever the price. But for the moment, it is necessary to yield to Hitler, to be content with keeping Roehm in prison, and to warn Goering, Heydrich and Himmler in Berlin. It is necessary for the moment to wait, to accept what the Führer has offered: the death of five of the SA leaders imprisoned at Stadelheim.

The SA leaders wait in their cells. Despite the Führer's shouts of rage, despite his insults and the scorn of the SS, they cannot believe that they will die while Hitler is still in power, while they still wear uniforms covered with badges of rank and insignia proclaiming that they are power, that they, the SA, represent strength and force. The summer sunlight brightens their cells. Die? What is this madness?

Toward 5 P.M., Sepp Dietrich arrives at the prison. His brief orders are immediately executed. While he climbs to the second story of the prison, six SS noncoms assemble in the courtyard, which at this hour lies in the shadow of the high gray stone walls. An SS officer has them check their weapons, and line up ten yards from one of the walls. By now, Dietrich has entered the office of Director

Koch, and handed him the list of prisoners condemned to die. Koch hesitates. His mouth trembles. Since morning he has been afraid; the world has turned upside-down, and he has understood how fragile and threatened one's hold on life really is. He is afraid to decide—afraid to accept the order, afraid to refuse it. Out of his deep respect for regulations, he protests: the list is not signed. Therefore, Koch informs Sepp Dietrich, he cannot hand over the prisoners. The Gruppenführer makes no comment. He takes back the list, and a few minutes later his car returns to the Brown House. Perhaps he, too, wishes to be covered by higher authority. At the Brown House, Minister Wagner signs the list unhesitatingly, and the stay granted the SA officers is over.

The firing squad is drawn up in the empty courtyard. Sepp, escorted by two SS, goes to the first cell, and the dry click of the turning lock startles the prisoner, who stands up. Dietrich salutes: "You have been condemned to death by the Führer for high treason. Heil Hitler!" The two SS move on, and the prisoner, yesterday a man of power, controlling other men's lives and destinies, follows them down the corridor toward the courtyard. Soon he is standing with his back to the wall, perhaps watching the sunlight striking the glass of the offices on the second floor, while the orders ring out. "By order of the Führer," shouts the SS officer who commands the firing squad. "Ready, aim, fire!" The body falls.

The firing can be heard in the other cells. Nightmare has become reality.

When Dietrich presents himself to Obergruppenführer Schneidhuber, the latter cries out: "Comrade Sepp, this is madness! We are innocent!" The Gruppenführer simply repeats: "You have been condemned to death by the Führer for high treason. Heil Hitler!"

But Sepp Dietrich's determination does not save him from the nausea which attends repeated executions. Later he remembered: "Just before Schneidhuber's turn I grew sick of it, and left." Several more times the courtyard echoes to the sinister shout: "By order of the Führer. Ready, aim, fire!" And another body falls, as twilight descends over Munich.

"HEIL HITLER!"

Sepp Dietrich has returned to the Brown House to make his report. "The traitors have paid," he tells the Führer. Hitler, who had withdrawn into a long silence, seems startled, then suddenly recovers his raging anger and self-assurance. He says he will speak to the SA.

When Hitler's arrival is announced, the SA, gathered in one of the big rooms, cheer him with loud hurrahs. The Führer is skillful and tough. "Your leaders have betrayed your confidence," he shouts. "You manned the front lines, while your officers spent their nights carousing, living in luxury, dining in town."

The SA are silent, sensing that the Führer is giving them a way of dissociating themselves from their leaders, abandoning them. He continues: "It is now necessary to know whether you are with me or with those who deceived you and used your devotion to build their own personal fortunes. Acclaim your new leader, Lutze, and wait for my orders, which he will transmit to you."

Lutze steps forward and shouts, "Heil Hitler!" The entire room takes up the cry and then with Lutze sings the "Horst Wessel Lied," while the Führer stands, his arms crossed, staring at the crowd of faces, these men who have just denied their past. When Hitler withdraws, Lutze states that the SA are now free to leave the Brown House. "You will go directly and separately to your homes, and there remove your uniforms. You will not intervene in any public affairs until you have been informed that the SA has been reorganized, and is once again united."

With the exception of a few who are still being held, the SA are allowed to return home. In silence, one by one, they go out into the sunny streets of Munich. Passers-by turn to look at them, no longer marching with the provocative and martial air of their days of triumph, but with the heavy walk of defeated men hoping to make themselves inconspicuous. The Reichswehr troops and their officers, executing their hundred paces in front of Party headquarters, seem not even to notice these Brown Shirts who had imagined themselves one day organizing and commanding the eternal and invincible German Army.

A few minutes later an order ends the blockade of Briennerstrasse; the Reichswehr lifts the siege of the Brown House, and the street is once again open to normal traffic. Only a few SS are left near the Party building. They will remain until 7:30 P.M., when Hitler, accompanied by Goebbels, Hess and Sepp Dietrich, will return to Berlin by air. There is nothing more to do in the Bavarian capital: the Sturmabteilung is broken, its membership brought to their knees, its leaders executed or in prison. There remains only the old comrade, Roehm, disarmed, lying on a camp bed in his cell at Stadelheim Prison, his scarred chest rising and falling with his labored breath; Roehm, granted a stay because of the Führer's hesitation, a moment of hesitation which many of the Nazi leaders wish to bring to an end.

Driving at top speed through the streets, Hitler and the Nazi leaders are silent. They feel as if years had elapsed since dawn; yet it has only been fifteen hours since the Führer's Junker landed at the Munich-Oberwiesenfeld field, where they are now returning. On the field, half-visible in the half-light, there is the same sound of propellers and the same silhouetted figures moving toward the plane. Everything, except for the redness of the sky, is the same; there is even a cool breeze, as before, flattening the short, dry grasses between the runways. But in fact, nothing will ever be the same again in this Third Reich. In these few hours men have died, and others are waiting to die. Wilhelm Eduard Schmidt will never again write music criticism, and von Kahr, as the Führer's plane takes off, is a broken body, buried in mud. Violence in the Third Reich has reached new levels.

At 8 P.M., as the Führer's plane passes over the city of Nuremberg before turning east toward Berlin, the Munich Press Bureau of the National Socialist Party releases a communiqué giving the official version of recent events. Broadcast by local radio, the text astonishes the residents of Munich: with the exception of the few whose curiosity was aroused by the movement of troops and the barricades on the Briennerstrasse, they had suspected nothing. Now the radio announcer informs them in solemn tones: "For several months isolated elements have tried to foment conflict between the SA and the State. Chief of Staff Roehm, who enjoyed the Führer's special confidence, did not oppose these tendencies, but beyond all doubt actually favored them. His unfortunate tastes (which are all too well known) weighed so heavily on the situation that the Führer found himself caught in a grave conflict of conscience. Last night, at two in the morning, the Führer went to Munich and ordered the immediate cashiering and imprisonment of the leaders most heavily compromised. The arrests took place amid scenes so painful from a moral point of view that there was no room for pity. Some of the leaders of the SA had with them young men of peculiar morals: one was surprised and arrested in an absolutely repugnant situation."

The announcer pauses for a moment at this point, and then continues with greater emphasis: "The Führer has ordered this diseased abscess pierced and drained, mercilessly. He will no longer tolerate the endangering of millions of decent people by a few of morbid unhealthy passions. The Führer has ordered Goering, the Minister-President of Prussia, to take action in Berlin and in particular to seize the reactionary allies of this political conspiracy."

The decent people of Munich listen gravely, in silence or in anger against the perverts who have dishonored the German Reich. They congratulate their Führer for his perspicacity and decisiveness in breaking with such men, even if they are old comrades. The decent people are reassured; they pack their bags. Tomorrow, the first of July, the holidays begin. At Dachau, the coffin of Wilhelm Eduard Schmidt, the music critic, is nailed shut. At Stadelheim, the bodies of the executed SA officers are collected.

Decent people know nothing of all that. On the radio they can hear the Hitler Youth chorus singing the "Horst Wessel Lied."

5

Saturday, June 30, 1934
Munich, Gleiwitz, Breslau, Bremen . . .

Early evening in Munich is soft and gentle. In the spacious parks, the English Garden and the Old Botanical Garden, near the Hauptbahnhof, more people are out strolling than usual. Young people are going to the concert given by the Bavarian Folk Ensemble; they are drinking and laughing. The beer halls in old Munich are full, as always in summer. In the hot, smoky beer cellars, people are singing, and the waiters shout out orders. A dark space on the Frauenplatz interests passers-by: it is the front of the Bratwurstglöckl. A notice tacked to the door indicates that the famous restaurant is closed because of special circumstances. But if the Bratwurstglöckl is closed, there is still the Donisl, or the Peterhof, or the Rathskeller in the Town Hall. There are plenty of restaurants and cafés, plenty of beer and high spirits, this warm, June Saturday. No one knows that early in the afternoon Gestapo agents came for Herr Zehntner, the proprietor of the Bratwurstglöckl, his headwaiter and another waiter. Since then, the three men have not been seen, and the police have closed the restaurant. No one other than Zehntner and his employees knows that Roehm met Goebbels at the Bratwurstglöckl one evening in June. Zehntner, his headwaiter and waiter will not remember this meeting much longer. They are in the Stadelheim Prison.

In other towns and cities throughout the Reich, men and women, involuntary witnesses, force themselves to forget what they have seen. In many cities the men of Himmler and Heydrich have been busy since ten that morning. Everywhere, the silhouettes are the same: men with immobile faces, in long raincoats, their hats pulled down over their eyes, firing at men they have snatched from their families.

At Gleiwitz, about a hundred miles from Breslau, the black cars arrive toward noon as the workers pour from the factories. The team of killers asks to see Ramshorn, the prefect of police, who is a member of the Sturmabteilung, a Party deputy and a war hero. The Gestapo agents brush aside the factory guards and open fire on Ramshorn, who has just left his desk. He collapses onto the carpet, like Schleicher in Berlin, like Bose, like Klausener.

At Stettin, Himmler's envoys stop first at the Webersberger Café on the Paradeplatz. They sit quietly and sip beer before going to Gestapo headquarters, where they arrest Hoffmann, the local Gestapo head, a monstrous torturer whom the Reichsführer SS wishes to be rid of.

In Königsberg, against the pale blue Baltic day, agents seize Count Hohberg, head of the SS. In Silesia, Heines' brother is killed. Anyone considered a nuisance can be killed—SA, SS, anyone—it doesn't really matter who, the day is favorable for killing. It is enough for a name to appear on one of the lists drawn up by the organizers of the action. Sometimes in some woodland setting, one of the hunted is told to run, while the gunmen fix their sights and take aim. Sometimes one manages, in fact, to get away, only wounded. So it is with Paul Schulz in the Potsdam woods. Some districts are scarcely troubled: in Thuringia the police and SS are content to arrest a few SA leaders and send them to prison, or to

Dachau, for a few weeks. They will return thinner, their heads shaved, their sunken eyes still large with fear.

From Berlin, Heydrich sends out his trackers and killers once again. He seizes the opportunity to rid the Reich of his adversaries. He telephones, insists, multiplies his orders. He remains at Gestapo headquarters on Prinz-Albrecht Strasse, personally directing operations, filling out cards which his agents take to Goering and Himmler in the Leipzigerplatz. A number, a word—"shot" or "arrested" or "in process"—to inform the two leaders of the fate of their former friends and colleagues. The Gestapo's central switchboard has been sending out continuous messages to local headquarters: Heydrich allows his killers no rest. As soon as one man is dead, it is time to track down another. Between Saturday, June 30, and Monday, July 2, 7,200 telephone calls are made from Prinz-Albrecht Strasse. Sometimes, however, one of the intended victims manages to get away: Regendanz, the banker who arranged the Roehm–François-Poncet meeting and who for years has known how to fly, is mysteriously warned and flies to England in his personal plane Saturday morning.

Most of the time, however, the Gestapo and the SS are successful: the Berlin lawyer who had the audacity to plead against Max Amann is killed; Dr. Erwin Villain, Standartenführer SA, the rival of an SS doctor, is killed, as are SS Toifl and Sempach, who quarreled with Himmler. Sometimes the victims try to defend themselves. At Breslau, the SA open fire on the SS of Oberabschnittsführer Udo von Woyrsch, the son of a Reichswehr general, who has joined the SS. This short-lived resistance provokes the immediate intervention of the Army. On the Ring, and around the Rathaus and Stadthaus buildings, the Reichswehr trucks take up their positions. The soldiers are heavily armed. It is like the time of the Freikorps again, and the revolutionary threat of 1919–1921. But the gunners will not have to fire. Von Woyrsch and Brückner, the Party Gauleiter, manage to quell the resistance of the SA. They order their old comrade, brigade leader SA Wechmar, shot. Woyrsch and Brückner vie with each other to avoid any risk of being accused as accomplices of the Sturmabteilung: the Jews pay for this rivalry. Beaten and tortured, their bodies are thrown, along with other victims, into the Oder River. On the evening of July 1, the SS chief of Breslau is still saying: "We must liquidate all those pigs." The killing continues. Not only the men whose names are on the lists, but their wives as well. The bodies float to the surface of the black waters of the Oder a few days later.

The SS track their enemies into prisons where they have been languishing, some for months. They go into the concentration camps and drag their victims out for beatings, torture, death. So died Erich Mühsam, the writer, who took part in the Consular Republic during its brief moment of victory in Munich, before the Reichswehr crushed it the first of May, 1919. Fifteen years later, Mühsam is killed by the SS, protected by the Reichswehr.

From the liquidation of enemies, the killing moves on to the suppression of rivals: Oberabschnittsführer SS Erich von dem Bach Zelewski arranges the murder of Reiterführer SS Anton Freiherr von Hoberg und Buchwald. It doesn't matter that the old soldier has nothing to do with the Sturmabteilung, nor that the murder takes place before the horrified eyes of the Freiherr's young son. What matters is the post the murder frees for the ambitious Zelewski. The arrest of Obergruppenführer SA Karl Ernst likewise allows an ambitious SS to grab new power.

Ernst suspects nothing. He dreams of his honeymoon trip to Madeira. At Bremerhaven, with a child's delight or like a newly successful man intoxicated by the adventure of wealth, he has visited the *Europa,* pride of the German fleet, with his bride and comrades from the SA. On Friday, in Bremen, they drink and feast all night. At noon, Saturday, there is a banquet at the City Hall, and the prefect of police wishes the young couple "a long life for the happiness of Germany." Then they sing the "Horst Wessel Lied."

It is almost three in the afternoon. A small plane lands at Bremen Airport from Berlin. Its passenger, Hauptsturmführer

SS Gildisch, has had a busy morning in the capital. Now Goering has given him a new assignment. As Ernst is leaving the banquet, an SA tries to warn him. Ernst, flushed with power, the banquet, the singing and the flowers, shrugs his shoulders. At the hotel Gildisch waits with his Gestapo agents. He informs Ernst he is under arrest; he, Gildisch, has been ordered to take him to Berlin. Ernst protests, demands a telephone, shouts that he will miss his boat, demands to be taken to his comrade, Goering, to his friend Prince August Wilhelm von Hohenzollern, whom he addresses familiarly as Prince Auwi. The Prince is a Reichstag delegate like Ernst. They share a bench, sitting side by side. But Gildisch is not moved, and Ernst senses that for the moment there is nothing he can do. In Berlin, however, everything will be straightened out, because only a madman would imagine that in this Third Reich anything unpleasant could happen to Karl Ernst, personal friend of Prince Auwi, Reichstag deputy and SA Obergruppenführer. Ernst allows one of the agents to fasten the handcuffs. Gildisch shows him the car. He climbs in without protest, and soon the car is driving to the airport along the road bordering the Weser, lighted by the setting sun. The plane is ready to leave. Ernst climbs the short metal ladder. Like the Führer, who is just leaving Munich, he will fly to Berlin.

Throughout Germany, from the proud and ancient fortress of Königsberg to the dreaming castles of the Rhine Valley, from the sandy heaths of Brandenburg to the dark lakes of Bavaria, the long red twilight of a summer day begins.

⑥

Saturday, June 30, 1934
Berlin

The late afternoon sun lights the runways of the Berlin Tempelhof Airport. A huge disk, sharply outlined, yet somehow unreal, it sinks beneath the horizon. It is as if all sounds were muffled and life suspended, while the sun sinks, a bloody host, engulfing the earth. The SS are everywhere, black, heavy with steel, their helmets and weapons dully gleaming. They stand along the runways, in front of the hangars and on the roof of the control tower, outlined against the sky. Companies of the new, still clandestine Air Force of the Reich are drawn up in ranks, in the new blue-gray uniform chosen by Goering. Slowly the officials arrive: Goering, Himmler, Pili Körner, Daluege, Frick, SS officers, members of the SD and the Gestapo. Gisevius and Nebe are there too, standing apart, exchanging information, observing the scene. Goering walks toward the Air Force troops, then "planted firmly, on legs somewhat astride, he stands in the middle of the square, speaking to the soldiers of fidelity and the spirit of comradeship," Gisevius remembers.

While the Nazis are tearing each other apart, while comrades-in-arms devour each other, and the trap closes around the calm and then astounded men of the same party as their pursuers, Hermann Goering's speech is not without an aspect of macabre humor: "Soldiers, you should be proud that you are becoming an official troop, which one day will be remembered."

"Everyone," Gisevius writes, "guesses that this hypocritical scene has been improvised simply to kill time, to relax nerves. There are none of the usual projectors, photographers, loudspeakers. This incoherent speech takes place in the dusk, and no one really listens to it."

Goering speaks to break the silence, for after the day of tension, the waiting is unbearable. Gisevius and Nebe feel it too. Everyone is anxious for darkness to fall, as if it may somehow soothe the torment which has spread across the Reich since dawn.

Little by little, as the hours pass, the number of informed people has grown. Early in the afternoon, details begin to penetrate official circles in the capital. The bars near the Leipzigerplatz, patronized by journalists, do an exceptional business for a Saturday afternoon. Everyone comes to find out what he can; it is rumored that Roehm, Papen and Schleicher have been arrested, perhaps even executed. Journalists have found it difficult to enter the district where the ministries are concentrated. On the Charlottenburger Chaussee, which crosses the Tiergarten and ends at the Brandenburg Gate, it is almost impossible to move. There are police barriers and Army trucks, and as everyone must take this road—the Tiergartenstrasse being closed—traffic moves at a snail's pace. It is known that troops have occupied the southern part of the Tiergarten. Clearly a large operation is under way, and no one who lives in the west of Berlin—between Unter den Linden, the Wilhelmstrasse and the Bendlerstrasse—can ignore the house searches by the SS, the arrests, the killings, the troop movements. Employees of the ministries, like Gisevius—although they do not have a complete grasp of the situation—are beginning to perceive the magnitude of the purge, which has touched the entire opposition.

Even now the known circumstances of particular incidents make it possible to reconstruct particular moments of the day. It is known, for example, that Gottfried Reinhold Treviranus, former minister in the governments of Brüning and General Schleicher, the leader of that fraction of the Nationalist Party which in 1929 refused to yield to the demands of Hitler and Hugenberg, has, miraculously, managed to escape the assassins. The SS got to his house too late. They followed him to the Wannsee Tennis Club, but Treviranus, in the middle of a game, saw the four SS men talking at the entrance of the club. Understanding immediately that they had come to arrest him, jumping over the fence, he managed to reach Grunewald. Hidden by a friend, he escaped to England a few days later.

Most, however, have no chance. Gregor Strasser is immediately locked up with the other SA. No need to question him: what matters for Goering, Himmler and Heydrich is holding him. The SA prisoners surround the former leader of the Party; his presence reassures them. What can happen to them while Strasser is there, alive, with them? At five o'clock, an SS takes Strasser to a separate cell, its wall broken by a large hole. Shortly after his arrival in this cell, Strasser must have glimpsed a shadow aiming a pistol at him through the hole. He tries to dodge when the gun is fired, but he is wounded. Three SS enter his cell to finish him off. Blood pours from his wound, but his breath will rattle for a long time. If Heydrich had been told, he would have said: "Not dead yet? Well, leave the pig to bleed." Thus ends, in the cellars of the Gestapo, one of the original Nazis, a man to whom Hitler owed everything as the organizer of the Party, a man with enormous insight and a keenly political mind; a man of brutal honesty. Many times Strasser had condemned Hitler, Himmler, Goering and Goebbels— once his secretary, whom he had trained and who later abandoned him. The official explanation will be suicide.

Often a victim resigns himself to the killers, deliberately choosing death. Toward four o'clock that Saturday afternoon, General von Bredow, formerly of the Bendlerstrasse, and an intimate friend of General Schleicher, removed from the War Ministry shortly after the dismissal of his leader, appears at the Adlon. The people there, mostly government officials and diplomats, are astonished to see him still alive. The rumors of Schleicher's death are more and more insistent. Now Bredow is here at the Adlon, in the heart of the trap, this grand hotel on Unter den Linden, patrolled by the SS and the Gestapo. To a friend who asks him if he has heard the news, Bredow replies: "I wonder why the pigs haven't killed me yet." Several people come up to shake his hand or sit at his table—acts of courage, for everyone knows that the waiters also work for Heydrich and Himmler.

After a moment's hesitation, a foreign military attaché invites Bredow to dine at his house, to remove him from danger for a few hours. General Bredow shakes his hand warmly.

"I thank you," he says. "I left home very early this morning. I wish to go back there, now that I have had the pleasure of having seen my friends once more."

In vain, people try to change his mind, but Bredow feels a great sense of lassitude. The time, for him, is one of disgust and despair. "They have assassinated Schleicher," he explains, "and he was the only man who could have saved Germany. He was my leader. There is nothing left for me."

With a simple salute and a large tip for the servile waiter who is about to report to the Gestapo, General von Bredow leaves the Adlon to walk down Unter den Linden with its late-afternoon bustle. He is not seen alive again. In the evening, the killers ring his bell and open fire.

Bredow is the second Reichswehr general killed that day. However, at five o'clock, when Goering presents himself to the press at the Chancellory, the anxiety he and Himmler felt when they learned of Schleicher's death seems to have completely evaporated. In the crowded room foreign correspondents, editors-in-chief of the more important German newspapers and a number of political personalities have gathered; partially informed, they want to know more.

The heat is suffocating, and Gisevius notes that the atmosphere is one of "unbearable tension." "Goering arrives in full uniform," he writes, "and walks to the speakers' platform. He takes his place with an air of portentous importance. After a long pause that is extremely effective, he leans forward and, resting his chin in his hand, rolls his eyes, as if afraid of the revelations he has to make, as if he had practiced before a mirror. Then he begins speaking in the lugubrious tone and flat voice of a practiced funeral orator."

His manner is haughty. An official statement will be given to the press tomorrow; for the moment, he has no time to discuss details as the action is still in process, and he is directing it, by the Führer's order. "For weeks we have been watching; we knew that some of the leaders of the Sturmabteilung had taken positions very far from the aims and goals of the movement, giving priority to their own interests and ambitions, indulging their unfortunate and perverse tastes." Goering makes liberal use of long pauses; he strides up and down the platform, with his hands on his hips. "What seemed to us most deserving of condemnation," he adds, "is that the leadership of the SA raised the phantom of a second Revolution, allegedly directed against the reactionaries, but in reality partly allied with them. The principal intermediary between these groups was the former Chancellor of the Reich, General von Schleicher, who put Roehm in touch with a foreign power. . . ."

Goering whirls about on the platform, a pirouette of satisfaction.

"I have enlarged my mission by striking a heavy blow at these malcontents."

Goering prepares to leave the room. A foreign journalist stands up and begins a question concerning the fate of General Schleicher. Goering stops, smiles and turns back to the audience.

"Yes," he says, "I know you journalists are fond of fancy titles. Well, listen to me. General von Schleicher was plotting against the regime. I ordered his arrest. He made the mistake of attempting to resist. He is dead."

Goering is pleased by the surprise his announcement produces. Before leaving the room he pauses to observe the journalists' reactions. A Reichswehr officer distributes the text of a communiqué from General von Reichenau, expressing the official view from the Bendlerstrasse, and therefore of the Reichswehr. The text proves that Reichenau and his chief, Blomberg, make common cause with the SS killers and with the Gestapo, that they have decided to ignore the violations of law, and all the attacks on the prerogatives of the Officers' Corps. Schleicher, the Army General most listened to and respected, is vilified. This decision will weigh heavily on the future of the Reich and the German Army.

Reichenau, the traditional officer, dignified, wearing his monocle and holding himself stiffly erect in his perfectly fitting uniform, does not hesitate to write: "General Schleicher was suspected of involvement in the plot organized by Roehm, and two SS were sent to arrest him. Unfortunately, the General vehemently resisted arrest, and the police were obliged to use their weapons. Fire was exchanged and the General and his wife, who appeared unexpectedly on the scene, were mortally wounded."

Goering's assurance is easy to understand. In the streets of Berlin, everything has returned to normal. Unter den Linden is filled with people out for a walk, and the sidewalk cafés of the Kurfürstendamm overflow with the Saturday evening crowds, enjoying the fine, warm twilight of this last day of June. The barriers in the Tiergarten have been removed, and young couples again walk down the tree-lined lanes which converge at the Floraplatz. The evening editions of the large newspapers announce simply that Obergruppenführer Lutze has replaced Roehm as head of the Sturmabteilung. The news is on the fourth page. There is no trace of the statements of Goering and Reichenau, which were delivered too late for publication.

Nevertheless, in conversations conducted in lowered voices,

the names "Lichterfelde" and "Columbus House" keep recurring —the two places of detention for persons arrested during the day.

Executions take place at the military school at Lichterfelde. There, Air Force Captain Gehrt, formerly a member of Goering's squadron and a chevalier of the Order of Merit, is forced to wear his decorations, so that Goering can rip them from him. The firing squads are from Sepp Dietrich's Leibstandarte SS—comrades of the men executing the Sturmabteilung officers in the Stadelheim Prison in Munich. There, one salvo followed another throughout the afternoon, punctuated by shouts and cries, and sometimes a "Heil Hitler!" from a condemned man who doesn't understand why he is dying, and salutes the man in whom he believed, in whom he still does. This will be the case with Karl Ernst.

At Tempelhof Airfield, while they wait for Hitler's plane, officials see a single-engined Junker come down at the end of a runway. The plane rolls slowly toward the control tower. As soon as it stops, Hauptsturmführer Gildisch jumps to the ground; then, with an SS on each side of him, Obergruppenführer SA Karl Ernst. They have come from Bremen. Ernst is confident. "He seemed to be in a very good humor," Gisevius notes. "He jumped from the plane and into the car, smiling in every direction, as if to show the world that he did not take his arrest seriously." He certainly has no idea of what is really happening. He is to die at Lichterfelde, victim of a plot he doesn't understand, shouting out his belief in Hitler—perhaps even persuaded that he is dying for him.

Hitler's plane arrives shortly after Ernst's. The Junker flies slowly over the field and into the middle distance before turning back to land, touching down and taxiing almost exactly to the spot where the SS Honor Guard is waiting. The moment is exceptional: the Führer has been away from the capital for days. The details of this return are striking, and remain precisely engraved in Gisevius' memory.

"BRAVO, ADOLF!"

Goering, Himmler and the other officials walk toward the plane. Hitler appears first, and after the clicking heels and salutes come Brückner, Schaub, Sepp Dietrich and finally Goebbels, with his sinister smile. Hitler seems to be walking slowly, "painfully, with heavy steps, between the puddles. He looked as though he might collapse at any moment. . . . Everything he wore was dark: brown shirt, black tie, leather coat, and high, regulation boots. Bareheaded, his badly shaven face was as white as a sheet, deeply lined and puffy. His eyes were dull, set in a fixed stare, half-covered by his heavy lids." Gisevius adds: "He filled me with disgust."

Himmler and Goering accompany the Führer. When this group stops for a moment, the others stop too, keeping their distance. "Himmler pulled a long, wrinkled list from his sleeve," Gisevius records. "While Hitler looked at it, the two men kept talking. One could see Hitler following the list with his finger, stopping from time to time at a particular name. . . . Suddenly, Hitler threw back his head with a gesture of such profound emotion, not to say disgust, that everyone noticed it. Nebe and I looked at each other: we both had the same thought: he has just learned of Strasser's 'suicide.' "

The scene is one of symbolic violence, like the last act of a tragedy or an opera set, as Gisevius recalls, against "a red, Wagnerian twilight." As the group of important figures move toward the waiting cars, there is even an isolated cry from the top of a hangar where crews and maintenance men have collected to watch the Führer's arrival. The unexpected shout crashes through the silence: "Bravo, Adolf!" It is repeated: "Bravo, Adolf!" An ill-placed salute from the people, as in a Shakespearean drama, a moment of farcical counterpoint, as if to remind these powerful men, victors at the close of this bloody day, of the mocking and provisional character of their triumph.

7

Saturday Night, June 30;
Sunday, July 1; Monday, July 2, 1934

The official cars have left Tempelhof; the SS and Air Force units are beginning to drive off. The silence of the empty airfield is broken occasionally by brief, guttural orders. The sun has disappeared below the horizon; nothing is left but a red glow streaked by gray clouds.

Before returning to the Ministry of the Interior, Gisevius eats a quick dinner in a little restaurant on the Kurfürstendamm, where many civil servants from the different branches of government often eat. There, at a discreet table at the back of the room, Gisevius sees Colonel Hans Oster, one of the heads of the Abwehr, who, Gisevius knows, has had consistent reservations about the Nazis. Gisevius sits down opposite Oster, and the two men quietly exchange information over dinner. Gisevius writes: "I realized then that at the War Ministry they were still unaware of most of the shootings." In fact, if some officers have remained on the sidelines, it is because Reichenau and Blomberg had bought them off with favors and advancement. Naturally, Oster is among those who were kept in ignorance; now he expresses his indignation to Gisevius over the methods used by Reichsführer Himmler and Heydrich. Gisevius agrees with what he says; as they part, the two anti-Nazis foresee that "The Gestapo will have to account for what it has done; this time it has definitely gone too far."

.But the reign of the Gestapo is only just beginning; for Himmler and Heydrich the day has been a crucial stage in the irresistible rise of the forces they control.

On Saturday night, Himmler and Heydrich are at the Chancellory with the Führer and Hermann Goering. After a few moments, Heydrich leaves Hitler alone with Goering and Himmler. They speak freely, evaluating the success of the day: the number of men executed before they even understood what was happening to them is proof of the victors' determination. Goering is the first to mention Roehm, still alive in his cell in Stadelheim. Hitler's hesitation makes them anxious. Does it mean that he plans to turn the argument against them, presenting himself as an impartial arbiter with clean hands, letting the blood fall on them alone? They must push him to the final decisive act forever linking his destiny with theirs. They remind him of Roehm's responsibilities, his dissolute morals, which caused a new scandal to break out almost daily; for instance, the suitcase which the Chief of Staff left on the staircase of a brothel, and all the subterfuges which had to be used to keep the affair from bursting into public notice. The Army also demands his head: yesterday he was excluded from the Officers' Corps by Blomberg, and today, now that Schleicher has been killed, how can the Reichswehr accept Roehm's survival? Justice cannot make exceptions. Justice —the word fills Goering's mouth—in the name of justice, Roehm must die. Hitler still hesitates, and when Goering and Himmler leave the Chancellory, nothing has yet been decided about the leader of the Sturmabteilung, who is dozing fitfully in the heat of his cell.

It is between eleven and midnight, Saturday, June 30, 1934. At Lichterfelde, the executions are suspended: the residents of the houses near the Cadet School are at last allowed a respite from the anguish of those gunshots punctuated by orders and cries which all day have broken the silence of this remote district. In the center of Berlin, the cafés are gradually emptying; quiet family groups who have walked to the Brandenburg Gate return along Unter den Linden, past the Ministry of the Interior of the Reich. Although everything in that large building seems calm, the senior civil servants who work there are afraid. Daluege, the head of the Prussian police and a general, is talking to Gisevius and Grauert, who are drawing up a balance sheet of the day's events, preliminary to a report. Then he announces that, considering the situation, he is going to set up a camp bed in his office for the night. Gisevius decides to do the same, and chooses the office of an absent colleague: who would think of looking for him in the Ministry, behind a door marked with someone else's name? Before settling in, he chats for a moment with Daluege's ADC. "I made him understand that our chief's decision to spend the night in his office was proof of his zeal. 'What?' replies his loyal aide. 'Zeal? Zeal?' His face suddenly turns bright red, and his voice trembles. 'He's afraid . . . that's why he's not going home tonight.' "

In every town of the Reich there are men who are afraid. In the cells of ·Stadelheim, Lichterfelde, Columbus House, or in the cellars of Prinz-Albrecht Strasse, they wait for the footsteps of the SS who may come at any moment to shoot them, or lead them to the firing squad. They listen in the darkness to catch the steps of soldiers lining up, the sounds of guns being loaded. They are afraid, and their terror is all the greater because they know none of the reasons which have brought them to their present situation, helpless before the will of a regime they know is without pity. They had been part of this regime, and their astonishment at being turned upon adds to their fear. In strange apartments, in borrowed clothes, with false identities, other men are trying, in anguish, to escape the killers; wounded men, who have miraculously evaded search parties, walk doubled over, through the woods around Berlin, their faces distorted by pain and fear. Still others, who seem to be safe, are afraid because they have learned that arbitrary whim is the sovereign rule of the Reich, and that tomorrow, or even today, they themselves may be the next victims.

Fear, terror and anguish mark this short night for thousands. And at seven in the morning, while Germany fills with clear, joyous light, the excited, metallic voice of Joseph Goebbels enters the homes of thousands, uttering insults, threats and death. Over the radio, Goebbels gives an account of the Night of Long Knives, which crushed its victims, his former comrades:

"They have discredited the honor and prestige of our Sturm-abteilung. By a life of unparalleled debauchery, by their parade of high living, by their feasting and carousing, they have damaged the principles of simplicity and personal decency which our Party supports. They were close to tainting the entire leadership with their shameful and disgusting sexual aberrations."

Tens of thousands of German families, on their way to church, feel a sense of calm indignation at Goebbels' account of the shocking debauchery. Fortunately, Hitler, a righteous leader, has punished them. "They thought," continues Goebbels, "that the Führer's tolerance was weakness. . . . Any warning was greeted by a cynical smile. As kindness proved useless, stern measures became necessary. The Führer can be great in his goodness; he can also be great in his severity. . . ."

Children rise from their beds to hear this voice. Mothers prepare breakfast. In the country, the heady smell of hay comes through the open windows. German life continues, calm, docile, respectful: the Night of Long Knives seems to have taken place somewhere else.

"Millions of members of our Party, the SA and the SS congratulate themselves for this storm of purification. The entire nation can breathe easier, delivered from a nightmare."

And it is true that on this Sunday morning there are many who feel delivered. They buy the papers and find the list of five

SA Obergruppenführers who have been shot; they read that Lutze has replaced Roehm. The SA have been brought to their senses. The drunken carousing, brawls and scandals which have disturbed the peace of countless small towns are now over, and order—the order for which Germans voted in the Nazis—is about to be established. They were not mistaken to put their trust in the Führer. As Goebbels said on the radio: " The Führer has decided to act without pity when the principles of decency, simplicity and public propriety are at stake; and the punishment must be all the greater when the persons concerned occupy the highest positions."

The respectable readers of the respectable *Deutsche All-gemeine Zeitung* are reassured. There will be no more talk in Germany of the second Revolution, so dear to the SA. "An energetic government has struck in time," they read in their paper. "It has struck with staggering accuracy, and has done all it could to assure the tranquillity of every patriot, who no longer need fear any harm or disturbance. . . . We now have a strong, consolidated and purified state. We need not dwell on the repulsive details which constituted the background of that pseudo revolution."

Everything is calm. Berlin looks magnificent in the summer sunlight; the parks are full of children at play. The American Ambassador, Dodd, drives slowly about the city in his car. Twice, he passes the residence of Franz von Papen, but except for a police car parked near the house, everything seems normal. The official news agency, DNB, has been sending out extra bulletins, which are broadcast, seeming to confirm that everything in Germany is perfectly normal.

"In Silesia," the first communiqué states, "the actions necessary to end the attempted revolution were carried out in perfect calm and tranquillity. The majority of the SA remained loyal to the Führer. The night between Saturday and Sunday was peaceful throughout Silesia. The SA sent a telegram to the Führer declaring their loyalty. The Gauleiter also sent a telegram to

Adolf Hitler to assure him of Silesia's loyalty." The SA leader, Wilhelm Scheppman, commander of the Niederrhein and Westphalian groups, also telegraphed: "We continue along the road toward the goals assigned to us by the Führer. We feel certain, in this way, of our service to the German people." Kaufmann, the Gauleiter of Hamburg, assures the Führer of his district's fidelity, and Loeper, Reichsstatthalter of Braunschweig-Anhalt, reaffirms his blind obedience to the Führer; Marschler, Gauleiter of Thuringia, swears loyalty to the Führer. "The Führer and his work cannot be touched," he writes. Streicher, Gauleiter of Franconia, declares that only noxious and dangerous persons have been arrested: "The Führer has triumphed, and we swear our loyalty to him."

Every leader of every Nazi organization sends a telegram of submission, and the officers of the Sturmabteilung are among the first. They have survived; no matter that they are on their knees.

The Führer's victory is thus complete Sunday morning, and the Reichswehr congratulates him. On the surface, the Reichswehr has won. In his order of the day, dictated to Lutze, Hitler stresses that ". . . above all, each SA officer must conduct himself toward the Army in a spirit of perfect honesty, loyalty and fidelity."

Roehm's ambition—to make the SA the core of a new Army of the Reich, has been thoroughly destroyed. The arms accumulated by the SA are handed over to the Reichswehr. On July 5, after inspecting the Sturmabteilung stores, General Liese, head of military supplies, exclaims: "I won't need to buy any more guns for a long time!" General Blomberg's proclamation of July 1 to the troops is the price the Army pays for Hitler's work. A copy is displayed in every barracks and officers' mess, and is read aloud to the men as they stand at attention:

> With military determination, and exemplary courage, the Führer himself has attacked and crushed the rebels. The Army, bearing arms for the entire nation, has remained aloof from the internal political struggle.

> The Army expresses its gratitude through devotion
> and fidelity. The Führer requires good relations be-
> tween the Army and the new SA. The Army will apply
> itself to the furthering of these good relations in full
> awareness of our common ideal.

Thus the Führer has carried the day: he is held up to the
common soldiers by the Minister of Defense as a prime example
of soldierliness, a model to emulate. The blood of Generals
Schleicher and Bredow has dried quickly: the upheaval seems
over.

However, when Ambassador Dodd tries to telephone von
Papen, there is no answer: the line is still cut. And in the Lichterfelde district, suddenly, in the middle of the morning, the sound
of firing breaks out anew: the executions at the Cadet School
have begun again. Every twenty minutes, one hears the shouted
command before the burst of firing; then, separated by the space
of a few seconds, the dry crack of the *coup de grâce*. For the
families of officers living in the barracks the tension is so unbearable that many leave their apartments to take refuge with relatives
in Berlin.

(Sunday, July 1, 1 P.M.)

Despite appearances, therefore, the affair continues. How
can it be over while Ernst Roehm is still alive? Late in the morning, Himmler and Goering return to the Chancellory, where the
Führer's flag with its huge swastika is flying. Berliners out for the
Sunday sights applaud the official cars. No one among these people
holding up their children to see General Goering and the Reichsführer SS could guess that these two men are going to try to
obtain from Hitler the promise of Roehm's death.

In the Chancellory the discussion is long and heated. Hitler,
refreshed after a long night's rest, is disposed to resist. He cannot

admit that alive Roehm is a weapon which may be used against Goering and Himmler. He recalls Roehm's services in years past, but these are feeble arguments, as they could just as well have been used for Heydebreck or Ernst, Schleicher or Strasser. Hitler yields, little by little, and shortly before one o'clock in the afternoon Sunday, July 1, he gives in. Goering stands up and walks about the room, radiating satisfaction. Himmler, more modest than Goering, appears to be meditating—hiding the harsh joy he feels.

A few minutes later, the Führer telephones the Ministry of the Interior in Munich, which has become, in effect, the headquarters of the repression. The officers of the SS Leibstandarte Adolf Hitler have established themselves there, as has Theodor Eicke, Commandant of Dachau, one of the first people to be warned by Heydrich of what was coming. He has been waiting at the Ministry for orders from Berlin. When they come, they are precise, and directly from Hitler. Roehm is to be killed. He is to be invited, first, to commit suicide.

Immediately, Eicke chooses two absolutely reliable SS: Sturmbannführer Michael Lippert and Gruppenführer Schmauser. The three men check their weapons, and proceed to the Stadelheim Prison.

1 P.M. A large crowd is waiting in front of the high doors of the Chancellory in Berlin. Children shout joyfully, escaping momentarily from their parents. The SS police good-naturedly accept the jostling of the crowd: the changing of the guard at the Chancellory is one of the most popular attractions in Berlin. Now the relief unit arrives, like mechanical puppets of flesh and blood, marching in parade step, stamping their metaled heels on the pavement. A huge drum major twirls a flag, its pole fitted with bells, and the band plays the "Horst Wessel Lied," then, while the soldiers go through their paces, the "Deutschland Lied," and the "Badenweilermarsch." At last the Führer appears in the Chancellory window on the first floor—the window at which he has appeared so often since his first days as head of the gov-

ernment, when he saluted enthusiastic crowds and torchlight parades. The crowd sees him and greets him with cries of joy. The Führer looks rested, his hair is neatly combed, he speaks with animation to General Litzmann, the Commandant of the guard, and to Minister Frick. He salutes the crowd and leaves the window with apparent regret. The crowd cheers again and then disperses, while the soldiers execute their meticulous quadrille. Many of the parents and children go on to the Tiergarten, and its cool, shadowy walks, as the afternoon begins, heavy and hot.

At 2:30 P.M. Eicke, Lippert and Schmauser arrive at Stadelheim Prison. The building seems to be sunk in sleep. The SS on guard salute their officers, who proceed immediately to the office of the director, Dr. Koch. Koch has had hardly any rest since the day before, and his face is marked with fear and fatigue. When he admits Oberführer Eicke, and Eicke demands that Roehm be handed over, Koch seems stunned. As he did before with Sepp Dietrich, Koch insists on a written order. Minister of Justice Frank, consulted with by telephone, gives verbal approval. Eicke protests, storms, speaks to Frank, and finally Koch yields. A prison guard is ordered to take the three SS officers to Roehm's cell—No. 474. Roehm, still naked to the waist, has apparently lost his will. He watches Eicke come in, watches him put a copy of the *Völkischer Beobachter* on the table. It reports the dismissal of Roehm and lists the names of the executed SA. Eicke also places a revolver on the table, loaded with a single bullet. Then he leaves.

In Berlin, at the Chancellory gardens Hitler gives a tea party for diplomats, ministers and high-ranking Reichswehr officers. Uniformed waiters offer a variety of drinks; there is the sound of laughter, and Goebbels' children run through the Chancellory. Outside a crowd cheers, unaware of the events continuing at Lichterfelde, where every twenty minutes shots ring out, unaware that at Stadelheim Roehm has been given the chance to kill himself. Hitler, smiling broadly, goes to the window and

269

salutes the crowd. Gisevius is there with his chief, Daluege, for whom the death of Ernst has meant the leadership of the SA of Berlin, Brandenburg and Pomerania. Hitler catches sight of Gisevius: "He turned aside, and raised his hand to greet me with the same motionless attitude I had seen him assume twice before. He looked at me as if I myself were an admiring crowd. I felt myself shrink under his Caesar-like gaze; it occurred to me that if he could read my innermost thoughts, he would have me shot. But he seemed to wish me no ill. He simply wanted to play his role to the full."

Then Hitler goes back to the middle of the room, and Gisevius, who still watches him, concludes: "At this moment I understood how tense he was that day, how he was trying to escape his inner agony by taking refuge in the pose which had become his most effective weapon." In the middle of the room, surrounded by elegant women who laugh at his slightest joke, Hitler almost dances with excitement. It is clear that he enjoys the deferential attention he is getting from everyone, and in his white shirt and uniform jacket with the Iron Cross and swastika armband, he seems very different from the man who walked across the airfield at Munich-Oberwiesenfeld yesterday at 4 A.M.

What Roehm had seen was more than a tragic vision or nightmare. He remains sitting in his cell; he has not moved. After ten minutes, SS Lippert and Eicke open the door. "Roehm, make yourself ready," Eicke shouts. Lippert, his hand trembling, fires twice. Roehm still has time to murmur, "Mein Führer, mein Führer," before a third bullet kills him.

In Berlin, to the cheers of the crowd, Hitler appears at the Chancellory window a third time. As he steps back, an SS officer hands him a message, informing him of Roehm's death. Hitler turns quickly to his guests, and then a few minutes later goes to his private apartment. Himmler and the SS have won. The Goerings, Heydrichs, Goebbels, Bormanns and Buchs—all the con-

spirators—can now, without fear of disorder in the streets and the
general violence of the SA, dominate Germany. The SA has lost
its head, Roehm lies in a pool of blood. Hitler has once again
chosen order, and broken with his old comrade. Those who will
speak up to Hitler, like Frick, are very rare indeed. "Mein
Führer," Frick said, "if you do not act as radically with Himmler
and the SS as you did with Roehm, you will simply have replaced
the devil with Beelzebub."

But the SS will be a much more difficult problem than the SA.
Moreover, on this Sunday, July 1, it is still a question of finishing
with Roehm and his supporters. The radio announces that Gruppenführer von Obernitz, head of the SA of Franconia, orders:
(1) that Roehm's name be removed from all swords of honor;
(2) that all portraits of Roehm be disposed of; (3) that the Ernst-
Roehm House be renamed; henceforth it is to be designated the
Administrative Service of the SA of Franconia.

In Party printing houses the decision has already been made:
all photographs of Roehm, every memory of him, must disappear.
As for the SA, they are told again that they are on leave: "This
leave," a communiqué states, "granted to all the SA, will be
respected, by order of Chief of Staff Lutze so that members of the
SA, after a year and a half of rigorous service, may rest and spend
time with their families." The death of Roehm, in effect, means
the end of the Sturmabteilung as an autonomous force. It is also
the signal for the deaths of a certain number of SA so far spared,
but who are now sought out in the cells of the Lichterfelde
school, or at Columbus House.

With fixed bayonets, the SS accompany the condemned men
to the wall. There is the brief command: "By order of the
Führer. Aim. Fire!" Sometimes prisoners from Columbus House
are driven by car to Lichterfelde, and executed there, in the courtyard of the Cadet School. This is to be the fate of Gruppenführer
SA Karl Schreyer. But when the moment comes to take him to
Lichterfelde, the car has not yet arrived. When Schreyer is finally
pushed into the car, a wide, black Mercedes suddenly drives up

at top speed, and brakes violently in front of Columbus House. It is about four o'clock Monday morning, July 2, 1934. The Standartenführer who jumps from the car announces that the Führer has just put an end to all executions. Perhaps Hitler has decided that the number of victims—at least a hundred, perhaps a thousand or more—is now enough. He must now play the moderate, just and magnanimous. Perhaps, too, he fears a reaction from old Marshal Hindenburg.

To be sure, the President is completely isolated on his vast estate at Neudeck. To make it doubly secure, the SS are on guard among the trees in the park, checking all visitors. Furthermore, the Chamberlain, Count Schulenburg, sees that orders are followed scrupulously. When a friend of Hindenburg, Count von Oldenburg-Januschau, a Junker neighbor alerted by Papen, tries to see the President to tell him what is happening in Berlin, he is sent away: Hindenburg is ill, he cannot receive visitors. But Hitler is cautious. Since the SA is broken, its top leaders dead and so many old adversaries liquidated, why continue the purge? A few SA pamphlets may have been distributed in Berlin during the night of July 1, but their appeal—". . . Comrades of the SA, do not allow yourselves to be disarmed; hide your weapons, never allow yourselves to become the executioners of the working class" —enlists no one. Everything is calm and submissive. The elite, the Army, the Party all applaud, the people approve or are silent. And since the principal victims have been executed, mercy is now possible.

Forty-eight hours earlier, Roehm, Spreti, Heines and his young SA were resting in the little rooms of the Pension Hanselbauer. Schleicher, Bredow, Schmidt and Kahr slept or worked peacefully in their homes—as did others like them, innocent or guilty—who would be killed without trial during those forty-eight hours of high summer, the Night of Long Knives.

EPILOGUE

On Monday, July 2, 1934, toward eight in the morning, a
motorcyclist from the Bavarian Ministry of the Interior stops
in front of a middle-class house in a suburb of Munich to deliver
an envelope to one of the tenants. It contains a long telegram
from the central office of the Gestapo in Berlin, and the sender—
a member of the SD—has participated in the actions, arrests and
executions of these last forty-eight hours. His wife reads the message aloud to their children:

> My dearest, we have had to mount a huge effort
> because of Roehm's mutiny. We have worked until 3
> or 4 in the morning; after that, telephone calls every
> ten minutes. We are so tired we could drop, and yet,
> also, freed from a nightmare. I embrace you. Your
> Papa.

Undoubtedly, the Gestapo agent is asleep at the moment
his family is informed of his activities, relieved to know that he

is safe and has done his job, as he himself is relieved at last to be able to sleep. Nazis are not often troubled by conscience.

This Monday morning, fatigue crushes everyone who has played an active part in the Night of Long Knives. Now it is necessary to begin living again as though nothing had happened, and yet everyone knows that a great deal has happened. The wives of the victims haunt the ministries, asking for news of their husbands, begging that at least they be given the body, for proper burial. Usually, the widows are roughly turned away, because the dead men themselves, with the exception of the ten or so mentioned in the press, do not exist, or exist only in the imagination of the foreign press, or the émigré organizations, bombarding the German people with appeals which they cannot and do not wish to hear. The exiled Social-Democrats declare in a manifesto:

> The gang of criminals who have thrown themselves on Germany are drenched in mud and blood. Hitler accuses his closest collaborators, the very men who brought him to power, of the most shameless moral depravities. . . . But it is he who required of them terror and assassinations. . . . He tolerated and approved their atrocities, called them his comrades. . . . Today he allows them to be assassinated, not because of their crimes, but to save himself. . . . One hundred thousand satraps in brown shirts have rushed across Germany like a cloud of locusts. . . .

The citizens of the Reich are unaware of this text. On Monday morning, July 2, they go to work as usual. The subway stations at the Wilhelmstrasse and Unter den Linden disgorge ministerial employees as usual; at the sound of the siren, the day shift floods into the sheds at Krupps. Everything proceeds as if nothing extraordinary had happened.

In the Berlin subway, in the streets of Munich, in Frankfurt, Germans read in their papers only the official bulletins, which announce that "the traitor, Roehm, refusing to accept the consequences of his acts, has been executed." The *Kreuz-Zeitung* writes: "We shall never be able to repay entirely our debt of gratitude to the Führer." All the papers, with occasional reservations largely ignored by the majority of readers, approve the repression. The Frankfurt *Gazette,* with more reservations than most papers, nevertheless writes: "All Germans must conclude that the unprecedented severity of the punishment corresponds to an unprecedented crime."

Life continues as if nothing has happened; the crimes must leave no trace. On Monday morning, Gisevius finds himself, completely exhausted, in his office at the Ministry. He is brought a message delivered to the Ministry by mistake. He reads:

> The Minister-President of Prussia and the Head of the Secret Police have assumed complete police authority. By highest order, all documents relating to the action of the past two days must be burned. Report immediately after executing this order.

"Should we burn our radiograms too?" the messenger, a police officer, asks Gisevius.

He holds out a bundle of little white slips on which questions and information from all parts of Germany have been recorded, preserving an hour-by-hour development of the action.

"Of course. They should be destroyed at once," Gisevius replies.

"Somewhat roughly," he remembers, "I snatched the bundle from his hands. As soon as his back was turned, I locked it in my strong box."

Thus a few traces are preserved for history. But ordinary Germans know nothing of all this—an ignorance often deliberate, as when a colleague or neighbor who has vanished, like Tschirschky, for instance, reappears with a shaven head, or when the wife of Bose, mother of two young children, suffers a nervous collapse upon learning that her husband is dead as she is handed

an urn containing a few ashes. Even a corpse can reveal something
of how a man died, but ashes are totally mute. If relatives insist,
if they know the right people, they will sometimes be sent these
small gray urns. The widow of Oberführer Hoffmann receives an
urn marked No. 262; Gregor Strasser's is No. 16.

"YOU HAVE SAVED THE GERMAN PEOPLE"

Conformism and terror weigh down Germany, but no one
wants to know it. The prisoners themselves are silent, horror
revealed only on their faces. When they speak, it is to praise the
Gestapo, its prisons and methods and the just, magnanimous
Führer. Even the close associates of President Hindenburg are
afraid. On Monday, July 2, the papers print a telegram dated
Neudeck, signed by Marshal Hindenburg:

> To the Chancellor of the Reich, the Führer, Adolf
> Hitler:
> According to reports sent to me, it appears that,
> thanks to the firmness of decision and courage which
> you showed, exposing your own person, the attempted
> high treason was crushed. You have saved the Ger-
> man people from grave danger. I am obliged to ex-
> press to you my profound thanks and recognition.
> REICH PRESIDENT FIELD MARSHAL VON HINDENBURG

The highest authority in the Reich, its greatest living military
man, this old man of eighty-seven years, symbol of Germanic
tradition, thus approves all the violations of right, all the assassinations carried out during that long night, and Hitler becomes the
sacred savior of the German people. On the same day, Hindenburg thanks Hermann Goering:

> I wish to express to you my gratitude and recogni-
> tion for your energetic action crowned with success in

the crushing of this attempted high treason. I send you
fraternal greetings.

VON HINDENBURG

Perhaps these messages were not sent out by Hindenburg
himself. Later, in 1945, when Papen, Goering and Marshal Keitel
were reunited in a cell at Nuremberg during the War Crimes
Trial, Papen raised this issue: "When I asked Goering whether,
in his opinion, Hindenburg had seen the telegram of congratulations sent in his name to Hitler, he quoted a sally of Meissner,
Secretary of State to the Presidency. On several occasions, speaking of this telegram, Meissner asked, with a meaningful smile:
'By the way, Mr. Prime Minister, were you satisfied with the
wording of the message?' "

But what matters is that the message establishes a link between the old Marshal, General Goering and his thugs. The chain
of complicity stretches from Hindenburg to Hauptsturmführer
Gildisch, shooting defenseless men in the back. The conscience
of the German people, calmly going about their affairs on this
Monday morning, is imprisoned by Nazism.

Thus Monday, July 2, brings new success to the Führer: the
road to the Presidency of the Reich is now wide open. The final
barrier will fall at Hindenburg's death.

Life continues. Tanned from their Saturday and Sunday
outings on the shores of the lakes around Berlin, workers return
to their offices to find everything as usual except perhaps a member
of the secretariat who whispers that two or three people will not
be in; they disappeared on Saturday. No one asks questions. The
machine is running smoothly again. As Gisevius writes: "The
second of July, the law and bureaucratic routine are restored;
everything once again resumes its normal functioning. Hard-work-
ing officials manipulate legal formulae to cover the events of the
past few days."

The parades have begun again too. In Essen, early that
evening, the police clear the streets of traffic. Official city and

Party cars, with SS on the running boards, and loudspeakers on the roofs, drive slowly through the foggy streets, palely streaked with July sunlight. It is hot and humid, as if a storm is about to break; a heavy cloud of industrial fumes and dust hangs over the city. Tirelessly, the loudspeakers repeat their proclamation: "People of Essen, Germans of the Third Reich: the city of Essen will celebrate the victory over criminal revolt, high treason and reaction by decorating the city with a massive display of flags: hang out your flags!"

It is an order. Shortly after the cars drive through the streets, they are followed by teams of men handing out huge flags, which will soon hang down the fronts of buildings. At 8:45 sirens wail: it is still light enough to distinguish the colors of the uniforms, and the red armbands. SA units are grouped in various squares through the town; the SA Standarte 219 has assembled on the playing field near Kopfstadtplatz. But the glory of the day belongs to the SS and the Party, assembled on the Adolf-Hitler Platz. A crowd is there too—large, disciplined, less lively, more passive than in Berlin. Employees of the metallurgical firms, factory workers, women, children, they press up behind the SS and SA. At exactly 8:45 Gauleiter Terboven stands up on the platform erected in the square. He looks serious, and proud, as he has since the Führer came to his wedding just a few hours before striking down his enemies. His speech is broadcast to five sections of town, from the Kopfstadtplatz to the Pferdemarktplatz. Through the loudspeakers one can hear the applause of the crowd which often threatens to drown his words.

"Loyalty is fundamental," Terboven declares. "The abscess has been drained. Naturally, there is still some corruption, as in any place, at any time. But what matters is to know how to act against the gangrene."

From time to time, the crowd interrupts Terboven to applaud, and when he shouts "Sieg Heil," the SS and SA roar in overwhelming reply, echoed in every square. Other officers and officials speak, then the parade begins, while the SS bands, dressed in black, beat time on their drums hung with the death's-head. They play "Im Ruhrgebiet marschieren wir" ("Marching Through the Ruhr"). As the SS march by at the head of the parade, the watching crowd, knowing no details, understands it is seeing the new face of Hitler's Reich. Throughout Germany the SS is being honored. The crowd silently scatters into the hot summer night, and the SS units, cheered and flattered, return to their camps. The men and officers of the Black Guard know they have emerged victorious from the Night of Long Knives.

That evening, Frau von Papen and her daughters return to Berlin. They are worried: Frau Tschirschky has told them of her husband's arrest, and they do not know what is intended for the Vice Chancellor. The police car is still parked in front of von Papen's villa, and the captain in charge is still there, guarding the entrance. But Franz von Papen is alive, beside himself with fury, cursing the Nazis and this retreat which has been forced on him. The next day, Tuesday, July 3, his telephone is restored—temporarily. The first call to come through is from Hermann Goering. "He had the effrontery to ask me why I was not at the cabinet meeting which was just about to begin," Papen recalls. "For once, I replied in a voice considerably too sharp for a diplomat. Goering expressed his surprise to hear that I was still more or less under arrest, and begged me to forgive this oversight. A short while later, the men who had been guarding me were withdrawn, and I was able to go to the Chancellory."

In the hall where ministers meet to discuss affairs of government, Chancellor Hitler is moving from one man to the next. He seems to be relaxed and at the top of his form. Today, more than twenty-four hours since the last shots were fired, with the congratulations of General Blomberg and Marshal Hindenburg behind him, and the passive acceptance of the assassinations by the German people, he is sure that he has won another victory. His clarity of vision enabled him to make the right decisions at the right moment, destroying his adversaries in one decisive move.

Destiny has protected him, and he is now indeed the Führer. Everyone approaches him with an air of deference, confirming his power. Karl Schmitt, the Nazi jurist, reordering the law, adapting it to new circumstances, will not hesitate to write in recalling the events of the preceding days: "The Führer's action was a matter of simple jurisdiction, not subject to the processes of law or justice; the Führer himself is law and justice."

The Führer can do anything. The Minister of Justice has drawn up a law for the July 3 meeting of the Council of Ministers, whose adoption is certain. Its single article states: "The measures which were undertaken June 30 and July 1 and 2 conformed entirely to law, and were carried out against threats of high treason which endangered the nation's security."

No legal opinions are required. The Führer's wish is sufficient reason for killing anyone, in any way.

When the Vice Chancellor enters the room, Hitler walks over to him, radiating friendliness. "As he invited me to take my usual place," Papen remembers, "I told him it was out of the question and demanded a private interview." The two men move into the next room. Hitler seems understanding, and full of good will. As on previous occasions when he has achieved a desired result, he seems ready for concessions, presenting himself as a reasonable man, a healer of rifts.

"I told him sharply," Papen continues, "what had happened at the Vice Chancellory and at my house and demanded an immediate inquiry into the actions taken against my colleagues."

The Führer is silent. This could mean several things: that he knows nothing of the matter, that he will order an inquiry, that he is mocking Papen or that he agrees with what Papen has said. But when the Vice Chancellor reveals his intention to resign and to make the announcement public, Hitler refuses to allow it.

"The situation is too tense," he says. "I cannot accept your resignation until everything is calm again. While waiting, would you at least do me the favor of attending the next meeting of the Reichstag, where I will account for my actions?"

It is Papen's turn to refuse. "I do not see any possibility of taking my ministerial seat," he says.

However, the Führer has obtained what he needed on the crucial question of Papen's resignation: it will remain secret. The public will know nothing of the differences of opinion between the Chancellor and the Vice Chancellor. The unity of the government of the Reich, from Hindenburg to Papen, from Blomberg to Rudolf Hess, seems complete: Roehm and the other victims were killed by unanimous consent. It is the façade which matters to the Führer. If Papen is not at the Reichstag session, sitting on the government bench, there will be time to deal with that. The session has been called for July 13, at the Kroll Opera House.

Hitler returns to the meeting hall alone and calm. Generals Blomberg, Hess, Goering and all the other ministers have taken their places around the long rectangular table. Hitler, standing with his fists pressed against his papers, will offer his version of the events.

As he talks, a feeling of violence grows. "Under the aegis of Roehm," he says, "a clique was formed, united by personal ambition and peculiar predispositions. . . ." His voice rises in anger and contempt. "Many times Roehm gave me his word of honor. I had always protected him, but he betrayed me, the Führer, outrageously, treacherously." Murdered, Roehm can only be guilty, and is. "Roehm had revolting private proclivities . . ." (which Hitler had known about for years, and which have only now become intolerable). "He surrounded himself with men, all of whom have suffered heavy and degrading penalties. . . ." Roehm's blood, as it ran, had purified Nazism. "Roehm wanted to betray his country. . . . Secret connections had been established between Roehm, Schleicher, Herr von Alvensleben, Gregor Strasser and a French diplomat. . . ." Hitler hammers out the names and then falls silent a long moment, before finally explaining that he, the Führer, had decided on immediate action the details and the success of which were known to members of the government.

He sits down, his face covered with sweat. He has just relived the Night of Long Knives, replaying the scene in which justice punishes treason, rehearsing his long upcoming speech to the nation. General Blomberg rises to answer him—grave, dignified and calm. In his sober uniform, with his modest decorations, Blomberg inspires the respect due a noble and generous warrior of the Reichswehr, imbued with the senses of honor and duty.

"In the name of the government," Blomberg announces, "I thank the Chancellor, who, by his determined and courageous intervention, has spared the German people the horrors of civil war."

Blomberg pauses. All eyes are fixed on him. The Führer, too, is staring at him, but perhaps does not see him.

"As a statesman and a soldier," Blomberg continues, "the Chancellor has acted in a spirit which has created in the government, and in the entire German people, the solemn expectation of great future exploits, through his fidelity and proof of his devotion in this grave and perilous hour."

Then the Minister of Justice states that the Führer has protected the law against violation, that he has created law when it was required, by virtue of his powers as Führer and Supreme Justice.

The Führer's attention seems to be elsewhere, as he listens with a vague, ironic and mistrustful smile on his lips. The generals, jurists and aristocrats, the men with stiff collars, bourgeois, monarchists, professors, Junkers, diplomats, all are with him, approving him, flattering him—including Franz von Papen, who protests, yet yields.

The Council of Ministers comes to an end, and Hitler sees the ministers to the door, respecting the custom of a Chancellor who esteems his colleagues.

A few hours later, he receives Hermann Rauschning, the President of the Senate of Danzig, with whom he enjoys talking. In his drawing room, with a few intimates, he allows himself to speak freely, alluding to the approaching death of Marshal Hindenburg. His words pour out in a torrent of violence and contempt.

"They are wrong . . . they think I am at the end of my rope

... but they are wrong. They don't know me. Because I come from humble people, because I have risen from the 'dregs of the population,' as they put it, because I lack education, because my manners and methods shock their bird-brains . . ."

Hitler laughs loudly. "They" are the von Papens, von Blombergs, von Hindenburgs—the Junkers and graduates of the Cadet School, the members of the Herrenklub.

"If I were one of them, I would be a great man today. But I don't need them to come and certify my greatness, my capacity. The insubordination of the SA has cost me a great many advantages, but I have others. I will know what to do if things go badly."

The monologue continues; Rauschning takes mental notes, and his fear grows as the Führer speaks. As one of Hitler's intimates for years now, an unquestioning ally, he is discovering the workings of a mind in the grip of a passion for power which nothing can stop, and which each success pushes toward greater confidence, greater contempt for others. Hitler stands up, his diatribe gaining in violence. "They haven't the slightest grasp of reality, these worthless careerists, with their petty bureaucratic mentality.

"Did you notice," Hitler adds, "how they trembled, how they humiliated themselves in front of me?"

The Führer's satisfaction is intense: the satisfaction of a self-made man who has gained power over those accustomed to advance through a slowly changing hierarchy.

"I've upset all their calculations. They thought I wouldn't dare, that I was afraid. They thought they had caught me in their net, that I was just their tool. Behind my back, they mocked me, they thought I was finished, that I had even lost the support of my Party."

His face radiates joy; his mouth twists into a vengeful smile. "I've given them a beating they'll remember. What I've lost through the purge of the SA I've won back by getting rid of those feudal plotters and adventurers, those Schleichers and their fellow conspirators."

So the Führer turns the situation to his own advantage. He

has sacrificed the men who had formerly constituted his strength —Roehm, Strasser and the SA—but he has also rid himself of the menace from certain conservatives: the deaths of both "Rightists" and "Leftists" will allow him to move toward absolute power.

"The plans of these elegant gentlemen will not succeed," he shouts. "They will not be able to go over my head when it comes to a successor to the old man. . . . Come on then, Herr von Papen, Herr Hugenberg: I'm ready for the next round."

Papen is aware of the Führer's contempt and senses the hostility behind the respectful façade. He tries to fight against them, to exert some sort of braking influence. After telling Hitler he is resigning, he drives to the Bendlerstrasse. The Ministry of War is still under heavy guard, as if a coup is expected at any time. Barbed-wire barricades are still in position in the courtyard, and the numerous sentries are heavily armed. In the corridor, the Vice Chancellor runs into the ADC of General Fritsch—"an old acquaintance from the happy days when I rode in the steeplechase. He looked at me as if I were a ghost. 'God,' he said, 'what happened to you?'

" 'As you can see,' I replied, 'I am still alive. But we shall have to put an end to all this *Schweinerei*.' "

The Vice Chancellor is taken to the office of Werner von Fritsch, his friend, but the General can only tell him what has already happened: the assassination of Schleicher and his wife.

"Fritsch admitted," Papen recalls, "that everyone had wanted the Reichswehr to intervene, but that Blomberg had been categorically opposed. As for Hindenburg, Supreme Commander of the Armed Forces, no one could reach him. Moreover, the President had almost certainly been badly informed."

Actually, Fritsch must have known that Reichswehr trucks, arms and barracks had been lent to the SS; that in Munich the Reichswehr had surrounded the Brown House of the SA, and that in officers' messes the night of July 2 champagne had flowed to celebrate the end of Roehm. General von Witzleben had even voiced his regret that the Army had not been allowed to intervene against the SA "rabble." "I wanted a part of the action," he shouted, lifting his glass to the future of the German Army.

The Reichswehr conservatives are powerless to act. They chose alliance with Hitler when he was weak and can only accept the situation as it has developed. Papen can write letters of protest to the Führer, he can confront him demanding the release of his colleagues, but Hitler will not retreat. On the contrary, on July 13, facing the Reichstag, he will say: "I accept complete responsibility for what happened." Papen had written to say that he would not attend the meeting of the Reichstag. But what difference does that make? The Opera House is full of Nazis—those who are anxious or afraid foremost among them—interrupting the Führer's speech with wild applause.

Next to Karl Ernst's empty seat sits Prince August Wilhelm von Hohenzollern, who had submitted to harsh interrogation, as an SA leader and friend of Ernst. In full uniform, he displays the most sincere enthusiasm, standing up several times as Hitler shouts out his words, while the entire nation listens and the Tiergarten fills with crowds: "I ordered the leaders of the guilty shot. I also ordered the abscesses caused by our internal and external poisons cauterized until the living flesh was burned. I also ordered that any rebel attempting to resist arrest should be killed immediately."

Prince Auwi claps as hard as he can: he is clapping for his life, he is gripped by fear.

How many others in the red armchairs of the brilliantly lit Kroll Opera are in the same position? How many others, who deny themselves, betraying the memories of their murdered comrades, bowing down before the triumphant power of the Führer? And how can Hitler feel that these men, ready to abandon so much, are anything but despicable? He believes them capable of following him no matter what he proposes, even when he is rash or wrong.

During the first two weeks of July, Franz von Papen also receives a visit from Dr. Lammers, Secretary of State to the Chancellor. The conversation is polite. On behalf of the Führer, Lammers offers Papen the post of Ambassador to the Vatican. Naturally, Lammers specifies, if the compensation seems inadequate, Papen may fix for himself whatever amount is commensurate with his capacities. The intention is clear. Hitler is brutal in his dealings with people.

Papen, his breath taken away by the audacity of the proposition, explodes: "Do you think you can buy me?" he shouts. "That is the most flagrant piece of impudence I've ever heard. Go tell that to your Hitler!" And Papen shows Hitler's envoy to the door. However, less than a month later, he becomes the Third Reich's Ambassador to Vienna.

It is not gold which seduces Papen. The night of July 25 there is violent pounding at the front door of his villa. Three SS are there, standing in the shadows. Since the Night of Long Knives, Papen has understood how little protection the law affords. His son opens the door, a revolver in his hand. But the SS have not come that night to kill: they inform Papen that the Führer at Bayreuth requests that Papen telephone him immediately. As it is almost two in the morning, it seems strange, and Papen is uneasy, wondering if the request is not a stratagem to get him into a telephone box where he can be swiftly dispatched by a burst of machine-gun fire.

But the Führer himself answers the phone.

"Herr von Papen," he says in a nervous voice, "you must leave for Vienna at once, as my Minister Plenipotentiary. The situation is alarming. You cannot refuse."

Papen knows nothing of what has been happening in Vienna that night—an Austrian version of the Night of Long Knives. Directed by Nazi Party Inspector Habicht, the Austrian Nazis have tried to seize power, and have assassinated Chancellor Dollfuss without hesitation.

July 25, 1934: less than a month after the German assassinations, more murder. Is someone trying to force Hitler's hand? It is astonishing that with the Third Reich still staggering from the shock of Roehm's liquidation, Hitler should fling himself into an enterprise as risky as the Anschluss. However, everything during these weeks between the meeting with Mussolini and the assassination of Dollfuss is surprising. Perhaps someone wishes to use an international incident as a means of getting rid of Hitler; or perhaps, more plausibly, the Austrian attempt is only a premature adventure undertaken by a few local Nazis.

The putsch fails, and Mussolini masses troops on the Alpine frontier. Hitler is forced to withdraw. He receives the news of Dollfuss' death as he listens in a state of ecstasy to *Das Rheingold* in Bayreuth.

"By the end of the performance," recalls Friedelind Wagner, who was sitting beside Hitler, "the Führer had reached a pitch of excitement terrible to see. Although he could scarcely hide his exultation, he took care to order dinner in the restaurant as on other days. 'I must appear in public,' he said, 'or people will think I am involved in all this.' "

As further news arrives from Vienna, the Führer's mood darkens. When he telephones Papen, he sounds like a man with his back to the wall: "It is a second Sarajevo," he shouts hysterically. He asks Papen to join him at Bayreuth to save Germany from disaster.

At Bayreuth, Papen meets Hitler, with Goering, Goebbels and Hess. The Nazis are anxious; Hitler curses the stupidity and brutality of the Austrian Nazis who have put him in such a terrible position. He begs Papen, for the good of Germany, to accept and go as his envoy to Vienna. Papen yields and serves the Nazis. "By acceding to Hitler's request," Papen writes, justifying himself, "I could still be of service to my country, on condition that at the outset I be given certain specific guarantees." Naturally, Hitler agrees to them. He knows how to give in when he has to. So in the end it is not gold which seduces Papen, but once more the idea that in serving Hitler he is serving Germany. Earlier, in January, 1933, when the Nazis took power, patriotism was the prime excuse: in July, 1934, it serves again. Meanwhile, however, the Reichstag has burned, the wooden huts in the concentration camps have been built at Dachau and at Buchenwald; Schleicher, Jung, Bose and Klausener have been assassinated, and during the Night of Long Knives the true face of Nazism has been unmasked as the brutal face of an implacable killer. And Papen knows all this.

Tschirschky has returned from Dachau, his head shaven, and Papen, at the cemetery with Frau Bose and her children, has delivered a eulogy for his colleague, summarily executed, as if by gangsters. But Papen submits to serving the Nazis because he wants to believe he is serving Germany. He also understands that going to Vienna—later he will go still further, as Ambassador to Ankara —is to take shelter. In the case of von Papen, as with so many Germans, there is that mixture of fear and illusion which is, ultimately, the strength of Nazism.

THE NAZI REICHSWEHR

On July 15, in the flowering countryside north of Berlin, the Army goes on maneuvers. The new units prove to be particularly effective, well trained, and equipped with new matériel. The French military attaché is impressed: the German Army is rapidly becoming a force to be reckoned with. Above all, it has rallied, without reservations, to Hitler. "The sentiments of the German officers," the French attaché writes to Paris, "as well as those of the government employees we lived with, and those of the common soldiers with whom we were able to speak, seemed unanimous: complete approval of Hitler's action. One sensed that they were fully satisfied with the triumph of the Reichswehr."

For them, the Night of Long Knives simply represents the victory of General von Blomberg over Roehm. They want to forget the part played by the SS, executors of ugly necessity. Undoubtedly they think they have skillfully managed to use the Black Guard to overcome an adversary, that they themselves have kept their integrity and remained faithful to the Reichswehr code of honor. After all, Schleicher and Roehm were not killed by the Army. Hitler has flattered and seduced the Officers' Corps, and has forced what is left of the SA to accept Army authority. In military matters, General Reichenau is now in charge of the SA, and is responsible for their reorganization.

"A Reichswehr officer whose anti-National Socialist views are well known to me," writes the French military attaché, "told me and many of my colleagues: 'Last year the Reichswehr was perhaps 60 percent Nazi; a few weeks ago, perhaps only 25 percent; now, at least 95 percent.' "

The common soldiers, indoctrinated by their officers and Blomberg's proclamations, even exceed the zeal of their officers. Toward the middle of July, Hitler, reviewing the maneuvers, drives down a long infantry column. It is high summer; the Führer is in an open car, the soldiers are sweating under their heavy helmets. Suddenly, cries of enthusiasm rise from the marching ranks: they have recognized the Führer, and from line to line the cheers rise up, harsh and virile, an outburst of youth on the march. Having discussed this incident with Reichswehr officers, the French military attaché concludes: "This type of spontaneous demonstration is not usual in the German Army; even the German officers were impressed by it."

Thus Hitler wins in men's hearts: youth follows him, the Army approves of him, and he controls the Party, the SS and the SA. Soon, in a final stroke of fortune, the death agony of President Marshal Hindenburg begins. Events follow each other in rapid succession, as if history has changed its pace, but in Berlin, Paris and London many refuse to understand the significance of the sequence. Hindenburg's death agony begins, and the will he has drawn up under Papen's influence, providing for the restoration of the monarchy, is a dead letter, even before his life has run out.

A cabinet council is hastily convened at the Chancellory on the first of August. Hitler presides. He agrees to a law, to go into effect as soon as the old man is dead, which combines the functions of the President and the Chancellor. Trembling at the thought of this triumph, now so close, Hitler goes to Neudeck. The old aristocrat is lying on his hard, austere bed, the bed of a Prussian soldier. The Führer is brought into the death room by Oskar von Hindenburg.

"Father, here is the Chancellor," the Marshal's son announces. Hindenburg opens his eyes, but does not recognize Hitler.

"Probably," Papen writes, "he thought that the Chancellor who had come from Berlin was named Papen." But this humiliating mistake makes little difference to the Führer. Hindenburg is about to die, and nothing can stop Hitler from becoming the next President of the Reich.

On August 2, at nine in the morning, salvos of artillery fired at regular intervals announce that the old fighter of Sadowa and Sedan, the Prussian soldier who was present in the Hall of Mirrors at Versailles when the German Empire was proclaimed, Marshal von Hindenburg, President of the Reich, is dead. Papen goes to Neudeck at once, to sit for a moment beside the old Marshal, "lying on a Spartan camp bed, his hands folded over a Bible, his face stamped with the wisdom, goodness and resolution I had so venerated."

A few hours after the announcement of Hindenburg's death, it is clear that the Nazis will use the funeral ceremonies being organized to mount an impressive mass display. The crowds will commune with the spirit of Nazism, abdicating their will as the law bestows the President's powers upon the Führer. When Papen brings Hitler Hindenburg's letter, which is in effect the old President's testament, Hitler declares: "Our lamented President has addressed this letter to me personally. I shall decide later if and when to authorize its publication." Papen can only plead for immediate publication; in the end, he has to accept Hitler's will. What else can he do? President Hindenburg died at nine in the morning of August 2. The law declaring Hitler his successor was in fact adopted during the evening of August 1, and by 9:30 the Reichswehr has sworn loyalty to the new Chief of State.

Thus the arrangements perhaps drawn up on the cruiser *Deutschland* in the Baltic fog have been respected: Roehm is dead, Hindenburg is dead, and Hitler succeeds to the Presidency of the Reich.

The evening papers appear framed in black. They print accounts of the dead Marshal's services, and often repeat the first verse of the German Army song of remembrance: "Ich hatt' einen Kamaraden!"

Officers publish accounts of their dead leader's heroic past. Simultaneously, the papers print the text of the new oath which General von Blomberg now requires of all members of the Reichswehr.

"I pledge before God my sacred oath of absolute obedience to the Leader of the Reich and the German people, Adolf Hitler, the Supreme Commander of the Wehrmacht. I swear to conduct myself bravely and to be always ready to sacrifice my life rather than break this oath."

On this same August 2, in every unit, officers and common soldiers begin taking this oath. They swear fidelity to the Führer, officers first, and then men in groups. The young recruits, their emotions high, their throats tight, hold out their hands above the flag. For them, and for many officers who have grown up in the belief that a sworn oath must not be violated, this new one is a bond they can never break. It is also one behind which they can take refuge, as they march in blind obedience to one man.

Thus Hitler wins the second round, as he predicted he would to Rauschning. When he receives Blomberg's telegram informing him that "the officers, noncommissioned officers and common soldiers of the Wehrmacht have solemnly sworn loyalty to the Führer and Chancellor of the Reich," he knows that he has definitely won.

All that remains for him to do is to preside at Hindenburg's funeral, to march behind the coffin of the old soldier, over which hundreds of flags and banners from every regiment in the Reich are lowered, to proclaim in the language of prophecy that Hindenburg will enter Valhalla, and to organize the plebiscite of August 19 in which 88 percent of the Germans will approve the law, already in effect, making him Chief of State.

Finally, on August 20, he is able to send a letter of thanks to General Blomberg. The Army has kept its word and sworn loyalty to him. He will not be ungrateful.

"Even as officers and soldiers," Hitler writes, "have sworn loyalty to the new state represented by me, so shall I always consider it my most sacred duty to defend the existence and integrity of the Wehrmacht, to execute the testament of the late Marshal and to remain faithful to my own desire, anchoring the Army solidly to its unique role as the military organ of the nation."

The Führer savors his triumph, and celebrates it at Nuremberg on September 4. In the enormous Luitpold Hall, decorated with thousands of flags stamped with the swastika, Hitler walks down the central aisle. The band plays the "Badenweilermarsch," and the room echoes with the shouts of "Heil Hitler!" The Führer walks slowly to the platform. Who remembers that gray dawn at Munich-Oberwiesenfeld and the forests he had to cross to reach Bad Wiessee? Adolf Wagner, perhaps, in whose office that Saturday morning, June 30, Hitler had insulted Schneidhuber and sent him to his death? But Wagner is here, beside Hitler. It is he who reads the proclamation opening the Nazi Party Congress:

"The shape of German life has been fixed for a thousand years to come. The crises of the nineteenth century have ended with us. There will be no further revolution in Germany for a thousand years to come."

For the first time, the High Command of the Reichswehr, plus the staffs of all the large units, are present at a Party Congress, beside the Führer. Scores of old-line officers, impassive and stiff in their uniforms, attend this day dedicated to military exercises: the Army is officially linked to the Party. In the evening, while the streets are noisy with the songs of the Hitler Youth, the officers drink to Eternal Germany, to the New Wehrmacht, which, in the New Reich, will remain the unchanging soul of the country, as the Prussian Army was before it.

(July 20, 1944)

Another time, another night, ten years later. To the bodies of Roehm, Schleicher, Wilhelm Eduard Schmidt, the innocent Munich music critic, millions of others have been added. The Gestapo and the SS no longer return the ashes of their victims to their families. Now these ashes rise into the low skies over Dachau, Buchenwald and Auschwitz. Another time, another night: from his headquarters, the Wolfsschanze—Wolf's Lair—Hitler speaks to the German nation:

"I am speaking to you today, first, so that you can hear my voice and know that I am unhurt and in good health, and to inform you of the most monstrous crime in German history. A small clique of ambitious officers, as irresponsible as they were stupid, organized a plot to eliminate me and the High Command of the armed forces. A bomb placed some two yards from me by Count von Stauffenberg exploded. . . . I received only a few scratches and bruises. I consider this a confirmation of the task entrusted to me by Providence. . . . This time we shall settle the account in the manner customary to National Socialists."

Thus begins a new Night of Long Knives. In a Reich in ruins, the SS, Gestapo and SD—the forces which rose to power in June, 1934—are still present, a hundred times more powerful than before, nourished through the commission of countless crimes. At least 4,980 persons are killed and thousands sent to concentration camps. And the victims are the very officers who thought they had won on June 30, 1934.

Here is Reich Marshal Erwin von Witzleben. The night of July 2–3, 1934, he had celebrated the victory of the Reichswehr over the SA, regretting that he had not been able to take part in the action. Now he is in the dock, without even the right to a belt to hold up his trousers. And Party Judge Freisler shouts at him: "Don't keep pulling at your trousers, Witzleben. It's disgusting. Can't you hold them up?"

Witzleben, Hoepner, Stieff, Hagen, Hase, Bernardis, Klausing, York von Wartenburg—all Wehrmacht officers, generals, commanders-in-chief or simple lieutenants—condemned to execution and torture. They were hung with piano wire, slowly strangled by the gradually tightening cord, which can take twelve minutes to kill. The cameramen are there on the Führer's orders to film their agony. A black sheet hides their faces, but their legs remain visible, so the spectators can watch the victims' spasmodic struggles. Reichswehr officers all, they are the same men who allowed the assassination of Schleicher, Bredow and Klausener on June 30, 1934; who swore fidelity to Hitler, and then, on another June night ten years later, rebelled. In every country in Europe lie their victims by the millions, each having met death "in the manner customary to National Socialists."

They had thought, during the Night of Long Knives, that they were winning, as others, the von Papens and von Hindenburgs, had thought they were winning on January 30, 1933. They forgot that Nazism could not be held at arm's length like a hooded hawk, obediently returning to the wrist once the chase and killing are over. They did not understand that Nazism drew its strength from violent mythologies, seeking out and manipulating dark instincts buried deep within each human being; that this new order, with its symbols, shouts, parades and killers, was an old barbarism surging up from an ancient past, its strength multiplied tenfold by the inventiveness of the times. They forgot that the end of barbarism is barbarism itself.

Paris–Nice
1969–1970

APPENDICES

I. Extracts from a Speech by Minister of State and Chief of Staff Ernst Roehm to the Diplomatic Corps and Foreign Press, Berlin, April 18, 1934

Under the sign of the Swastika the new National Socialist Germany has nothing but friends in this world. Much has been said and written on this subject. . . . Most foreigners have failed to understand either the direction or the nature of the German Revolution. The fact that it was not simply a change of political leadership is usually forgotten.

. . . The National Socialist Revolution signifies a spiritual rupture with the thought of the great French Revolution of 1789.

This thought, which takes into account only measurable and enumerable elements, has seen raised against it in National Socialism a new form of idealism before which democracy senses its own disarray, because, by natural necessity, democracy is incapable of understanding the internal principle of National Socialism.

To replace the values of democracy, National Socialism substitutes powers which cannot be precisely measured or weighed, and which cannot be understood by reason and calculation alone: powers deriving from the soul and the blood.

The moral universe of National Socialism and that of democracy, therefore, are located on different conceptual levels. . . .

I am going to speak to you of the SA. The SA is the heroic incarnation of the will and thought of the German Revolution. One can understand the nature and task of the SA only if one understands the nature and goals of the National Socialist Revolution. . . .

The German Revolution began by destroying the internal forms of the Weimar Republic. In place of the red and black system of November, the Revolution substituted the National Socialist regime, which is the incarnation of the political authority of the State.

But as a conception of the world—and the first and final aim of our struggle all these years has been to impose an entirely new conception of the world—National Socialism is not a constitutional problem, and there is no causal link between it and the external form of the State, whatever that may happen to be. . . .

The SA, let us repeat, is the heroic incarnation of the will and thought of the National Socialist Revolution.

The National Socialist Revolution is a process of moral pedagogy. It has been going on for a long time, and will not be finished until the last German incarnates and manifests National Socialism through his acts and thoughts.

When Hitler began his struggle, he was a soldier: combat, combat and more combat have marked his life. Also, by the very nature of the struggle, he subordinated all other considerations to military ones.

To guarantee the execution of his political line, he founded the Brown Army of the Revolution on the basis of two solid supports: the authority of the leader and discipline.

Only one decision in the SA is voluntary: to enter the ranks of the assault troops of German renewal. From the moment a man puts on the brown uniform, he submits himself without restriction to the law of the SA.

That law is: "Obedience until death to the supreme leader of the SA, Adolf Hitler. My goods and my blood, my strength and my life, everything that I have belongs to Germany."

From the first, Hitler has not fought for small ends. . . . From the first day, when seven men without names, allies, publicity or money dreamed of lifting Germany from its ruins, the whole power of the State was at stake.

In this struggle, his weapon has been the SA.

The SA is not a band of intrepid conspirators, but an army of believers and martyrs, agitators and soldiers, necessary in this gigantic struggle in which the soul of the German people is at stake.

As circumstances required, Adolf Hitler created a new type of combatant: the soldier of a political idea. To these political soldiers he gave the red flag with its swastika, the new symbol of the German future, and the Brown Shirt, clothing the SA in combat, honor and death.

By its color, the Brown Shirt distinguishes the SA from the masses. It is this fact which justifies it: it is the distinctive sign of the SA, allowing friends and foe alike to recognize immediately those who profess the National Socialist conception of the world.

. . . The SA is the incarnation of National Socialism. With their fists, the SA have opened to the ideas of National Socialism the road leading to victory. And in their progress the SA have drawn the skeptical and the hesitant into this prodigious mass rising of the nation.

The assault of the brown wave under the sign of the swastika calls to those on the sidelines who are waiting to see what will happen: "Come and join us, comrades!"

Without the SA, hundreds of thousands of workers would not have rediscovered the way of the Fatherland. . . . It is the SA which lifted them from the street, from hunger and from unemployment. These brown battalions have been the school of National Socialism. For in their ranks there are no privileges due to birth, rank or fortune: only the man counts, and the services he has rendered the movement.

Today, the National Socialist State rests on solid foundations. By the millions, the political soldiers of National Socialism watch over this new State, which is their State.

. . . Unfortunately, in the train of the National Socialist Revolution, reactionary elements attached themselves to us. Of course, they were correctly "aligned," and had even pinned the swastika to their lapels to prove that they had always been Nationalists.

However, we did not make a Nationalist Revolution only, but a

National Socialist one, and we stress the word "Socialist." . . . With amazing mercy, the new regime, on taking power, did not pitilessly eliminate all the representatives of the former system, or of the one which preceded it. . . . We will wring their necks without the slightest pang if they dare to put reactionary principles into practice.

Reactionaries, bourgeois conformists, specialists in denigration—all these, by natural disposition, consider the Revolution a monstrosity. In return, we feel like vomiting when we think of them.

But as an unshakable bastion of the Revolution, the SA rises up against reaction, denigration and conformism. The SA incarnates all the qualities which make the spirit of the Revolution.

During the years of struggle, the Brown Shirt was a formal uniform. It was also a shroud. After our victory, it became the symbol of National Socialist unity, it became the uniform of Germany, which it will remain.

The order and discipline of the SA were, from the outset, a necessity. The SA forged the unity of the revolutionary forces, which, to begin with, were only a loosely linked aggregate. Later, the SA became an instrument of education and the cement of our national community, which can exist only if the individual suppresses himself in every aspect of his life.

Today, it is the expression of a new style of German life. This new style, with its origins in the SA, will impose itself on every aspect of German life.

The SA is the National Socialist Revolution!

II. Extracts from a Speech Delivered by Chancellor Hitler before the Reichstag, at the Kroll Opera House, July 13, 1934

Deputies, Men of the German Reichstag:

At the request of the government, your President, Hermann Goering, has called you together today to give me the opportunity to present to our people before the most highly qualified forum in the nation explanations of events which will, I hope, remain in our history for all eternity, a memory as instructive as it is tragic.

As a result of a series of circumstances and personal faults, of the inadequacies of certain men and the dispositions of certain others, a crisis broke out in the bosom of your young Reich, which, in a future which would have come all too quickly, could have had only destructive consequences. The aim of my speech will be to present to you, and thereby to the nation, the origin and development of this crisis. My explanations will be frank and blunt, with the exception of a few reservations imposed by the interests of the Reich and by a sense of decency.

When, on January 30, 1933, Marshal Hindenburg, President of the Reich, entrusted me with the leadership of the new German government which had just been organized, the National Socialist Party took charge of a state which, in both the political and the economic realms, was highly decadent. All the political formations of the past epoch had contributed to this decadence, and therefore bore their share of responsibility. Since the Emperor and the German princes retired, the German people found itself delivered into the hands of men who, as representatives of political parties, consciously encouraged this decadence, or accepted it out of weakness. From the revolutionary Marxists through the Catholic center to the bourgeois Nationalists, all parties and their leaders have demonstrated their incapacity to govern Germany.

The thirtieth of January, 1933, therefore, marked not the simple transfer of powers from one government to another, but the definitive liquidation of an intolerable state of affairs—a liquidation longed for by the entire nation.

The restatement of these facts is necessary because (as events have shown) some people seem to have forgotten that the opportunity once existed for everyone to realize his political capacities. No one in Germany can reproach the National Socialist government for having barred the road to any political force in which some hope could still be placed.

For impenetrable reasons, destiny condemned our people to serve for fifteen years as a field of experimentation, as guinea pigs for politicians of every sort.

It was perhaps interesting, as well as amusing, for our group to follow these experiments, but for the German people they were as painful as they were exhausting. One has only to recall that period, and the men who succeeded one another as Chancellor of the Reich. We National Socialists were, rightfully, no part of this succession. On January 30, 1933, we did not, as had been the case on so many occasions, form a new ministry; on that date a new regime rejected an outmoded epoch.

This historic act, which liquidated the worst period in our nation's history, was legitimized by the German people itself. For we did not, like the men of November, 1918, take possession of power by usurpation, but by legal means. We did not, like unscrupulous anarchists, make a revolution, but, as executors of the national will, we rejected the regime which had given us an insurrection. We did not feel that we had to secure our power with bayonets; we planted it in the hearts of our countrymen.

If I read today in a certain foreign paper that I am extremely concerned, that I am especially anxious about the economic situation, I have only one reply for this scribbler: Yes, I have worries, but that has always been so. It was because we were concerned for our people that we defended them when a war was imposed upon them for which they were in no way responsible. Later, after the disaster, concerns which were even more serious turned us into revolutionaries. And when, finally, after fifteen years we assumed the leadership of our country, our anxieties and concerns did not drop away. On the contrary. But you must believe me when I say that so far I have felt no concern for myself; rather, since the Marshal's confidence has placed me where I am, I am aware only of a great concern for the present life of our people and its future. For on January 30 we did not take over a healthy state, but an economic and political chaos which those same men who criticize me today were then declaring irreparable. As for us, we have dared to undertake the struggle in every area against a destiny which seemed inexorable.

The lesson of a year and a half of National Socialist government is significant and clear. Any judgment of our success will be fair only if the present is compared with what would have happened if we had not won. Only those who still see the direction in which our country was going before January 30 can measure the greatness of our work. We were not content simply to halt the course of destiny. We were able to reform it in every aspect.

When I moved into the Wilhelmstrasse offices as Chancellor, governmental authority was no more than a myth. . . . Today, the German Reich is no longer simply a geographic region, it is a political entity as well. And, even as we have known how to ensure the internal unity and future of the German people, externally, too, we have known how to make its rights respected.

But to rescue the people from these political convulsions was not enough. After six months of the National Socialist regime, our former political life and our party quarrels were forgotten. With each month the German people have drawn farther away from a period which has become incomprehensible to us. There is no need for me to insist on this point; every German today realizes it: the mere thought of a return to a regime of political parties is as inconceivable as it is absurd.

Opposed to this positive Germany, this embodiment of all the virtues it possesses, there is also, and naturally, something negative.

There were those who took no part in the work of German revival:

1. The small group of international subversives who, as spokesmen for doctrinaire political and economic Communism, fight against everything orderly, attempting to provoke chaos. We see all around us obvious evidence of the actions of this international conspiracy. The flames of insurrection are rising in several countries. Incidents in the streets, battles, barricades, panic, and the use of destructive propaganda today trouble almost every country in the world.

In Germany, too, a few madmen or isolated criminals still carry on their pernicious activities. Since the disappearance of the Communist Party, we have recorded one attempt after another—although they have become increasingly feeble—to found and activate Communist organizations more or less anarchist in character.

The method is always the same. As they present our actual situation as insupportable, they praise the Communist paradise of the future, which, in reality, would only lead to a battle for Hell. The consequences of their victory in a country like Germany would be more destructive than anything else could be. But fortunately, the German people is now so well informed about them that the great majority of German workers has gotten rid of these international Jews, these "benefactors of humanity." If necessary, the National Socialist State will undertake an internal war of a hundred years' duration to extirpate and exterminate the final remains of a movement which spreads poison and madness among the people.

2. The second group of malcontents is composed of those political leaders who, on January 30, saw an end to their future prospects and who have not been able to resign themselves to admitting that this fact was irrevocable. As time went by, as they fell into oblivion, the more they felt they had the right to recall themselves to the memory of the nation. But as their impotence was not solely due to circumstances, but was also innate, they are still incapable even today of demonstrating their value through some useful work. They felt they had done their work when they had delivered themselves of criticism as perfidious as it was untrue. The National Socialist State cannot really be threatened or troubled in any way by such people.

3. A third group of destructive elements consisted of those who lost their positions in 1918 and could find nothing else to do except become revolutionaries. Being a part of the Revolution, they wished to turn it into a permanent condition. We all suffered during those tragic hours when those of us who were disciplined soldiers, faithful to our duty, found ourselves faced with mutineers who claimed to have become the State. We had all been brought up to respect laws and obey the representatives of the State. . . . But we could not respect those usurpers. Our honor demanded that we refuse to obey them, and so, we, too, became revolutionaries. Even as revolutionaries, however, we did not consider ourselves freed from our obligation to respect the natural laws imposed by the sovereign power of our people. When, finally, we were legitimized by the confidence of this people and when we had reaped the consequences of our fourteen years of struggle, we had no choice but to create a new order, which would be better than the one it was replacing. . . . For us, revolution was not a permanent condition.

Among the innumerable documents I have had to read during the past week I found the diary of a man who, in 1918, had been led to resist the laws, and who ever since has lived in a world in which the law—whatever it might be—was something to be destroyed. That diary is a troubling document, revealing the state of mind of the eternal conspirator, which opens insights into the mentality of people who without admitting it have become nihilists.

Incapable of collaboration, determined to assume positions against all established order, filled with hatred toward the authorities, who-ever they might be, many of these adventurers, born conspirators, were with us during our struggle against former governments. Most of these, however, well before January 30 had withdrawn from a movement whose prime characteristic was discipline. These undisciplined men had only one quality in common: they never thought of the German people, but only of struggling against all institutions and order. . . .

The inquiry has shown that among some of the superior officers of the SA tendencies had come to light which could only give rise to the gravest anxieties.

Other findings were made before the connection between them all became clear:

1. Contrary to my direct order and to the declarations made to me by former Chief of Staff Roehm, the Assault Sections were filled with elements which risked destroying the homogeneity of the organization.

2. The instruction of new militiamen in the principles of National Socialism was increasingly relegated to a level of secondary importance among the preoccupations of certain of the higher authorities.

3. The natural relationship between the Party and the militia was slowly relaxed. There were indications of a systematic tendency to turn the Assault Sections further and further from the mission I had assigned to them, and to use them for other tasks, or to place them in the service of other interests.

4. The promotion of the leaders of the SA was too often dictated by purely external considerations. The great mass of loyal veterans was increasingly overlooked in these promotions while the class of 1933, which had never been particularly esteemed in the Party, was incomprehensibly heaped with advantages. Often, it was enough to have belonged to the SA for only a few months to obtain important positions which an old SA leader was not able to achieve after years of service. . . .

The decision of the directorate of the Party to put an end to the excesses of which I have just spoken provoked a vigorous reaction on the part of the Chief of Staff. Veterans of our struggles, among whom some had been fighting with us for fifteen years, and others who had represented the Party in high functions of State, were referred to tribunals of honor composed in part of very young Party members, or even of people who did not belong to the Party at all. . . .

As a result of all this, there were serious discussions between Roehm and myself. It was during these talks that, for the first time, I began to have doubts about the loyalty of this man. . . .

Beginning in the month of May, there was no doubt that Chief of Staff Roehm was involved in ambitious plans which, if realized, could lead only to most serious change.

If I was slow, during these months, to reach a decision, I had two reasons:

1. I could not, without further proof, accustom myself to the idea that the relations I had built up in mutual confidence rested on a lie.

2. I always nourished the secret hope that I might spare my SA the shame of such a revelation, and that I might reduce the damage without having to fight. . . .

Gradually, three groups formed inside the leadership of the SA. First, a small group of elements with similar dispositions or vices and who, ready for anything, were entirely in Roehm's hands. Foremost among these were the SA leaders Ernst in Berlin, Heines in Silesia, Hayn in Saxony, and Heydebreck in Pomerania. Beside these was a second group of men who actually did not belong to this clique, but who considered themselves obliged to obey Roehm out of a sense of discipline. Opposed to these two groups was a third: its leaders made no secret of their aversion to what was happening. For this reason they found they were not given responsible positions, and in many cases were completely ignored. At the head of this group were Lutze, the present leader of the SA, and Himmler, the leader of the SS.

Without ever telling me, or giving me the slightest hint of it, Chief of Staff Roehm had entered into relations with General von Schleicher through the intermediary of a corrupt adventurer, Herr von Alvensleben. Schleicher was the man who gave a concrete form to Roehm's plans. He decided that:

1. The present German regime could not last.

2. The Army and other national organizations should be placed under a single leader.

3. The only man qualified to be this leader was Roehm.

4. Herr von Papen must be dismissed, and he himself should take Papen's place at the Chancellory—which would also mean other changes in the government. . . .

For fourteen years I have consistently stated that the Storm Troopers were political organizations which had nothing to do with the Army. It would, in my eyes, have been a disavowal of my previous statements and of all my policy to have put an officer at the head of the Army other than the man who was the leader of the SA, Captain Goering. . . .

The supreme leader of the Army is Marshal von Hindenburg, President of the Reich. As Chancellor, I have sworn loyalty to him. His person is sacred to us. . . .

Within the State, only the Army bears arms, and only the National Socialist Party thinks politically. Roehm's plan was conceived so as to provoke resistance:

1. First, it was necessary to create conditions favorable to a second revolution. The propaganda services of the SA spread the rumor that the Reichswehr desired their dissolution, and that it had won me over, which was nothing but a lie.

2. To guard against this attack, the SA must make a second revolution, to get rid of the reactionaries in their organization and seize power themselves.

3. Thanks to collections taken up in the name of charity, Roehm had managed to amass some twelve millions to further his designs.

4. In order to wage decisive battles without scruple or hesitation, special groups of mercenaries had been organized, ready for anything. These groups were called the "Guards of the General Staff."

The political preparation for internal action was entrusted to Herr von Detten, while General Schleicher undertook external arrangements, acting personally, as well as through the mediation of his courier, General von Bredow. Gregor Strasser was also involved in the plot.

At the beginning of June, I made a final effort with Roehm. I asked him to come to my office, and we talked together for nearly five hours. I told him I had the impression that certain conscienceless elements were preparing a Nationalist-Bolshevik revolution, which could only lead to miseries beyond description. I also told him that I had heard a rumor that the Army was to be involved in this action. I said to the Chief of Staff that those who thought that the SA should be dissolved were entirely mistaken, that I myself could not prevent the spread of this falsehood, but that any attempt to spread disorder in Germany would be met by my immediate personal opposition, and that whoever attacked the State must consider me his enemy. . . .

If one could still prevent this misery, it was only by striking with the suddenness of a bolt of lightning. Only a ferocious and bloody repression could nip the revolt in the bud. There could be no question of wondering whether it was better to annihilate a hundred rebels, traitors and conspirators, or to allow ten thousand innocent SA to be killed on one side of the barricades, and ten thousand innocents on the other. For once the movement of the criminal, Ernst, had got under way in Berlin, the consequences would have been incalculable. As the rebels had made use of my name, they had succeeded in obtaining from the police four light armored cars.

At one in the morning I received this last news. At two I flew to Munich. Minister-President Goering, meanwhile, was ordered to act in Berlin and in Prussia. With his steel fist, he crushed the attack against the National Socialist State before it even began. . . .

Mutinies are judged by their own laws. If someone asks me why we did not use the regular courts I would reply: at that moment I was responsible for the German nation; consequently, it was I alone who, during those twenty-four hours, was the Supreme Court of Justice of the German people. In every time and place, rebels have been killed. Only one country has not used this provision in its military code, and this country is Germany. I did not want to expose the new Reich to the fate of the old.

I ordered the leaders of the guilty shot. I also ordered the abscesses caused by our internal and external poisons cauterized until the living flesh was burned. I also ordered that any rebel attempting to resist arrest should be killed immediately. The nation must know that its existence cannot be menaced with impunity by anyone, and that whoever lifts his hand against the State shall die of it. Similarly, every National Socialist should know that no circumstances can shield him from responsibilities, and, consequently, from punishment. . . .

A foreign diplomat states that his encounter with Schleicher and Roehm was entirely inoffensive. I need not argue this question with anyone. Absolute opinions on what is or is not inoffensive never coincide in politics. But when three men capable of high treason organize a meeting in Germany with a foreign statesman, a meeting which they themselves characterize as a "working" meeting, when they send the servants away, and give strict orders that I should not be informed of their meeting, I have those men shot, even if in the course of those secret conversations the only subjects discussed were the weather, old coins and similar topics.

The cost of these crimes has been high: nineteen superior officers and thirty-one junior officers of the Storm Troopers and members of their squads have been shot. Further, three senior officers of the SS who participated in the plot were also shot. Thirteen SA leaders or civilians lost their lives in attempting to resist arrest. Two others killed themselves. Five Party members who did not belong to the SA were shot for their participation in the plot. And finally, three more SS were shot for mistreating prisoners.

The action was completed during the night of Sunday, July 1, and normal conditions have been re-established. A series of violent acts which have no connection with this action will be referred to the regular courts. . . .

I had hoped that it would not be necessary to defend the State by force of arms. Since this could not be the case, we must all congratulate ourselves for having been sufficiently fanatic to have preserved in blood what was acquired by the blood of our best friends. . . .

BIBLIOGRAPHY

In addition to German archives, various oral accounts, and the newspapers of the time, numerous publications were consulted, as listed below.

I. Documents

Archives of the Institut für Zeitgeschichte, Munich.

Forschungsstelle zur Geschichte des Nationalsozialismus, Hamburg.

International Military Tribunal, Nuremberg: *Trials of the Major War Criminals,* Baden-Baden, 1947–1949.

Protokoll des Schwurgerichts in dem Strafverfahren gegen, Josef Dietrich und Michael Lippert, Munich, May 6–14, 1967.

Weissbuch über die Erschiessungen des 30 Juni, 1934, Paris, 1934.

Norman H. Baynes: *The Speeches of Adolf Hitler, 1922–1939,* Oxford, 1942.

Charles Bloch: *La Nuit des Longs Couteaux* (a collection of documents including previously unpublished texts), Archives, Paris, 1964.

II. Memoirs and Eyewitness Accounts

André François-Poncet: *Recollections of the Berlin Embassy*, Paris, 1946; *The Fateful Years*, London, 1949.

Ruth Andreas-Friedrich: *A Berlin sous les Nazis*, Paris, 1946.

Hans Bernd Gisevius: *Jusqu'à la lie*, Paris, 1948; *To the Bitter End*, Boston, 1947.

————: *Où est Nebe?*, Paris, 1967.

Joseph Goebbels: *My Part in Germany's Fight*, London, 1935.

Adolf Hitler: *Mein Kampf*, Paris, 1938; also Boston, 1943.

Franz von Papen: *Memoirs*, Paris, 1953; also New York, 1953.

Hermann Rauschning: *Hitler m'a dit*, Paris, 1939; *Time of Delirium*, New York, 1946.

Ernst Roehm: *Die Memoiren des Stabschefs Röhm*, Sarrebruck, 1934.

————: *Die Geschichte eines Hochverräters*, 1934.

Ernst von Salomon: *Les Réprouvées*, Paris, 1931.

————: *Les Cadets*, Paris, 1969.

Otto Strasser: *Hitler et moi*, Paris, 1940.

III. Miscellaneous Studies

William Sheridan Allen: *Une Petite Ville Nazie*, Paris, 1967; *The Nazi Seizure of Power: The Experience of a Single Town, 1930–1935*, New York, 1965.

Gilbert Badia: *Histoire de l'Allemagne Contemporaine*, Paris, 1962.

H. Bennecke: *Die Reichswehr und der Röhm-Putsch*, 1957.

————: *Hitler und die S.A.*, 1959.

J. Benoist-Méchin: *Histoire de l'Armée Allemande*, Paris, 1938.

Karl Dietrich Bracher: *Die Nationalsozialistiche Machtergreifung*, Köln, 1960.

Alan Bullock: *Hitler, ou les mécanismes de la tyrannie*, Paris, 1963: *Hitler: A Study in Tyranny*, New York, 1962.

Georges Castellan: *Le Réarmement Clandestin du Reich*, Paris, 1954.

————: *L'Allemagne de Weimar*, Paris, 1969.

Jacques Delarue: *Histoire de la Gestapo*, Paris, 1962.

Jean François: *L'Affaire Röhm-Hitler*, Paris, 1939.

BIBLIOGRAPHY

Walter Hofer: *Die Diktatur Hitlers bis zum Beginn des Zweiten Weltskrieges,* 1960.

Heinz Höhne: *L'Ordre Noir, Histoire de la SS,* Paris, 1968; *The Order of the Death's Head,* London, 1969.

Roger Manvell et Heinrich Franckel: *Hermann Goering,* Paris, 1962.

———: *Goebbels,* Paris, 1964.

William L. Shirer: *Le Troisième Reich,* Paris, 1961; *The Rise and Fall of the Third Reich,* New York, 1960.

Otto Strasser: *Die deutsche Bartholomäusnacht,* 1935.

J. Wheeler-Bennett: *Le drame de l'armée allemande,* Paris, 1955; *The Nemesis of Power: The German Army in Politics, 1918–1945,* London, 1953.